Soccer Culture
in America

Soccer Culture in America

Essays on the World's Sport in Red, White and Blue

Edited by YUYA KIUCHI

McFarland & Company, Inc., Publishers
Jefferson, North Carolina, and London

LIBRARY OF CONGRESS CATALOGUING-IN-PUBLICATION DATA

    Soccer culture in America : essays on the world's sport in red, white and blue / edited by Yuya Kiuchi.
       p.   cm.
    Includes bibliographical references and index.

    ISBN 978-0-7864-7155-3
    softcover : acid free paper ∞

    1. Soccer—United States.   2. Soccer—Social aspects—United States.   I. Kiuchi, Yuya.
    GV944.U6S62 2014
    796.3340973—dc23   2013041717

BRITISH LIBRARY CATALOGUING DATA ARE AVAILABLE

© 2014 Yuya Kiuchi. All rights reserved

No part of this book may be reproduced or transmitted in any form or by any means, electronic or mechanical, including photocopying or recording, or by any information storage and retrieval system, without permission in writing from the publisher.

Front cover image © Zoonar/Thinkstock

Manufactured in the United States of America

McFarland & Company, Inc., Publishers
  Box 611, Jefferson, North Carolina 28640
    www.mcfarlandpub.com

To Tsuneo Kiuchi, my father,
who introduced me to soccer
by buying a small
soccer ball as my first toy

To Nichole Kramer-Kiuchi, my wife,
whom I met thanks to soccer

Table of Contents

Acknowledgments   ix

A Note on Terms   xi

Introduction   1

PART I: SOCCER AS AN AMERICAN PHENOMENON

  1. Making the Mainstream: The Domestication of American Soccer
     DAVID KEYES   9

  2. Individualism vs. Community: The Globally Strange Relationship Between the U.S. Soccer System and the U.S. School System
     ANDREW M. GUEST   25

  3. New Traditionalists: The Emergence of Modern America and the Birth of the MLS Coalition
     DENNIS J. SEESE   43

PART II: AMERICAN SOCCER ECONOMICS

  4. It's All Fun and Games Until No One Gets Hurt: European Soccer Leagues, Capitalism and the Movement Towards a Socialist American Model
     CLIFF STARKEY   71

  5. A Resounding Soccer Success ... in the U.S.?
     DWIGHT BRANCH   84

6. "Fast-Kicking, Low-Scoring and Ties": How Popular Culture
   Can Help the Global Game Become America's Game
   BENJAMIN JAMES DETTMAR 95

PART III: SOCCER IN AMERICAN SOCIETY

7. Perceptions of Hooliganism in American Soccer
   CEDRICK G. HERAUX 121

8. Becoming Apple Pie: Soccer as the Fifth Major Team
   Sport in the United States?
   GLEN M.E. DUERR 143

9. Pitch Perfect: How the U.S. Women's National
   Soccer Team Brought the Game Home
   DANIELLE SARVER COOMBS 160

PART IV: INTERVIEWS

10. Scholarship and Soccer: Alex Galarza 179
11. Japanese Referee in the MLS: Toru Kamikawa 192

Conclusion 205
About the Contributors 207
Index 211

Acknowledgments

This book would not have been possible without the hard work of my contributors. I truly appreciate their generosity in sharing their experiences, knowledge, and passion for soccer. I have my fair share of understanding of the game, but what makes this book valuable is the versatility that these authors bring to this collection in the pages that follow. I offer a big thank you to Emily Bolton for her crucial role in transcribing an interview.

My wife, Nichole, also deserves recognition. Writing or editing a book is not only time consuming but also space-consuming work. Our home office became filled with books and papers, which slowly but surely found their way to our living room table. "No work books or articles on the living room table," I had promised. But when essay manuscripts began to arrive, she kindly looked the other way and focused on her *New York Times* crossword puzzle. Now that this project is completed, I promise our living room will be free of work-related documents (until my next project begins). Thank you, Nicki.

I want to express special thanks to my father, Tsuneo Kiuchi, who is not here with us to read this book. He was the one who introduced me to soccer. I can't even remember it, but he bought me a small soccer ball as my first toy. My childhood is filled with memories of playing and watching soccer with him. May he rest in peace.

A Note on Terms

In this collection, the words "soccer" and "football" are used interchangeably. When "football" refers to American football, it is clearly stated. I did not change essayists' use of terminology in this respect.

As the introduction discusses briefly, the American soccer lexicon is filled with inaccurate terms. Although more popular sports such as American football, ice hockey, and others may have "sidelines," "endlines," shoot-outs," and "penalty boxes" and so on, these are not proper terms according to the Laws of the Game, annually revised and published by soccer's international organizing body, FIFA. Although these "American" expressions have begun to influence soccer communities outside of the U.S., and members of various continental associations and FIFA have used them, this collection uses only expressions, phrases and terms that appear in FIFA's official publication materials.

Introduction

Yuya Kiuchi

Even before I can remember, soccer has been a part of my life. The first toy I received as a little boy in Tokyo, according to my mother, was a soccer ball from my father. When I told my mother I was not doing well in baseball in my junior high school physical education class, she said to me, "I wish your father had played catch with you once in a while when you were little. All he told you was 'Yuya, try to kick that ball.'" I remember watching my father play on his company team. I remember even playing in one of the games as a preschooler — I only made one touch on the ball. What a proud boy I was. I attended or watched on TV numerous games with him. We went to the Toyota Cup games, now the FIFA Club World Cup. We watched Japan play in World Cup qualifiers late at night on TV. So it was natural that I decided to join my elementary school soccer team as soon as I was in the third grade, the earliest I could join the team. A day before sign-up, as excited I was, I was kicking the ball around in the school yard before classes began in the morning even though students were not allowed to play soccer until after school. My homeroom teacher told me if I continued to break the rule, I might not be allowed to play for the team. Three years later, on a rainy day, I was playing soccer with a few friends. We did not think anyone would catch us because it was a downpour and we were playing under trees in an attempt to remain somewhat dry. We wound up getting in trouble, but there was something special about kicking a ball around with friends.

I also remember asking my father about the flags that the linesmen (now called assistant referees) used. He brought home a pair that belonged to his soccer team and I would play with them. I pretended to be a linesman. I was probably only five years old. My father, just like most players, was not a huge fan of referees. But I was mesmerized by the flags. As I played for my elementary school and junior high school, when opportunities arose, I would volunteer to help my coach as a linesman. When I learned I could be certified as a referee, I looked into it. At the time, you had to be eighteen to take an introductory class. I wrote several letters to the soccer association asking for an exception, because I was only fifteen. I heard back and was told that I could take a class. Until I graduated from high school, I was a soccer player and a referee, but I soon realized I was not a very talented soccer player. I was, however, doing well as a referee. Since then, I have been fortunate enough to officiate international, professional, and intercollegiate matches on three different continents.

I tell the story of my childhood because this project is a product of the gap I felt between my childhood and what I later observed as I pursued my academic career in the U.S. Probably because soccer had always been a part of my life and it appeared to be a part of my friends' lives, it was a big surprise when I came to the U.S. as an exchange student to Boston College, at age twenty-two, to see how little my friends knew about soccer. It was right after the 2002 World Cup. Although my roommate, Dwight Branch, who is also a contributor to this book, was an avid soccer fan, "football" (not the right kind in my mind), ice hockey, basketball, and baseball, for sure, were much more popular than the sport that seemed to bind the world. At the time I did not have many friends to talk about soccer with. It was not easy to find a bar where Dwight and I could watch important soccer fixtures from Europe. Soccer seemed to escape the attention of most Americans. I studied in Boston to learn about American culture. Following soccer, it seemed, was probably least American thing to do.

The more I thought about the meaning of soccer in American culture, however, I began to realize soccer might be a very American sport. There are strong communities of soccer players, fans, coaches, referees, and many others both online and offline. American national teams, both men's and women's, have been doing very well at the international level. As Toru Kamikawa explained in his interview that is included in this book, the women's national team has won world championships. The men's national team has performed well in the World Cups too. When I go to a local park on a weekend, I see youth soccer games. "Soccer mom" is a very common expression. Soccer may very well be American.

I have asked my students at Michigan State University for the past seven years if they have played soccer. Almost all of them raise their hands. Furthermore, a majority of them have played for a team, not just casually in the backyard. But when I ask if they have played ice hockey, basketball, or American football, considerably fewer students say yes. This has been the case consistently. Students, regardless of gender, are more likely to have played soccer than any other sport. However, these same students watch less soccer than other sports, and they are unaware of how their university soccer team did in the past year in their conference even though they seem to be able to recount every play of a non-conference American football game. They cannot even list half of the Major League Soccer teams.

What do I make of this? On the one hand, it is an unquestionable fact that most of my students have played soccer. There are reasons to believe soccer is very American. But at the same time, few of my students know about soccer. To make matters worse, so-called experts on ESPN do not even know proper terminology. "Handball," "endline," "sideline," "penalty box," and "offsides" are not proper soccer lexicon. "Handling," "goal line," "touch line," "penalty area," and "offside" are. Some new referees explain that they had sent off a player for "punching," even though it is not one of the reasons why a referee could show a red card to a player (it has to be called "striking"). Soccer and the U.S. seem to have a complicated relationship. This is why I had to question what soccer means in American culture.

That is where this book began. If I define "American" as a suburban white lifestyle, soccer can only be American among youth. But if I use a more inclusive definition of "American," there is no doubt soccer is a very American sport in any segment of American society. Tom Weir has said,

> The World Cup draw is Sunday and admit it, you don't care. And no matter how much this event gets crammed down your throat... you still won't care. But don't feel guilty about it. There is a good reason why you don't care about soccer, even if it is the national passion in Cameroon, Uruguay, and Madagascar. It's because you are an American, and hating soccer is more American than mom's apple pie, driving a pickup or spending Saturday afternoon channel-surfing with the remote control.

But the reality is different, as Douglass Massey has correctly pointed out,

> Although migrants belong to a variety of voluntary organizations in the United States, the most important is the soccer club.... Although [soccer club's] manifest functions are recreational, its latent functions are to strengthen and expand the social connections within the network, thereby supporting the migrant enterprise.... [The game] is the place where dates are made, work obtained, friends located, new arrivals welcomed, and news of the town exchanged.... Townspeople meet to watch soccer and to socialize [105].

As I mentioned earlier, I have refereed at various levels of play. Countless Sunday afternoons have been spent refereeing men's soccer games. Family members of players gather by the local soccer field an hour or two before the match to start a BBQ. I have seen a cooler filled with sport drinks on top of ice, but underneath were numerous cans of beer for post-game merriness. Frequently, I do not understand what players are saying to each other, because it is not one of the languages I speak. I only understand them when they complain about my calls, or lack thereof. Teams are based on national identities. A men's game between Croatians and Serbians in Detroit was almost more intensive than any professional games I have ever had, even though the game was just an amateur in-state match. Soccer in the U.S. is a unique phenomenon. The essays in this book explore what soccer means in American culture.

The book is divided into four parts. Part I: Soccer as an American Phenomenon examines unique features of American soccer culture. David Keyes' essay, "Making the Mainstream: The Domestication of American Soccer," is a gateway to understanding of how soccer became the sport it is today in the U.S. Keyes points out that it has been a youth sport since World War II. Before the mid–1940s, it was predominantly played by immigrants. The concurrent rise of soccer's popularity among American families and post-war suburbanization was not coincidental. The American Youth Soccer Organization (AYSO) attempted to redefine this foreign sport as one that was part of an American way of life. Keyes suggests that this effort was a three-part domestication process. He claims that the AYSO translated the "foreign" to "American," configured it as a "safe" sport, and marketed it as a family sport and event. Even though some of the adaptations that the AYSO made to make the game more acceptable to American families turned some traditionalists off, we continue to see the AYSO's success at local soccer fields around the country on weekends.

Andrew M. Guest's "Individualism vs. Community: The Globally Strange Relationship Between the U.S. Soccer System and the U.S. School System" is a combination of historical and ethnographic analysis. In the first essay, Keyes discussed the AYSO, entry-level soccer. What happens once players decide to play at a slightly more competitive level or on a high school team? Guest answers this question by opening his essay with the fact that men's and women's U.S. national teams have an extremely high educational attainment level. Seven starting players on the men's World Cup team in 2010 had college-level education. Every starting player of the women's Olympic team in 2012 attended a four-year college. These are unique examples among other teams representing nations where soccer players mostly focus their youth on the game and not on education. Guest suggests that this difference reflects a tension between individualism and communal identity. He argues that soccer in the U.S., at least at the youth level, is not really about soccer. Even as we witness an increasing popularity of club teams that are not associated with schools, soccer is where America's traditional emphasis on community takes place. As Guest shows, players often consider high school, college, or Under 18 soccer their ultimate career goal as soccer players. Athletic experiences gained at these levels do not compete with aspiring to play on the national team since age seven and dedicating youth ages to soccer. Communal experiences in the U.S. context are, however, fulfilling because to play at a high school soccer field on a weeknight or to represent, even at the Division Three level, one's school is an end of its own.

"New Traditionalists: The Emergence of Modern America and the Birth of the MLS Coalition" by Dennis J. Seese is an interesting study of soccer with a dualistic framework that integrates "the modern U.S." and "the traditional U.S." Seese argues that there is a cultural battle between a traditional American identity represented by baseball and emergent and more modern American identity as represented by soccer. In other words, accepting soccer in American culture is to accept what the contemporary U.S. is beginning to represent: true progress toward diversity rather than tokenism, decline of white, male-dominated, heteronormative idealism, and more liberal ideas. This parallel between the cultural battle (soccer vs. baseball) and political battle (traditional vs. modern) is key in understanding soccer's role in American society in the twenty-first century.

Part II: American Soccer Economics begins with Cliff Starkey's "It's All Fun and Games until No One Gets Hurt: European Soccer Leagues, Capitalism and the Movement toward a Socialist American Model," a comparative investigation of European and American soccer business models. Starkey accurately points out that despite America's anti–Communist and anti-socialist history, its sports leagues are built on a Socialist model, whereas its European counterparts tend to follow a more Capitalist model. In the U.S., salaries are capped. Profits are shared. Teams, at least in theory, should have equal chance to win a championship. Its draft system often is part of this scheme. In Europe, however, the winner takes all. Big teams have repeatedly won domestic and continental championships. To make the sport interesting to as many fans and teams, Starkey argues, European "soccer-preneurs" may eventually resort to America's socialist sport business model.

"A Resounding Soccer Success ... in the U.S.?" by Dwight Branch focuses on the Seattle Sounders FC to understand how the team built on a history of interest in soccer in the region and utilized a strategy to maximize fan engagement. As a result, Seattle quickly broke MLS attendance records and has experienced consistent success, even though the team lacked superstars. The strategy was to make sure that the team delivered a compelling, relevant, quality product and that fans felt highly connected to the team. Branch posits that extending and customizing this approach may represent MLS's best opportunity to expand itself to make soccer a core part of the U.S. sports and cultural landscape.

"'Fast-Kicking, Low-Scoring and Ties': How Popular Culture Can Help the Global Game Become America's Game" connects the history of media culture to the development of soccer culture in the U.S. Breaking the history of U.S. soccer into six phases, Benjamin James Dettmar captures some key events. Comparing it to general sport history in the U.S., Dettmar argues that televising games has helped basketball and football become staples of American life. Advertisements, movies, and other examples of popular culture have also assisted this process. Although he agrees with other contributors that American youth have been and will continue to be the key to the success of future American soccer, what Dettmar terms "middle-aged medium of television" will also be key factor.

Cedrick G. Heraux opens Part III: Soccer in American Society with "Perceptions of Hooliganism in American Soccer." Heraux examines violence associated with soccer in its historical context in Europe and contemporary examples in the U.S. to explore the perception and characterization of hooliganism among MLS supporters. On the one hand, there have been cases of hooliganism in MLS. They were highlighted in the media because David Beckham and Landon Donovan were targeted. Furthermore, there seems to be a moral panic about soccer culture as an unfamiliar culture that is mistakenly associated with fictional images of hooliganism. One of the major challenges for MLS as it strives to expand is, in addition to improving its quality of play to the level of top European leagues, to handle this fear of violence around the soccer field.

"Becoming Apple Pie: Soccer as the Fifth Major Team Sport in the United States?" by Glen M.E. Duerr considers the current status of soccer in American culture as he envisions how it might develop. In contrasting to existing work on the topic, Duerr argues that three major factors could influence the sports future: the growth of MLS, the popularity of soccer among immigrant communities, and youth participation. The essay suggests that the growth of the professional league has a strong correlation to the building of soccer-specific stadiums. Establishing an environment in which fans can enjoy games seems to help the teams. Duerr also shows that immigrant and youth participation has been and will be the key to the success of the game. While this general argument might be no surprise to many scholars of soccer, Duerr provides solid evidence that such a common assumption would be a matter that the stakeholders might need to pay close attention to.

Danielle Sarver Coombs, in "Pitch Perfect: How the U.S. Women's National Soccer Team Brought the Game Home," focuses on the U.S. women's national team. As she traces the history of the U.S. women's national team, showing that it epitomizes the reversal of a common view — men's sport as the norm and women's sport as inferior. This is seen in the team's greater success than its counterpart and in its general popularity in the U.S. Coombs not only considers the recent victories at the 2012 Olympics in London or the 2011 silver medal in Germany but points out accurately that playing soccer is an appealing option to many young American women including those in immigrant communities where males are typically the soccer players. The essay suggests that these potential players could influence the future of women's national team in the years to come.

The final two presentations are interviews. The first is "Scholarship and Soccer: Alex Galarza." Galarza's main research topic has been Argentinian football, but he has also been active in launching and taken the leadership role in the Football Scholars Forum. Galarza explains where soccer scholarship has been and where it might be headed, and stresses that the accessibility of soccer scholarship is especially important. As high-quality books and articles on soccer written by not only academics but also by those with backgrounds in journalism, it is clear, he suggests, that those in this scholarly field must keeps others involved in soccer in mind as they write. Their academic output should be readable even for non-academics.

The book ends with "Japanese Referee in the MLS: Toru Kamikawa." Kamikawa is the chair of the Japan Football Association Referee Committee and a member of the Referees Committee of Fédération Internationale de Football Association (FIFA) and the Asian Football Confederation (AFC). Kamikawa discusses his experience in the referee exchange program between Japan's professional league, J-League, and its American counterpart, Major League Soccer. He shares his thoughts on how U.S. soccer may evolve, as well as cultural differences both on and off the field in Japan and the U.S.

Despite the wide variety of expertise and knowledge that the contributors bring to this book, it does not capture every facet of soccer culture in the U.S. There is much that needs to be discussed. But it is my hope, and I am sure that colleagues old and new would agree, that this book will make it clear how relevant soccer is in the U.S. It may not be the most popular sport in the country, and hating it could be as popular as liking it. But the undeniable reality is that soccer is here to stay and to prosper. A quick trip to a local sports complex, a brief review of the program listings on your cable or satellite channel guide, or a stroll through a sporting goods store will show its relevancy to many Americans. And, of course, so will the essays that follow.

Works Cited

Massey, Douglas S. "The Social Organization of Mexican Migration to the United States." *Annals of the American Academy of Political and Social Science* 487 (Sept., 1986): 102–113. Print.

Weir, Tom. "Soccer Always on Wrong Foot in USA." *USA Today* 17 Dec. 1993, final ed.: 3C. Print.

PART I: SOCCER AS AN AMERICAN PHENOMENON

1

Making the Mainstream

The Domestication of American Soccer

DAVID KEYES

David Andrews calls the post–World War II rise of soccer "America's silent sporting revolution" (37). "No longer a 'mini-passion' of suburban America," he writes, "youth soccer participation has emerged as a defining practice at the core of American life" (31). Today, nearly 14 million people in the United States play soccer, of whom nearly 60 percent are below the age of 17 (SGMA). Unlike other sports in the United States, youth soccer has existed primarily since World War II. Prior to that, soccer was played almost exclusively by immigrants and largely seen as a "foreign game" (Markovits and Hellerman; Wangerin, *Soccer in a Football World*; Wangerin, *Distant Corners*).

How, then, did soccer move beyond immigrant communities to become the cultural juggernaut that it is today? This change was made possible only once the sport was no longer seen as a foreign game. One of, if not *the* most important, organization in reshaping the image of soccer in the United States was the American Youth Soccer Organization (AYSO), based in Los Angeles. The leaders of AYSO sought to redefine the sport so that it would not be seen as a foreign game, but instead as the perfect game for the newly ascendant suburbs. Through this redefinition, soccer became what David Andrews and colleagues call a "sporting practice and symbol of fin-de-millennium suburban America" (Andrews et al. 263).

The explanation for the changing meanings associated with soccer in the United States, and thus the sport's growth lies in its domestication, meaning that soccer has been made "American" (domestication number one) by presenting it as a "safe" sport (domestication number two) and moving it into the domestic sphere (domestication number three). The domestication of American soccer has been, in large part, a process of stripping the "residual ethnicity" from soccer. By making the sport safe and moving it into the realm of the family, AYSO transformed the game, making it no longer seem foreign. Below, I trace out the role that this organization played in the 1960s and 1970s in the domestication of American soccer, and thus the growth of the sport.

Background

One of the major questions that those who study soccer raise in the United States is what I call "residual ethnicity." Drawing from Raymond Williams' concepts of emergent, dominant, and residual, soccer's shift from an emergent to a dominant cultural form has required an attempt to jettison the residual ethnicity of its past. Many have asked how much soccer today continues to be "associated with ethnic Otherness" (Andrews 35). While some see residual ethnicity as central to explaining why soccer, especially at the professional level, has never quite "made it" in the United States (Markovits and Hellerman; Wangerin, *Soccer in a Football World*; Wangerin, *Distant Corners*), others, especially those who study suburban youth soccer, suggest that the sport has moved beyond such associations (Foer; Andrews et al.). If it is true that youth soccer has come to shed most, if not all, residual ethnicity, how did this process take place?

Soccer in the United States has long suffered from the perception that it is a "foreign" sport. Andrei Markovits and Steven Hellerman have argued that during the late nineteenth and early twentieth centuries, when the American sport space was being developed, "soccer was perceived by both native-born Americans and immigrants as a non-American activity at a time in American history when nativism and nationalism emerged to create a distinctly American self-image" (52). While soccer remained an ethnic curiosity, the popularity of sports such as baseball and football, whose foreign roots (in rounders and rugby, respectively) were intentionally obscured by promoters who sought to present them as distinctively American games, boomed.

Soccer remained a marginal sport in the United States in part because of the reluctance of its leading officials to "Americanize" the sport. David Wangerin writes that "in a country whose national motto, *e pluribus unum* (out of many, one), articulated a desire for assimilation, leaving soccer in the hands of what [President Teddy] Roosevelt, [Senator Henry Cabot] Lodge and their ilk disparagingly referred to as 'hyphenated-Americans' was tantamount to marginalizing it for good" (*Soccer in a Football World* 33).

But Americanizing soccer was never a goal of those in charge of the sport. The main reason they were involved with the game was to provide a connection to their ethnic community in the United States and, by proxy, to their home country. David Trouille describes soccer clubs in early twentieth-century Chicago as "play[ing] a crucial role in helping to alleviate the alienation many immigrants felt by providing a release from the often grim experiences at work and in the neighborhood.... Beyond their social function, many teams also provided important community services, such as helping players acquire jobs, housing and loans" (805). For most involved with soccer, there was never a choice between leaving soccer to be seen as a foreign game and Americanizing the sport; soccer connected them to their fellow immigrants and their homeland — and that was exactly why they loved it.

But the boom in youth soccer in the post–World War II period indicates that a change has taken place. Soccer today, especially youth soccer, is no longer seen, in most cases, as a foreign game (for exceptions to this, see Grey; Zirin). How this change has taken place is ultimately a question that gets at the definition of the nation. Implicit in the statement that a sport is foreign are the boundaries of an imagined national community.

Much study of the nation takes as its starting point the work of Benedict Anderson, who argues that the "nation is always conceived as a deep, horizontal comradeship" (7). Anderson's work has been fundamental in allowing scholars to see that the nation is less a concrete thing and more a boundary drawn by people, who imagine themselves a member of a national community. The road that Anderson starts us on — seeing nation as a process of boundary making — takes us only part of the way. In the words of Ana Maria Alonso, "Anderson does not go far enough in identifying the strategies through which 'the imagined' becomes 'second nature,' a 'structure of feeling' embodied in material practice and lived experience" (382). If the nation does indeed become part of people's material practice and lived experience, then it is possible to see the maintenance of the nation as a salient boundary through its performance. Many scholars have built on Anderson's work to demonstrate that performance is central to the process by which the nation continues to be a relevant boundary in people's lives.

Katherine Verdery describes the nation as "an aspect of the political and symbolic/ideological order and also of the world of social interaction and feeling" (37). If the nation is both political and symbolic/ideological order as well as a world of social interaction and feeling, then how might we study the connection between the two? How is the nation made part of people's social interaction and feeling? Several scholars have argued that examining the performance of nation is one way to do so.

Among the most articulate proponents of this perspective are Jon Fox and Cynthia Miller-Idriss. They write that "nations are not just the product of structural forces; they are simultaneously the practical accomplishment of ordinary people engaging in mundane activities in their everyday lives" (554). Andrew Thompson echoes this view, writing that "nations do not just exist, they are made real to the individual by the individual in the course of her/his deliberations and interactions" (24). Consumption practices, in particular, provide "important modalities for the production of national sensibilities. They provide people with occasions for establishing, upholding, and reproducing national difference in ways that follow not from elite designs but rather correspond to the contingencies of their daily lives" (553).

Fox and Miller-Idriss look at sports and holidays as two areas in which the consumption and performance of a nation takes place. These performances, the authors argue, do not always fit with the boundaries of a nation that those in power would prefer. Thompson suggests that the scant work on studying people's understandings of nation can in part account for this, as researchers rarely ask people what the nation means to them, and thus have no basis to compare it with that promoted by the state or other entities. By studying the performance of nation, it is often possible to see the boundary-making process in action.

Rogers Brubaker goes furthest of all scholars in arguing for treating nation *only* as a "category of practice" that exists in certain contexts. He argues that approaches which treat the nation as more concrete than it is miss its true nature.

> Nationalism can and should be understood without invoking "nations" as substantial entities. Instead of focusing on nations as real groups, we should focus on nationhood and nationness, on "nation" as a practical category, institutionalized form, and contingent event. "Nation" is a category of practice, not ... a category of analysis [7].

Drawing from the work of Brubaker and others, I argue that the debate about the American-ness of soccer is, at its core, a debate about the boundaries of the nation. If soccer has shed itself of residual ethnicity and come to occupy a place firmly within the mainstream, it has done so not only by changing how it is presented, but also by redefining the boundaries of the foreign and the mainstream. The mainstream is not an unmoving core separate from all around it. Instead, the mainstream is a process, a constant shifting of social boundaries to determine who and what are inside of it and who and what are outside of it.

The domestication of soccer has been a process whereby the sport has not only fit into a newly developing mainstream, but also has defined the boundaries of this new mainstream. In post–World War II suburbia, this new mainstream was defined by increased concerns with safety and a rise in the importance of the nuclear family. In what ways has soccer sought to fit into a changing mainstream? And in what ways has soccer actually shaped this changing mainstream?

This type of question is one that few scholars have taken up. Also absent is an explanation for why the dramatic growth in youth soccer in the United States has taken place over the last half-century? Why has no one asked how youth soccer, today firmly rooted the mainstream of American life, come to occupy this place? This is perhaps the case because many more scholars focus on professional soccer in the United States (see, for example, Markovits and Hellerman; Sugden; Wangerin, *Soccer in a Football World*; Wangerin, *Distant Corners*) than youth soccer. Even among the few who do study the youth game, the growth of the game and the sport's move from the ethnic margins to the mainstream has never been studied in-depth. Soccer has been used as a lens to examine racial segregation (Andrews et al.), gender norms (Messner), class differences and consumer lifestyles (Andrews; Swanson, "Soccer Fields of Cultural [Re]-Production: Creating 'Good Boys' in Suburban America"; Swanson, "Complicating the "Soccer Mom")", and the so-called "culture war" (Foer). But rarely, if ever, asked is why youth soccer has exploded in the post–World War II United States, a question I begin to answer here. The American Youth Soccer Organization sought consciously to shed the residual ethnicity attached to soccer by reframing the sport, a move that has led to the game's growth over the last half century.

The Founding of AYSO and the Domestication of American Soccer

In 1956, Bill Hughes had high hopes of establishing a youth soccer program in Los Angeles. That year, he worked to set up a youth program affiliated with the Greater Los Angeles Soccer League (GLASL), a league established in 1903 and which had long served as a social outlet for waves of immigrants settling in the city. Teams such as Los Angeles Magyar and San Pedro Croat had been a central part of ethnic communities for adults in Los Angeles, and leaders of the GLASL hoped a youth program could be set up to pass the game they loved on to their children. Hughes, a Brit who had been involved with the GLASL's Los Angeles Scots club, and other league leaders established nine teams in the first season, eight of which were affiliated with adult ethnic clubs. Hughes' team was the only one not to be organized along ethnic lines.

Hope for the youth program quickly turned to disappointment. The ethnic-based teams in particular struggled to stay together. Bringing in the children of a single ethnic community proved a problem as players were forced to travel many miles for practices and games, a task made difficult by the rapid growth of Los Angeles at the time, including a steep rise in traffic. Teams also struggled to stay together because they stockpiled players from a single ethnic group, which led to rosters containing over twenty players in some cases, leading some children who were given few opportunities to play to lose interest.

Four teams disbanded after the first season, leaving only five in the league. At a meeting of the GLASL leadership, Bill Hughes made a series of proposals that he felt could improve the situation, including limiting distances to be traveled and capping rosters at fifteen, but his ideas were voted down. The leaders decided to play a further six weeks, a final hurrah before the league would disband. One year after the hopeful meeting between Bill Hughes and the GLASL leadership, the youth program was dead.

The Greater Los Angeles Soccer League continued without a youth program for the next seven years until then–GLASL president Duncan Duff approached Bill Hughes to try again. But Hughes was wary, concerned that the same issues that had doomed the previous attempt would resurface. In spite of his concerns, Hughes attended a meeting with the GLASL leaders in 1964. At that meeting, Hughes was introduced to four other men who had an interest in establishing a youth soccer program: Hans Stierle, Ted McClean, Ralph Acosta and Steve Erdos. These men talked and decided that they did want to move forward with starting a youth league. But they agreed that doing so under the GLASL umbrella was likely to lead to similar problems as had occurred nearly ten years earlier. Instead, they decided to form their own youth soccer program, independent from GLASL or any other ethnic league. They settled on a name: the American Youth Soccer Organization.

The goals that Bill Hughes, Hans Stierle, Ted McClean, Ralph Acosta and Steve Erdos had in creating AYSO in 1964 were very different from those involved with the ethnic leagues. While for those in ethnic communities, soccer was about providing a connection to fellow immigrants and to their homelands, from the beginning AYSO was focused on growing the popularity of the game in Los Angeles and throughout the United States.

As Clay Berling, longtime editor of *Soccer America*, puts it, "The ethnic groups were concerned with having a team that won championships. That was what they grew up with" (Berling). In contrast, "The AYSO contingent had an entrepreneurial spirit that the ethnic groups didn't have." Former

AYSO executive director Tim Thompson has gone further, describing the organization as having a "religious zeal" (McLeod). Like an evangelical church, the non-profit AYSO was run by leaders who saw it as their mission to convert others to this new game of soccer.

Domestication Number One: Making Soccer American

In order to grow soccer, AYSO's leaders believed, they had to change the sport's image. They were very much aware of the perception of soccer as a foreign game and were determined to change this. If the game were to increase in popularity, they determined, it would have to appeal not only to those in ethnic communities, but to a broader public. Soccer would have to be "made American."

One of the ways that AYSO sought to carry out this first domestication was by having the organization remain independent from any existing United States Soccer Football Association (USSFA) league or team, all of which at that time in Los Angeles were run by and for ethnic communities. Joe Bonchonsky, whose sons played in the first ever AYSO game and whose extensive later work with the organization would see him elected to the AYSO Hall of Fame, sums up the founding of the organization as follows: "AYSO started at the request of a [USSFA] organization. Bill Hughes had tried it before under their direction and failed because it had been too ethnic-oriented. So he said, 'we'll start but not in an affiliated manner. We'll be independent completely'" (Bonchonsky).

The structure that the ethnic leagues like the GLASL had created was, in the eyes of AYSO leaders, a barrier to the growth of soccer. These leaders were explicit in seeing the ethnic nature of soccer as a problem, and used the language of national boundaries to lodge their complaints. In a letter published in *Soccer America* in 1973, Bill Hughes described the problem, as he identified it, in his typically energetic fashion: "Practically all soccer teams formed between 1860 and 1960 were given *foreign* titled [sic], thereby giving support to the myth that soccer is a foreign sport!!!" (Hughes).

One of the earliest policies that AYSO put in place to Americanize soccer was in direct response to this situation. "As a co-founder of AYSO," Hughes continued, "it was one of my suggestions that *foreign-sounding* names be banned for the good of soccer." And so it was that when two teams took the field in the first ever AYSO game in February 1965, they were not called the Magyars or the Macabees, but instead the Bulldogs and the Hornets. Bill

Hughes and the other AYSO founders went further in Americanizing the sport. An early draft of the AYSO rules said, "The use of a language other than English by a coach, official or participant during AYSO competition or activity shall not be permitted" (it is unclear whether this rule ever actually went into effect).

When nominated to be the organization's first president, Hughes refused, arguing that he, as a foreigner, would not be the right face to put on an organization attempting to Americanize the sport of soccer. Instead, the founders chose Hans Stierle, the only American-born individual among them. Stierle was as adamant as Hughes about the need to Americanize soccer in order to grow the sport, writing in a 1968 report to the AYSO board: "Too many good sports — from Europe — have been relegated to second class status or oblivion." The founders and early leaders of AYSO, in an extremely overt and explicit way, saw the foreignness of soccer as a problem to be overcome. They did not tip-toe around the issue; they attacked it head-on. A radio spot that AYSO ran in 1969 said, "Soccer is fun — but soccer American style is more fun."

But making AYSO independent from the ethnically-oriented USSFA, prohibiting the use of foreign-sounding names, forcing the use of English, and choosing the American-born Hans Stierle to be the face of the organization was not sufficient for youth soccer to grow. This first domestication — making soccer American — depended on two other domestications, making the sport safe and connecting it to the nuclear family.

Domestication #2: Making Soccer Safe

If the first domestication dealt explicitly with national boundaries, the second and third domestications did so more subtly. While promoting soccer as a safe sport and connecting it to the family did not necessarily imply a shifting of national boundaries, this did move soccer out of the realm of the foreign and into the newly developing mainstream.

A 1972 article in *Soccer America* by Norm Nielsen (who later head up CalSouth, the youth wing of the USSFA and, at least initially, a rival youth soccer organization) summed up the popular perception of the sport:

> There seems to be little question about it: soccer is a violent sport, which is capable of seducing a common, ordinary peaceful citizen into bouts of hysterical frenzy and mob mayhem. Or is this just the image presented most often by the media to the American public?
> Item: Picture in the *Los Angeles Times*, October 18: Enraged fans chasing an Italian soccer player who scored the winning goal against their team; one fan appears to be biting the player on the arm, while another is swinging a chair at

his head. The referee appears to be lying on his knees, battered and bruised, in the background.

Item: Lead article, font page, *L.A. Times*, October 24: Title: "Kill the ref (umpire) — and Israeli fans mean it!" The article, in great and excruciating details, goes on for 40 column inches about the violence and destruction perpetrated by players and, particularly, fans in Israeli soccer [Nielsen].

Soccer had an image problem to overcome. To change the perception of soccer as a dangerous and violent sport, AYSO leaders began a concerted effort to promote youth soccer as a safe sport on two levels: the physical and emotional. Soccer would no longer be the sport of rioting mobs in Europe, but instead the sport that children could safely play on a Saturday morning in a supportive environment.

In its promotional materials and quotes given to the media, AYSO leaders emphasized that soccer was a safe sport. A 1968 AYSO fact sheet trumpeted the fact that "in the four years of existence the most serious injury reported and recorded was one (1) broken ankle." AYSO also emphasized that physical size was not an obstacle to participation in soccer. A 1970 article in the Los Angeles area *Daily Breeze* newspaper, headlined "Small Size is No Handicap in Soccer" quoted thirteen year-old Tom Basen, a short but talented forward for the Torrance Bruins AYSO team, saying, "that's why soccer is so cool. You can be small and still be good." Although quotes such as these only sometimes mentioned other sports directly, the contrast between soccer and other sports— football and basketball especially — that require physical size to be successful, and to be safe while playing, was clear.

If soccer was promoted as a safe alternative to other sports, it was also promoted as the ideal sport for physical fitness. As Pierre Bourdieu has written extensively, attitudes about the body and physical fitness vary tremendously based on class position: "It can easily be shown that the different classes do not agree on the profits expected from sport, be they specific physical profits, such as effects on the external body, like slimness, elegance or visible muscles, and on the internal body, like health or relaxation" (Bourdieu 211). Bourdieu writes that sports preferred by the working classes "demand a high investment of energy, effort or even pain (e.g., boxing) and ... sometimes endanger the body itself (e.g., motor cycling, parachute jumping, acrobatics, and, to some extent, all the 'contact sports')" while those in the middle classes choose sports that "cultivate the body" in what he calls a "cult of health" (Bourdieu 213). At a time in the United States which saw the rise of the suburban middle classes, it is perhaps not surprising that the sport this growing group of people signed their children up for was one which promised to cultivate the health of the body.

Safety, then, was not just about staying away from potential injury but also in maintaining physical fitness in a safe and healthy way. A 1966 promo poster for AYSO said, "Soccer's demands are agility, quickness and balance, and a good deal of running skill which is as important to soccer as skating ability is to hockey. The other needs come gradually as the game is being learned ... endurance and teamplay. Playing soccer is tantamount to being 'in shape.'" The contrast to other sports, though unspoken, was apparent throughout the promotion of AYSO in the early years: football can lead to injuries while baseball does not provide the physical fitness of soccer.

In addition to promoting soccer as a physically safe activity, AYSO leaders also structured their organization in a way that prioritized emotional safety. Many of the regulations that AYSO put in place (they called them their "philosophies") were both reactions to what Bill Hughes, Hans Stierle and the other founders saw as the problems of soccer in ethnic communities and an attempt to promote soccer as an activity that was emotionally safe for children. The idea of "open registration," for instance, allowing anyone who wanted to play to do so, was a response to the organization of ethnic clubs, which often excluded those not from that ethnic community. The philosophy of "balanced teams" was a response to what the founders saw as an overemphasis on winning to promote ethnic pride. And the idea that "everyone plays" in every game was intended to differentiate AYSO from other youth soccer organizations (recall Bill Hughes' experiment with the Greater Los Angeles Soccer League in which teams often had twenty or more players on their rosters).

These AYSO philosophies were a key part of redefining soccer as a safe sport, something different from other iterations of soccer that had existed in the United States and in other countries. The AYSO leaders were clearly onto something when they sought to reframe the sport as safe. As Joe Bonchonsky puts it, "There were a lot of good rules introduced by AYSO that were not of the old, affiliated school. That was important to our growth" (Bonchonsky).

But it was not just that AYSO identified a new ethic of safety within society and defined soccer to fit within this ethic. Instead, AYSO actually helped to create this ethic. If, as Michael Messner puts it, "youth sports are, among other things, an organized response to a culture of fear for our children's safety" (194), then AYSO did not just respond to this fear and create an organized activity to counter it but instead actually played a role in promoting creating the ethic of safety. But this was not enough to see the growth that AYSO and youth soccer in general experienced. A third domestication — bringing soccer within the domestic realm — was also necessary.

Domestication #3: Making Soccer Part of the Family

In his classic book *Crabgrass Frontier: The Suburbanization of American Life*, historian Kenneth Jackson argues that the rise of the suburbs saw the "privatization of social life" (272). The growth of suburban developments, he claims, led to the break-down of social life, once focused on neighborhoods but which would later come to be centered largely around the nuclear family. As people moved to the suburbs, without an existing structure in these new neighborhoods (or, indeed, many other types of social organizations), parents stepped into the void, playing a large role in shaping the activities that their children would take up. Instead of simply shooing their kids out the door to play this new game, many parents themselves played a central role in the activities they took up. For many parents in the newly booming suburbs of the Los Angeles area, soccer was the sport of choice for their children.

The geography of the suburbs necessitated parental involvement. With suburban developments spread over vast distances, children could not walk out their doors to play AYSO soccer. Suburbanization meant that parents had to drive their children to practices and games. But parents' involvement went well beyond chauffeuring. From the beginning, parents were recruited as volunteers for AYSO. A 1969 *Los Angeles Times* article described the situation: "[AYSO] depends on volunteers for its coaches and officials and is constantly seeking manpower. Coaches have been known to put their own team through a game, then go out and referee two or three more" ("Youth Soccer League Accents Participation"). Fathers served as coaches, referees, and administrators; mothers quickly became "team moms," providing orange slices at halftime and moral support throughout the game.

Many newspaper articles in the late 1960s and early 1970s quotes parents who claimed to have devoted all free time to their children's soccer practices and games. A 1971 article in *The Tidings*, a Catholic newspaper in Los Angeles, quoted a beleaguered father named Tom Donahue, who had become an AYSO coach for his son's team, the Eagles. "I love soccer, but it's ruined my golf game," exclaimed Donahue. "I haven't played a round in two years!" ("Soccer Comes Before Golf?"). In case it was not clear why Donahue's golf game had suffered, the newspaper clarified: "The Eagles eat up his spare time."

Mothers whose children played AYSO were not immune from the loss of free time. Sue Browder wrote in a 1970 article in the *Daily Breeze*:

> If the traditional song of baseball fans were rewritten to go, "Take me out to the soccer game," South Bay soccer players' mothers would have a theme song. In

fact, they already know the lyrics by heart, including the part about "I don't care if I ever get back" [Browder].

If fathers and mothers joked to newspaper reporters about losing free time for their own activities, it is also clear in their words that they loved being involved in their children's activities. A 1974 *Soccer America* article headlined "Kick It, Mommy, Kick It!" showed mothers, huge smiles plastered on their faces, trying out soccer for themselves. AYSO promoted this idea that soccer was an activity that was fun for the entire family. A 1966 poster for an AYSO "Soccer Jamboree" urged people to "bring the whole family."

In this way, soccer was moved into the domestic realm of the family. AYSO, conscious that soccer was seen as a violent, male-dominated sport (recall the *Los Angeles Times* articles about rioting fans in Italy and Israel), brought the sport into the domestic realm, a move to reframe the sport, making it seem safer to those who might take it up. Placed safely within the realm of the ever more important nuclear family, soccer was reframed for a growing suburban public in Los Angeles.

Conclusion

The three domestications laid out here are intricately related. Indeed, the residual ethnicity was stripped from soccer and it was "made American" (domestication number one) by reframing it as a safe sport (domestication number two) strongly connected to the domestic realm (domestication number three). Soccer was long perceived as a foreign game, not only because foreigners and immigrants were the main people involved with it (though this was important), but also because it was perceived as an unsafe game whose players, coaches, fans, and officials existed outside of the domestic realm. Before the youth soccer boom, violence at games was one of the ways in which soccer most often appeared in newspaper coverage. And this violence, unsafe by definition, carried out on fields far removed from the trappings of the domestic realm, led many to see the entire sport of soccer as foreign. The idea of the foreign, then, is a comment on national boundaries, but also a comment on two values: that of safety, physical and emotional, and that of the nuclear family.

AYSO leaders, whether they recognized it or not, clearly identified the rising importance of safety and the family in the post–World War II period. But they did more than this: they played a central role in the promotion of these values. AYSO did not just draw from the value of safety and the value of the nuclear family but instead made these into central values of the post–World War II suburban landscape in Southern California.

The leaders of AYSO started out with an obvious goal: to grow youth soccer in the United States. In so doing, they also ended up promoting a set of values. This fits with the work of David Graeber, who writes, "In working towards obvious goals, people also set up relations with other people and shape themselves" (64). Or, as Nancy Munn puts it, "Agents not only engage in action but are also 'acted upon' by the action" (14). By Americanizing soccer through making it safe and connecting it to the domestic realm, AYSO leaders, parents, and others involved with youth soccer came to hold these values themselves and promote them to others. AYSO did not just fit into this newly emerging mainstream, it also helped to the boundaries of the post–World War II suburban mainstream.

At the same time as this domestication brought soccer to the masses, it also excluded some who disagreed with the way AYSO was run. In particular, immigrants often saw the changes that AYSO put in place as an affront to the sport they loved, and they left to form their own leagues. If the process of domestication was necessary to grow soccer in the United States, it also left some out of the redefined sport.

Not all were enthused by what AYSO was doing. Soccer officials in the ethnic communities were particularly unimpressed. Adolfo Miralles, a native of Argentina, had enrolled a team in AYSO in 1967. But he and a group of mostly foreign-born coaches became dismayed with AYSO's attempt to Americanize the game, in particular with some of the rule changes. As Miralles put it, they "wanted to play by FIFA rules, not AYSO rules." He continued: "We thought it would be good to be part of world soccer instead of just being part of AYSO." For these coaches, it was more important to be part of the world's game than it was to see the game Americanized in order to raise its profile in the United States.

So Miralles and a small group of disaffected coaches met and decided to form their own league, which they launched in 1968. Called the Golden State Soccer League (GSSL), the new organization was affiliated with the USSFA and included many teams from ethnic communities put off by the changes AYSO had made. The experiences of Miralles and other early founders of the GSSL were not uncommon, as AYSO often met resistance when attempting to expand into ethnic communities. As Ric Fonseca, longtime soccer observer and former professor of history at Los Angeles City College, says, "AYSO tried to but was not successful in getting into the Latino community because of the philosophy that everyone plays." In particular, he said, Latinos were "more used to idea that you put a good team together and they stay together."

Despite the fact that some were put off by the Americanization promoted by AYSO, the organization grew quickly. From nine teams in the first season in 1965, it had over 200 by 1970. By the mid–1970s, ten years after its founding, AYSO had nearly 2,000 teams and over 25,000 players. Despite grumbling from some in the ethnic communities, AYSO quickly became the most prominent youth soccer association in Southern California.

Why did AYSO take off in Los Angeles in the 1960s and 1970s? Why did it start there and not in other parts of the country? And why did the rise of AYSO take place at this time period and not earlier or later? If AYSO succeeded in domesticating soccer, who were the people in Los Angeles who were open to this new sport?

Though difficult to imagine now, the growth of Los Angeles is a relatively recent development. Arthur Verge writes that "the city known today as the 'freeway capital of the world' did not have a single mile of freeway in 1939" (Verge 291). Verge argues that World War II was the catalyst for much of this change: "The Second World War's impact on Los Angeles proved to be nothing short of a social and industrial revolution" (290). Defense spending during the War turned the city from a "distant western outpost, isolated and separated by 3,000 miles from the nation's industrialized East" into "an industrial giant" (290). Defense spending continued beyond the end of the World War II, with the aircraft industry booming as the government sought to maintain its defenses in the Cold War. This, combined with a rapidly expanding entertainment industry, would see the city expand with incredible speed.

This growth saw the arrival of many newcomers, both from other parts of the United States as well as from around the world. And it is this mix that led to the growth of soccer. Specifically, the immigrants who had come from other countries to settle in Los Angeles brought knowledge of soccer with them. But this was not enough to see the game grow beyond ethnic communities, as countless examples throughout time in cities across the United States had shown. In order for the game to move beyond the ethnic communities of Los Angeles, an openness to new games was required. And Los Angeles had this openness in spades, as journalist Carey McWilliams put it in 1946. "Southern California is a great laboratory of experimentation.... It is a great tribal burial ground for antique customs and incongruous styles" (369).

AYSO pioneer Joe Bonchonsky says that many of the parents who signed their kids up for AYSO in the early years were these new arrivals from other parts of the United States. Having recently come to this new city, they looked around and said, "What do we do here?" When they heard about AYSO, from word of mouth, in flyers sent home in their children's backpacks, and in signs posted around their newly developed suburbs, they were open to trying out the new sport. With AYSO having created a newly domesticated version of soccer and new arrivals open to signing their kids up for a game that they didn't associate with ethnic otherness, the sport could grow, and grow it did.

Youth soccer ultimately "made it" into the mainstream by remaking the boundaries of the mainstream. As AYSO founders sought to strip the residual ethnicity from the game, they promoted soccer as a safe game connected to the family. In so doing, they stripped associations with foreignness from soccer, allowing it to be reframed as a sport central to the daily life of the growing suburban middle in post–World War II Southern California. The domestication of soccer — making the sport American by making it safe and connected to the domestic realm of the family — in the United States goes a long way to explaining the phenomenal growth of the sport over the last half century.

Works Cited

Alonso, Ana Maria. "The Politics of Space, Time and Substance: State Formation, Nationalism, and Ethnicity." *Annual Review of Anthropology* 23.1 (1994): 379–405. Web. 19 Oct. 2010.
Anderson, Benedict. *Imagined Communities: Reflections on the Origin and Spread of Nationalism*. London: Verso, 1991. Print.
Andrews, David. "Contextualizing Suburban Soccer: Consumer Culture, Lifestyle Differentiation and Suburban America." *Sport in Society* 2.3 (1999): 31–53. Print.
Andrews, David, et al. "Soccer's Racial Frontier: Sport and the Suburbanization of Contemporary America." *Entering the Field: New Perspectives on World Football*. Ed. Gary Armstrong and Richard Giulianotti. Oxford: Berg, 1997. 261–282. Print.
Berling, Clayton. Interview with Clayton Berling. 17 Apr. 2012.
Bonchonsky, Joseph. Interview with Joseph Bonchonsky. 20 Mar. 2012.
Bourdieu, Pierre. *Distinction: A Social Critique of the Judgement of Taste*. Trans. Richard Nice. Cambridge: Harvard University Press, 1984. Print.
Browder, Sue. "Their Kicks Are in the Stands." *Daily Breeze* 22 Jan. 1970 : np. Print.
Brubaker, Rogers. *Nationalism Reframed: Nationhood and the National Question in the New Europe*. Cambridge: Cambridge University Press, 1996. Print.
Foer, Franklin. *How Soccer Explains the World: An Unlikely Theory of Globalization*. New York: HarperCollins, 2005. Print.
Fox, Jon E., and Cynthia Miller-Idriss. "Everyday Nationhood." *Ethnicities* 8.4 (2008): 536–563. Web. 14 Mar. 2011.
Graeber, David. *Toward an Anthropological Theory of Value: The False Coin of Our Own Dreams*, 1st ed. New York: Palgrave Macmillan, 2001. Print.
Grey, M. A. "Sport and Immigrant, Minority and Anglo Relations in Garden City (Kansas) High School." *Sociology of Sport Journal* 9.3 (1992): 255–270. Print.
Hughes, Bill. "Letter to the Editor." *Soccer America* 26 Feb. 1973: 17. Print.
Jackson, Kenneth T. *Crabgrass Frontier: The Suburbanization of the United States*. New York: Oxford University Press, 1987. Print.
Markovits, Andrei S., and Steven L. Hellerman. *Offside: Soccer and American Exceptionalism*. Princeton: Princeton University Press, 2001. Print.
McLeod, Paul. "AYSO Nears 25 Years Building Youth Soccer." *Los Angeles Times* 2 Oct. 1988. Web. 5 Nov. 2012.

McWilliams, Carey. *Southern California: An Island on the Land*, 9th ed. Layton, UT: Gibbs Smith, 1946. Print.
Messner, Michael A. *It's All for the Kids: Gender, Families, and Youth Sports.* 1st ed. Berkeley: University of California Press, 2009. Print.
Munn, Nancy D. *The Fame of Gawa: A Symbolic Study of Value Transformation in a Massim Society*. Durham: Duke University Press, 1992. Print.
Nielsen, Norm. "Violence: The 'Mystique' of Soccer?" *Soccer America* 31 Oct. 1972: 14. Print.
SGMA. *Single Sport Report—2011 Soccer (Outdoor)*. Silver Spring, MD: Sporting Goods Manufacturing Association, 2011. Print.
"Soccer Comes Before Golf?" *The Tidings* 7 Apr. 1971: np. Print.
Sugden, John. "USA and the World Cup: American Nativism and Rejection of the People's Game." *Hosts and Champions: Soccer Cultures, National Identities and the USA World Cup*. Ed. John Sugden and Alan Tomlinson. Brookfield, VT: Ashgate, 1994. 219–252. Print.
Swanson, Lisa. "Complicating the 'Soccer Mom': The Cultural Politics of Forming Class-Based Identity, Distinction, and Necessity." *Research Quarterly for Exercise and Sport* 80 (2009): 345–354. Print.
_____. "Soccer Fields of Cultural [Re-]Production: Creating 'Good Boys' in Suburban America." *Sociology of Sport Journal* 26.3 (2009): 404–424. Print.
Thompson, Andrew. "Nations, National Identities and Human Agency: Putting People Back into Nations." *The Sociological Review* 49.1 (2001): 18–32. Print.
Trouille, David. "Association Football to Fútbol: Ethnic Succession and the History of Chicago-area Soccer Since 1920." *Soccer & Society* 10.6 (2009): 795 — 822. Print.
Verdery, Katherine. "Whither 'Nation' and 'Nationalism'?" *Daedalus* 122.3 (1993): 37–46. Print.
Verge, Arthur C. "The Impact of the Second World War on Los Angeles." *Pacific Historical Review* 63.3 (1994): 289–314. Print.
Wangerin, David. *Distant Corners: American Soccer's History of Missed Opportunities and Lost Causes*. Philadelphia: Temple University Press, 2011. Print.
_____. *Soccer in a Football World: The Story of America's Forgotten Game*. London: WSC Books, 2006. Print.
Williams, Raymond. *Marxism and Literature*. Oxford: Oxford University Press, 1977. Print.
"Youth Soccer League Accents Participation." *Los Angeles Times (1923–Current File)* 14 Sept. 1969: sg_b8. Print.
Zirin, Dave. "Glenn Beck's Blues: Why the Far Right Hates the World Cup." *The Nation* 13 June 2010. Web. 25 Oct. 2010.

2

Individualism vs. Community

The Globally Strange Relationship Between the U.S. Soccer System and the U.S. School System

ANDREW M. GUEST

When the captains of the U.S. and the English national teams shook hands before the kick-off of their group-stage match at the 2010 World Cup in South Africa, the men represented the pinnacle of soccer in each country. Both were established professionals in top European leagues with long records of success playing for club and country. But the English captain that day, Steven Gerrard, had reached the top of his country's soccer pyramid in a globally familiar way: by devoting virtually his entire life to being a professional soccer player. Gerrard joined a Liverpool FC youth academy team at age 9, spent years as a professional trainee, and officially signed his first professional contract (again with Liverpool) at age 17. Reflecting on his youth, Gerrard himself was blunt in an interview with Liverpool FC's media published at *lfchistory.net*: "Football was more important to me than school." His U.S. counterpart at the World Cup, Carlos Bocanegra, had a much more circuitous — and peculiarly American — path to the game's biggest stage. At the same age when Gerrard signed his first professional contract, Bocanegra was finishing four years of high school where he had been on three different varsity sports teams: soccer, American football, and track and field. He would spend the next three years playing soccer and studying for a history degree at one of America's top public universities, the University of California at Los Angeles. Sports may well also have been more important than school to Bocanegra personally — but the cultural oddity that is American soccer has historically made such distinctions blurry at the community level. The U.S. soccer system has long been intertwined with the U.S. school system in a globally strange way that is best understood as being more about American identity than it is about soccer itself.

The intertwining of soccer and schools in the U.S. is evident across the soccer spectrum: it is embodied by U.S. World Cup teams, and is simultaneously enacted in thousands of neighborhoods across the nation. At the World Cup level, the U.S. starting team on that 2010 day in South Africa included seven players with university-level education: almost certainly the most of any starting team at the 2010 World Cup. In fact, the only competitive international soccer team likely to have more combined years of education than the U.S. men's team is the U.S. women's team. Every single one of the starting players on the gold medal winning U.S. women's team at the 2012 London Olympics had attended four years of university — many at some of the best universities in the world such as Stanford, Notre Dame, and University of California at Berkeley. Further, virtually all of those players (on both the men's and women's sides) played for one of the 11,000 plus high schools across all fifty U.S. states that offer boys and/or girls soccer as a competitive interscholastic sport — a number that has been growing consistently for decades according to participation numbers reported by the National Federation of State High School Associations. Curiously, however, high school soccer in the United States is not about producing international class players; the best U.S. players always also play for elite club teams outside of school, and when they do play in high school it is more for the social experience than the soccer experience. But the simple fact that so many do play soccer at schools raises interesting questions about the American system.

The underlying philosophy of American schools has long held that whether a child is destined to be a business executive, a pipe fitter, a nurse, a soldier, or a World Cup player, he or she should be prepared broadly for both individual opportunities and social responsibilities. The way that philosophy is enacted is often deeply flawed, unequal, and contested, but in concept the U.S. school system is premised on balancing meritocracy and community. American schools promote for individuals the idea that anything is possible with hard work and dedication — that every child should be given every opportunity to cultivate their talents and to achieve their dreams — while simultaneously promoting the idea of America as a melting pot — offering shared socialization experiences to a diverse populace and serving as a hub for community interaction and identity. Much of the globally strange positioning of soccer in the United States can be understood as a byproduct of that broader philosophy.

From this perspective, it is useful to think of the peculiar intertwining of the U.S. soccer system and the U.S. school system as related to broader American tensions between individualism and democracy. Of course, formal analyses of these tensions, starting famously with Alexis de Tocqueville and continuing in much contemporary social science, rarely have anything to say about soccer in particular. Yet, sport and leisure more generally do offer useful sites for investigation. In his well-known 1995 essay and 2000 book *Bowling Alone*, for example, sociologist Robert Putnam took his title from the fact that "between 1980 and 1993 the total number of bowlers in America increased by 10 percent, while league bowling decreased by 40 percent" (70). Putnam saw this shift towards more solitary leisure pursuits as a sign of significant concern for the balance of individualism and community in the U.S. At least one response to Putnam, however, argued that mass participation in youth soccer leagues could be thought of as an evolving substitute for the communal function of bowling leagues: Nicholas Lemann titled his essay in *The Atlantic Monthly* "Kicking in Groups," taking heart in the fact that U.S. Youth Soccer "has 2.4 million members, up from 1.2 million ten years ago and from 127,000 twenty years ago" (25).

While the rest of Lemann's essay is not really about soccer — focusing more broadly on how social science conceptualizes the changing dynamics of social capital in American society — the present chapter will specifically consider the U.S. soccer system and its globally peculiar relationship with the U.S. school system as related to broader American ideologies and experiences. The first part offers a brief social history of sports in American schools, with particular attention to the relatively recent integration of soccer in an era of increasing globalization. The second part examines recent attempts to disentwine elite youth soccer from the school system, and the ensuing controversy from a requirement that elite players *not* play for high school teams. The third part draws on field research on youth development and sports in two distinct high schools to consider how two particular youth players experience the American soccer system. In the end, the essay will argue that each of these topics illustrates ways the peculiarities of soccer in the U.S. are explained by (and simultaneously help to explain) Americans underlying belief in sport as a space to balance the sometimes conflicting values of individualism and community.

Soccer vs. Schools: A Brief History of Sports in American Education

In his sociological overview of sports in American schools, Jay Coakley notes that "the United States is the only nation in the world where it is taken for granted that high schools and colleges sponsor and fund interschool or varsity sports programs" (472). Though there have long been parallel community-based sport systems in the U.S. with large numbers of participants, school sports have traditionally held sway in the popular imagination and in community life. Soccer, however, has been a relative latecomer to the American school sports tradition. Though a few schools and universities have had versions of soccer programs since the origins of formal school sports in the late nineteenth century, school soccer only became relatively mainstream in the last forty years. Nevertheless, its recent popularity is undergirded by much of the same social history as other games and activities.

Most accounts of the globally distinct school sports system in the U.S. start with the growth of university level sports in the late 1800s and early 1900s. Andrei Markovits and Steven Hellerman, in their book *Offside: Soccer & American Exceptionalism*, argue that the broad popularity of sports at colleges and universities came down to the distinct social role of universities in American culture:

> On the European continent, sports never entered the realm of the universities, since these were seen as research institutions, training grounds for state bureaucrats, or domains of the church. In all three cases, they remained strictly in the realm of the mind and had little, if any, tolerance for pursuits of the body. In England, Oxbridge did in fact engage in organized and competitive sports as part of its students' educational ethos. But this engagement remained confined to amateur, extracurricular, and purely a vocational pursuits, never leaving the realm of the gentlemanly. Not so in the United States. By dint of this country's meritocratic ethos and the proliferation of its institutions of higher learning — itself a consequence of this meritocratic ethos — sports became an integral part of university life and thus of public identity [43].

This "meritocratic ethos" also helps explain other contributing forces to the inclusion of school sports in early twentieth century American education such as the "high school movement," which vastly expanded access to secondary education,[1] and the "progressive education movement," which put an emphasis on educating the whole person — body and mind — through experiences both in and out of the classroom. Primary and secondary schools were also managing a large influx of immigrants, and public education took on an assimilative function that coincided with the growing popularity of sports as a tool for the positive socialization of youth. In fact, the first major interscholastic athletic league for primary and secondary schools in the U.S., the Public Schools Athletic League (PSAL) in New York City, was directed by Luther Gulick — who had been an influential early figure in the Young Men's Christian Association (YMCA) and a prominent American promoter of "muscular Christianity." In pursuing its mission to socialize and assimilate, according to Elliott

J. Gorn and Warren Goldstein, "the PSAL explicitly stressed the values of 'Duty,' 'Thoroughness,' 'Patriotism,' 'Honor,' and 'Obedience'" (176). The league proved extraordinarily popular, and by 1910, 17 other major U.S. cities had created their own interscholastic athletic leagues (Farrey 107).

The association between school sports and values such as "patriotism" also extended to regionalized allegiances. Markovits and Hellerman argue that school teams — particularly at the university level — offered a sense of imagined community within a diverse nation:

> Being a Sooners fan in Oklahoma, a Huskers fan in Nebraska, a Longhorns fan in Texas, a Wildcats fan in Kentucky, or a Wolverines fan in Michigan has been every bit the iconographic, spiritual, and affective equivalent to being an Arsenal supporter in North London, a Rangers fan in Glasgow, a Rapid supporter in the Hütteldorf district of Vienna, and a Barca fan in Barcelona. As in the case of major European soccer clubs with their clear identities, milieus, and networks, the football and basketball teams of American universities became essential representatives of the identity and culture of their respective regions, states, cities, and towns [43].

Of course, the contrast here between identification with American football or basketball teams and with European soccer teams highlights the distinct sporting foci of U.S. schools. For a variety of historical reasons Americans in the late 1800s and early 1900s, despite sampling from global football codes that were still in early gestation, ended up developing their own version of football and marginalizing soccer as an immigrant's game. Markovits and Hellerman do note, however, that school soccer has always been around in some form (sometimes played by schools as an alternative when American football was perceived as too rough). But soccer really only caught hold at the university level with the broader expansion of American higher education and college sports after World War II. Markovits and Hellerman found that where 86 colleges had varsity soccer programs in 1946, nearly 1,000 had varsity soccer by 1978 (123). That pattern quickly filtered down to the growth of soccer at the high school level.

Between 1972 and 2012 the estimated number of high school soccer players in the United States grew nearly tenfold: from 79,210 to 730,106 (National Federation of State High School Associations). The most dramatic portion of that growth came on the girls' side. In 1972 the National Federation of State High School Associations documented 700 girls playing high school soccer at 28 schools; in 2012 that number had increased to 370,975 girls at 11,127 schools. Not coincidentally, 1972 is the year Title IX was included as part of the Education Amendments to the 1964 Civil Rights Act, mandating that: "No person in the United States shall, on the basis of sex, be excluded from participation in, be denied the benefits of, or be subjected to discrimination under any educational program or activity receiving financial assistance." The original intention of Title IX had little to do with sports, but the particular history of sports being so closely linked with American education made school sports — primarily those at the high school and collegiate level — an important symbolic site for the application of Title IX. This application has associated with a massive increase in all types of high school sports participation by girls, from just under 300,000 participants in the 1971-1972 school year to over 3,200,000 in the 2011-2012 school year (National Federation of State High School Associations).

In specific regard to soccer, it is worth noting that the significant increase in girls participation in American high schools associated with Title IX — while potentially distinct globally in ensuring participation opportunities — has also corresponded with an increase in boys' high school soccer that is nearly as dramatic: during the 1971-1972 school year there were almost 80,000 boys playing soccer at 2,290 American high schools; during the 2011-2012 school year there were over 410,000 boys playing soccer at 11,600 high schools. In other words, forces well beyond Title IX have combined to increase the popularity of soccer in American schools.[2]

One such force is the popularity of soccer in relatively wealthy suburban communities where school sports offer social status and social capital. As Lisa Swanson described in an ethnographic study of suburban "soccer moms," upper-middle class American parents often devote much time and energy towards soccer "to produce cultural capital in and through their sons. As a result, these well-respected, skillful, team-oriented soccer players could then effectively gain what the mothers believed to be necessary social capital, that is, placement on the high school team" (412). In other words, for a portion of American soccer players, playing school soccer is the ultimate goal — in the same way as a professional contract might be the goal for a South American, African, or European youth.

At the same time, however, globalization and immigration have also meant that American schools still serve an assimilative function. But unlike the period of high school expansion in the first half of the twentieth century, when schools focused primarily on "Americanizing" immigrants, recent efforts at integration involve more complex tensions between assimilation and respect for diversity. In this context, school soccer can serve an important mediating function: immigrant children can play a game they know and love from their birthplace, while also engaging in the distinctly American ritual of school sports. One recent journalistic book on a successful American high school team comprised largely of Hispanic immigrants, *The Boys from Little Mexico* by Steve Wilson, even carried the subtitle *A Season Chasing the American Dream*. Such a book would be much harder to write about an elite club team detached from the U.S. school soccer system.

Ironically, the relatively inclusive nature of a high school soccer team and its ostensibly educational mission — the very things that can make high school sports emblematic of "the American dream" — often mean that elite athletic performance is secondary. School soccer seasons are short and compartmentalized within the school year. High school teams tend to draw players with a wide range of ability levels. School coaches are often teachers or counselors rather than soccer specialists. In general, the particular history and social positioning of U.S. school soccer makes it incompatible with the increasingly globalized professional game — and has put American school soccer on a collision course with its competition.

Schools vs. Clubs: Debating Models of Youth Development

The U.S. Soccer Federation, in its role as overseer of the U.S. national team program, has long struggled to reconcile the popularity of American school sports with the efficiency of professionalized talent development. In many other parts of the world where community based professional clubs have a vested stake in developing young talent, national federations can rely on extant structures to identify the best players.[3] In the U.S. where a limited professional soccer scene has historically put little emphasis on youth programs, the talent development system has traditionally relied on a hodgepodge of schools, youth clubs, and state level select teams (as per the U.S. Youth Soccer Olympic Development Program).[4] And while the popularity of school soccer teams offers wide breadth for a talent pool, it does not offer the depth necessitated by global competition. American school sports, as described above, operate with their own history and rules which are founded on the intention (however imperfectly actuated) to integrate sports with education rather than with professionalized talent development.[5]

In 2007, the U.S. Soccer Federation, in hopes of providing more depth for a relatively narrow segment of elite youth players, organized a group of sixty-four elite youth soccer clubs in twenty-four states and the District of Columbia into a "U.S. Soccer Development Academy." The stated intention was to intensify training, scouting, and competition for the very best Under-16 and Under-18 players.[6] American professional teams in Major League Soccer (MLS), along with some lower level professional teams, soon added "academy" teams as part of the national program and the season grew to ten months to model a European professional season. While this system caused significant upheaval in the American youth soccer world, which had traditionally organized competition between youth club teams at the state level with time off for the high school season, it was not until 2012 when the program made national headlines by requiring academy club participants to *not* play high school soccer.

The ensuing controversy was both implicitly and explicitly about American identity in the context of globalization. An article by Tod Palmer in the *Kansas City Star* newspaper, for example, cited U.S. National Team coach Jürgen Klinsmann — himself raised in the German professional system — as an advocate of the exclusive ten month schedule: "This is the model that the best countries around the world use for their programs … and I think it makes perfect sense that we do, as well." Palmer then immediately juxtaposed that perspective with that of a local high school coach in Kansas City: "We [in the U.S.] are a unique culture and the whole concept of high school soccer and the concept of high school in general is very different here.... It's a very special part of a young person's development. I'm not convinced taking that away from a young player is the best thing."

In explaining their decision through responses on their website to "Frequently Asked Questions" about the 10 month academy season starting in 2012, the U.S. Soccer Federation was quite explicit about trying to adapt to global norms:

> From the start of the Academy program, our goal has been to close the gap with the top footballing nations in the world. The 10-month schedule, from September through June, or July based on postseason play, is what a typical elite soccer player's schedule looks like around the rest of the world.... We are competing in a global marketplace. We are not just trying to prepare elite players for college and the pro ranks in the United States; we are trying to prepare players to compete against the best clubs and international teams from around the world. Therefore, our standard has to be higher.

Two things are worth noting in this explanation. One is the use of the term "footballing nations" without reference to "soccer" — when the latter is not only the American convention, but is actually in the name of the USSF as an organization. Identifying as a "footballing nation" eschews the notion of American soccer as historically distinct in favor of perceived global integration (though, it is worth noting, other nations ranging from South Africa to Australia also tend to prefer the term "soccer" over "football"). Second, the explanation highlights how U.S. Soccer sees youth development as a matter of "competing in a global marketplace." In this framing youth players are not people learning a game; they are commodities being prepared for competitive exchange — which is particularly significant when elite soccer clubs in the United States have long been an expensive endeavor funded by participation fees (development academy coach Alecko Eskandarian noted in an on-line article for *Sports Illustrated* that "some non–MLS academies charge each player more than $5,000 per year, and that's without the cost of travel"). These clubs support a substantial industry of "professional" youth coaches,[7] and the newer MLS academy teams have an obvious financial interest in finding top talents.

The distinction between youth players as individuals judged by their character and education and youth players as commodities judged by their sporting talents is an embedded tension in the "schools vs. clubs" debate. In the case of the Development Academy decision to ban participants from high school soccer, the National Soccer Coaches Association of America (NSCAA) took the position opposite from U.S. Soccer by emphasizing character and education rather than athletic talent. In direct response to the U.S. Soccer Federation and the Development Academy, the NSCAA posted speaking points on its web-site that listed benefits of high school soccer including:

- Experiences & values to last a lifetime
- Family environment is incapable of being replicated by clubs and provides unparalleled camaraderie
- Individual player development as extension of the classroom/integral to education of the whole child
- High school sports [are] often the fabric of community identity & pride
- Foreign exchange students from countries lacking high school sports find American high school sports environment exhilarating
- Nations without organized high school sports are envious of American high school experience & opportunities

Though the NSCAA speaking points offer no evidence to support claims such as other nations being "envious" of the American high school system, the organization is clearly drawing on a mythology of that system focused less on the sport itself and more on a distinctively American experience (further evidenced by citing in one word "Tradition" as a benefit of high school soccer). Another high school soccer coach quoted by Tod Palmer in the *Kansas City Star* was even more explicit: "My concern [about the development academy model] is that, at the end of the day, it's going to be only about soccer.... At the high school level, the focus isn't just on soccer but also the development as a student-athlete and human being. That's where the kids will be missing out."

Part of the tension here comes down to a question of defining youth development in the context of soccer — or really in any sport. Is youth development about maximizing specialized talents, or is it about gathering experiences that serve both educational and social functions? Is the goal of the U.S. soccer system to produce the most elite players possible, or is it to give a positive experience to the most possible people? The simple geographic reality is that the 80 current Development Academy clubs reside in less than half of U.S. states, whereas the more than 11,000 high schools that offer boys soccer in the U.S. reside in every state and city in the country.

But the other part of the tension in the "schools vs. clubs" controversy is the sense that in its elite structures the U.S. soccer system is moving closer to global models of professionalized talent development and away from American "traditions" emphasizing education. At the elite level, the U.S. soccer system is actively trying to disentwine from the U.S. school system. Yet, from the time of the founding of the U.S. Soccer Development Academy in 2007 to 2012 — when the high school ban was imposed — the number of boys and girls playing soccer in American high schools still went up from 715,631 to 782,732 (National Federation of State High School Associations). Statistics such as these suggest that at the broader societal level, it may be harder to disentwine the U.S. soccer system from the U.S. school system than any decontextualized analysis would assume. It may be that American soccer players still appreciate ways the U.S. soccer system allows them to meld their individual talents with broader community traditions.

Professional vs. Fun: Individual and Communal Experiences of High School Soccer

So do American soccer players actually appreciate the peculiarities of the U.S. soccer system? I had a chance to think through some such questions during the 2008–2009 school year through a mixed-methods research project undertaken in two distinct high school communities. The project was oriented by broader questions about the role of extracurricular activities ranging from community service and arts activities to sports teams towards youth development in different community contexts. For reasons of personal interest, one particular point of inquiry was with soccer teams — including observing and documenting a full season with a girls' soccer team at each of the two schools, and undertaking intensive case studies with a representative player on each team. Though these teams and players did not necessarily have explicit perspectives on soccer as a global game, many of the tensions in the U.S. soccer system were implicit in their experiences.

The first thing abundantly evident from spending a season at two distinct high schools and talking in-depth with two very different players is that high school soccer is not just one thing. The schools were both Catholic high schools in a large metropolitan area in the western United States, but they were intentionally chosen to learn about the role that social class plays in adolescents' developmental and educational experiences. So where one school was a reasonably large suburban school (here called SHS) serving a relatively homogenous upper-middle class community, the other was a smaller and more diverse urban school (here called UHS) with a mission of serving students from lower income families who might not otherwise have access to a college preparatory education. Both were good schools where the staff and families generally worked hard to ensure their children reached their potential — but as with so much of the American education system, the resources and opportunities available towards those ends differed dramatically.

The differences in resources meant that players on the soccer teams at each school sometimes seemed to have little in common besides the shared goal of putting a round ball in the back of a net. SHS was known throughout the region for its prowess in sports, and it had the facilities and staff to support that prowess. At the end of a Fall school day hundreds of students would rush from classrooms to locker-rooms, changing into practice gear provided through a sponsorship from a major national sportswear company, getting treatment in a well-appointed training room, and congregating with teammates to learn which of the school's four grass or two lighted all-weather turf fields would host their practice for the day. State championships were a tacit expectation at SHS, and the school attracted some of the most talented athletes in the region. UHS, in contrast, had no athletic facilities of its own other than a too-small gym that doubled as a lunch room and the school day was oriented by a workplace internship program designed both to help fund students' tuition and to give students exposure to professional environments that were often otherwise unfamiliar. Thus, at the end of a UHS school day students dispersed widely, with most of the athletes having to catch a bus to whatever city park was hosting their practice for the day and others having to skip practice entirely for the sake of their jobs. The sports teams were generally quite average; the athletes ranged from rank beginners to competent recreational players with one or two more serious athletes mixed in somewhat randomly.

Underneath these obvious differences, however, lay the shared foundations of American school sports. At SHS, for example, school administrators and coaches intentionally discussed soccer as one of many "co-curricular" (rather than "extra-curricular") activities in a way that belied the professional seeming environs. Players were encouraged to play other sports, or to participate in other types of activities ranging from choir to community service, and the main sporting challenge was to mesh talented players from different club teams into a cohesive unit that would represent the school proudly. And while UHS teams did not draw from the same talent pool, UHS administrators did explicitly promote sports as a way to generate "school spirit" and build community while simultaneously offering students a chance to engage competitively outside the classroom. Soccer at UHS was just one part of a palette of offerings designed to develop individuals within and through the school community. And at both schools the only potential post–high school goal for most sports endeavors was not a professional career but a college scholarship.

Amy Shorter, the pseudonym of a SHS soccer player, was well on her way to achieving that goal. Amy had excelled at all levels of American youth soccer; she was a regular on the state Olympic Development Program team, a captain for an elite club team, and an important midfielder for her state champion high school team. She had also "verbally committed" as a high school sophomore to attend a university with a highly ranked women's soccer program and would have been within her rights to aspire to more. Yet, she expressed no interest in playing the game beyond the university level either as a professional or as an international; for Amy, as for many elite American players, college soccer was an end of its own.

In some ways, soccer itself was only one of many possible avenues where Amy could have devoted her attentions. Growing up in an upper-middle class suburban family, she and her two siblings were immersed in a variety of activities from piano to dance but had a particular affinity for sports. At one point, Amy's mother explained with both pride and exhaustion, Amy and her two-years-older sister "played six sports, did ballet, tap and jazz and took piano lessons all at the same time!" Where Amy's older sister ended up focusing on volleyball, now playing with a prominent major university team, Amy herself whittled her focus down to soccer after her freshman year of high school—though she thinks she could have just as well continued in volleyball or basketball or several of her other sporting endeavors.

One reason she decided to focus on soccer was how much she enjoyed her club team, which drew elite players from around the region and had a professional coach who had worked with the same core group for nearly six years. When Amy talked about her favorite experiences in any type of activities, she focused first on winning tournaments with her club team—many of which required extensive travel to other states and regions of the country.

Further, when asked to identify people outside her family who have influenced her positively, she immediately endorsed her club soccer coach: "he's been my coach for a long time, like five or six years, and he has been really influential in my life.... I guess he has changed my perspective about soccer and how the world is ... he taught us a lot about good leadership, persistence and never giving up and courage and all that stuff. And how to deal with people and how to deal with problems. And it's not just telling us but the way he acts and the way he treats us."

When Amy talked about high school soccer she took on a much less reverential tone: "I mean it's obviously a fun experience. It's different cause you are playing with people from your school, people from other places, but it is kind of fun cause you get together with people you usually play against. And that's kind of cool. And it's also kind of cool to have your whole school come out and watch you and stuff like that. So I mean it's different atmospheres but ... [I] definitely cherish the club moments more. I don't know why; it's just more deep for me I guess."

One clue as to Amy's attitude towards high school soccer came from her parents' description of her club coach: [he] "just thinks high school soccer is worthless.... He thinks they should all go to some soccer academy and be educated through the soccer academy. I don't know if I am using the right word, but it would be because that's the way it is in other countries." Amy's mother had mixed feelings about that model: "that's all good and fine but I kind of like it the American way.... The social camaraderie part I think is great with high school sports. And, you know athletically, I don't think it hurts. At SHS it doesn't hurt." Amy's father, despite having himself been a collegiate basketball player, was less enamored with high school sports. But rather than focusing on an academy approach, her father focused on an interest in soccer as a tool towards a broader ideal: "When I look at Amy's development through soccer, is the end result that she kicks a ball well to another person? Absolutely not. And I think she sees—I mean she loves that part of it but she sees well beyond that so I think for her it wouldn't matter what the activity is. The leadership and using the gifts that God gave you to make everybody better around you in all ways would come out no matter what the activity was."

Megan Poway, the pseudonym of a soccer player at UHS, would likely agree with both Amy's mother and father: she loved the social camaraderie part of high school soccer, but also saw soccer as just one of many school-based activities she found worthwhile. Megan had played recreational soccer much of her life, but never had ambitions of playing at any kind of elite level: "I always played soccer for fun, not because I thought I would get a college scholarship or go be an amazing soccer player in the world—I just did it because it was fun, so I never saw the need to go join a professional, or not a professional but, like, a select team." Megan's conflating of select club teams with "professional teams," and the contrast with her own experience of playing "for fun," is meaningful. Even as a sophomore in high school she recognized that the soccer world is bifurcated between the "professional" and the "fun," and her own interests were firmly on the fun side of the divide.

Yet, Megan had wanted to attend UHS in significant part because it did offer competitive high school sports—her previous school had been an arts magnet that did not sponsor any competitive teams. Her parents had also long encouraged Megan to be active and engage in a variety of activities— her father had coached one of her childhood recreational soccer teams, and her mother had helped organize activities at the school as a way to volunteer and be involved with her children. But they had encouraged her to sample activities widely and saw no need for Megan to specialize in any particular sport. In fact, while the family was stable and supportive, they were of decidedly modest means and did not push Megan towards any particular professional ambitions: her father worked as a retail appraiser, and her mother had stayed home with their children due partly to never having found meaningful employment. When they thought of Megan's future they were skeptical that university level education, given the growing costs, would be a wise investment (her older brother had skipped higher education, eventually ending up in the military). Megan herself was interested in going to a university, but sports and soccer seemed to play no part in her thinking about that future.

Instead, through her broad palate of high school activity participation Megan had realized that her true passion was more for theater and drama rather than for soccer. In school she had also become a student-leader for an environmental club focused on promoting "green" initiatives, had been involved with school-based outdoors expeditions, and was an active member of the school track team. Her parents were just happy that she was involved with constructive activities of any sort, and while they enjoyed watching soccer themselves the game was decidedly secondary to their goal for Megan to be engaged and happy. When I talked with Megan's parents her mother, who had emigrated to the U.S. as a young adult from Europe, emphasized wanting all her kids to be involved in whatever activities they could find simply because in her own childhood she remembered feeling "totally bored."

Megan did feel engaged and happy with her high school soccer experience, but mostly because it "became a chance to hang out with my friends and make friends.... I never got any epiphanies or anything from playing soccer. I don't know if I'm supposed to or not?" When asked if there was anything she would change about her experience she again focused on friends and community: "I really wish we had a home field so ... people could come to our games and it could be more, you know, everybody's rooting for us." The reality, however, was that the UHS team was not particularly good and played in a not particularly good league — girls like Megan played the game because it was a fun part of high school life, not because of competitive ambitions or a passion for the game. Megan herself, exasperated with questions about the deeper meaning of her soccer participation, described the high school experience just exactly as it was: "we ran around the field trying to kick a ball and that is fun."

Ultimately, Megan Poway and Amy Shorter were on opposite ends of the American soccer pyramid. Megan was a recreational player with limited opportunities who enjoyed the game as one small part of a diverse palate of childhood activities and had few ambitions for her soccer career. Amy was an elite player with considerable resources who had devoted much of her adolescence to the game in a quest for both personal development and future prospects. Both had other things in their lives they found more meaningful than high school soccer — theater for Megan, club soccer for Amy — but both also thought of their high school experience as a "fun" way to engage a community. Importantly, however, neither girl thought about high school soccer as being about actual athletic performance and neither particularly cared about whether the U.S. national team was competitive at the World Cup.

Both Amy and Megan valued competition and wanted their teams to win, but the girls, their parents, and their coaches all talked about their high school team as about something other than on-field performance. In fact, when Amy's SHS coach — who was among the most successful high school soccer coaches in the state — addressed the question of whether there was anything particular about soccer or sports as related to his players' experiences he explained: "I don't think it matters a lot whether a kid is in ... drama [or] art or robotics or whatever and ... it's the same thing between baseball and soccer. You know to me it's that commitment, that involvement, that commitment to get better, that learning to work with other people, that leadership potential...." School soccer in the United States is, in other words, about lots of things. But even for the participants themselves it is not really about soccer.

U.S. vs. World: Negotiating American Identity on School Soccer Fields

So if school soccer in the United States is not really about soccer, then what is it about? The argument here is that school soccer, and school sports more generally, is best understood as a peculiar American "tradition"—one of many globally strange and potentially inefficient ways of working out the classic American tension between individualism and community. In the history of American school sports, in contemporary controversies pitting high school and club teams, and in the experiences of high school soccer players, the U.S. soccer system serves as a contested space where the global game mixes together with particularly American ideas about meritocracy and community. But that mix, like American identity itself, is far from a static blend.

This essay began by noting that U.S. national soccer teams have long been globally distinct for the number of players who have invested heavily in education — most have university educations rather than lengthy professional apprenticeships. But that is too is changing. Whereas seven of the first eleven on the aforementioned 2010 team had attended a university, the starters for the 1990 U.S. Men's World Cup team — the first U.S. team to participate in the World Cup since 1950 — had all attended a university (the majority for the full four years). Perhaps not coincidentally, the 2010 team was significantly better on the field than the 1990 team, which lost its opening game in embarrassing fashion (1–5) to a Czechoslovakia team stocked with seasoned professionals. The 2010 team, in contrast, advanced to the second round (topping England in the group table) only to lose in extra time to Ghana. Even on the women's side, the professional apprenticeship model that predominates globally may be starting to encroach on a school soccer system often lauded as responsible for much of the U.S. women's success on the global stage. In 2012 U.S. U-20 midfielder Lindsey Horan became one of the first elite female American players to forgo university soccer, signing directly out of high school with Paris Saint-Germain.

These changes at the elite level, the broader shift away from schools towards professional apprenticeships befitting the specialization encouraged by globalization, will almost certainly benefit the competitiveness of United States national teams. If more elite youth players dispense with high school and university soccer in favor of intensive specialization and professionalization from a young age, the U.S. national teams will most likely be able to find eleven excellent players to compete in future World Cups. Like much of the contemporary global economy, however, that system may also produce some deleterious by-products: only eleven players can step on the World Cup field, and global competition for lucrative professional careers will only continue to grow. In bypassing schools the U.S. soccer system is improving its global competitiveness while risking what makes it American: its integration with broader goals of merging broad opportunity and diverse community. There is a way in which American players who opt out of school soccer may identify more with the game than with whatever it means to be American.

Amidst such shifts at the elite level, however, it is worth re-emphasizing that the total number of American youth playing in the globally strange school soccer system continues to rise. Much of that rise is attributable to the broader growth of soccer in the United States at all levels, but some of it is also about the enduring appeal of school sports in American education. From the early missionary zeal of those promoting sports as part of a broad and democratic education, to the challenges posed by elite development academies affiliated with professional clubs, to the diverse experiences of youth players in contemporary high schools, the peculiar American ideal of a school playing field as a space where individualism balances with community endures.

Notes

1. In describing the "high school movement," Goldin and Katz note that in the 30 years between 1910 and 1940 the percentages of American 18-year-olds with high school diplomas went from 9 to more than 50—and attendance of at least some high school became the norm rather than the exception.
2. For more extensive discussion of related issues see *Soccer in a Football World* by David Wanterin.
3. Other countries do, of course, still employ national level training centers — such as the well-known "Clairefontaine" national technical center in France or St George's Park National Football Centre in England.
4. Though the U.S. Soccer Federation did start funding a residency program in 1999 for members of the Under-17 and Under-16 boys national teams at the IMG Academy in Bradenton Florida, that program only served approximately 40 players at a time.
5. It is clear, for example, that the three month season typical of a high school sport is not enough to significantly accelerate elite talent — but it is short enough to allow any one sport to be compartmentalized as part of a broader high school educational experience.
6. In 2012, the U.S. Soccer Federation also announced it would start an Under-13/14 division to start in the fall of 2013. At the time of this writing the specifics of this division are still being developed, so are not being discussed. The push to younger ages does, however, seem to fit the pattern of tension between American traditions and global trends towards increasing professionalization.
7. For more extensive discussion of related issues see *The Most Expensive Game in Town* by Mark Hyman.

Works Cited

Coakley, Jay. *Sport in Society: Issues and Controversies*, 10th ed. New York: McGraw Hill, 2008. Print.

Eskandarian, Alecko. "Debate Ignites Over Extended Development Academy Season." *Sports Illustrated*. 7 Sept. 2012. Web. 7 Jan. 2013.

Farrey, Tom. *Game On: The All-American Race to Make Champions of Our Children*. New York: ESPN, 2008. Print.

Goldin, Claudia, and Lawrence F. Katz. "Why the United States Led in Education: Lessons from Secondary School Expansion, 1910 to 1940." *Human Capital and Institutions*. Eds. David Eltis, Frank D. Lewis, and Kenneth L. Sokoloff. New York: Cambridge University Press, 2009. 143–178. Print.

Gorn, Elliott J., and Warren Goldstein. *A Brief History of American Sports*. New York: Hill and Wang, 1993. Print.

Hyman, Mark. *The Most Expensive Game in Town*. Boston: Beacon Press, 2012. Print.

Lemann, Nicholas. "Kicking in Groups." *The Atlantic Monthly* April 1996: 22–26. Print.

LFChistory.net. "60 mins with Steven Gerrard." LFChistory.net, n.d. Web. 7 Jan. 2013.

Markovits, Andrei S., and Steven L. Hellerman. Offside: Soccer and American Exceptionalism. Princeton: Princeton University Press, 2001. Print.

National Federation of State High School Associations. "Participation Statistics." NFHS.org, n.d. Web. 7 Jan. 2013.

National Soccer Coaches Association of American. "High School Soccer Speaking Points." NSCAA.com, 26 Apr. 2012. Web. 7 Jan. 2013.

Palmer, Tod. "Boys Soccer Standouts Forced to Choose Between School, Club Teams." *The Kansas City Star*. 25 Feb. 2012. Web. 7 Jan. 2013.

Putnam, Robert. "Bowling Alone: America's Declining Social Capital." *Journal of Democracy* 6.1 (1995): 65–78. Print.

Putnam, Robert. *Bowling Alone: The Collapse and Revival of American Community*. New York: Simon & Schuster, 2000. Print.

Swanson, Lisa. "Soccer Fields of Cultural [Re]Production: Creating 'Good Boys' in Suburban America." *Sociology of Sport Journal* 26.3 (2009): 402–424. Print.

U.S. Soccer Federation. "Frequently Asked Questions: Academy Starts 10-Month Season in 2012–2013." *U.S.Soccer.com*, 10 Feb. 2012. Web. 7 Jan. 2013.

Wangerin, David. *Soccer in a Football World*. Philadelphia: Temple University Press, 2008. Print.

Wilson, Steve. *The Boys from Little Mexico: A Season Chasing the American Dream*. Boston: Beacon Press, 2010. Print.

3

New Traditionalists

The Emergence of Modern America and the Birth of the MLS Coalition

DENNIS J. SEESE

On Election Night 2012, Fox News commentator Bill O'Reilly decried President Barack Obama's pending re-election as heralding the end of what he characterized as "a traditional America." Before the election was even decided, the popular pundit and self-proclaimed "Culture Warrior" noted, rather forlornly, on Fox's Election Night coverage, that "it's a changing country" where "the white establishment is now the minority" ("Bill O'Reilly"). O'Reilly's comment can be read as an explicit, open lament for the end of a "traditional" or orthodox notion of a patriarchal American society dominated entirely by heterosexual, white, Christian men. We know now that the President won re-election largely on the collective strength of modern "non-traditional" voting blocks and constituencies such as women, Latinos, Millennials, Asians, and African Americans. These groups combined to form what has become known as "the Obama Coalition," coalescing together to mount a serious challenge, electorally and culturally, to both the constructed symbolic entity that constitutes the identity of "traditional America" as well as the on-the-ground demographic and cultural realities of the United States in the twenty-first century (Teixeira and Halpin).

The construction of the narratives and symbols that constitute the conceptual grammar of "traditional America" has been fashioned and re-fashioned since the nation's inception. When sport is viewed as a powerful cultural force, there is an ongoing symbolic warfare between baseball and soccer. This is a conflict between America's "National Pastime" or key signifier/symbol of "traditional" America, and a signifier rich in symbolism with regards to an emergent "modern" America with an authentic, unique lexicon of its own. This represents a struggle that directly parallels the larger political and cultural battles constantly being fought rhetorically and, ultimately, electorally by Americans. Indeed, the tension and hostility generated by the discourse between the cultural messengers contesting the meanings of these two sports can be read as a microcosm of the larger political realignment resultant from the ongoing battle between the forces embodied by O'Reilly's "traditional" white American establishment, and the modern, multicultural face of America represented by the "Obama Coalition."

Franklin Foer observed the outlines of this burgeoning sociological rupture in his influential work *How Soccer Explains the World* when he noted that starting in the late 1960s significant numbers of affluent (largely white) middle class families adopted soccer as their own for a variety of socio-cultural reasons (235–248). The widespread adoption of soccer by this specific segment of American society had the unforeseen consequence of creating a new cultural (and eventually political) battleground. Foer writes, "When they adopted soccer, it gave the impression that they had turned their backs on the American pastime. This naturally produced even more disdain for them — and their sport" (239). Foer perceptively notes not only the initial stirrings of this conflict, but he also identifies a handful of other important characteristics that would come to define what is essentially a battle to define: disdain, the shifting political and cultural allegiances of middle-class suburbia, and the intuitive, almost subliminal, contrapuntal relationship between baseball and soccer in American thought.

Building from Foer, no one has articulated this rupture and the similarities between the parallel cultural (soccer vs. baseball) and political (traditional vs. modern) struggles to define America, specifically how they are identified and formulated, more explicitly than Gary Armstrong and James Rosbrook-Thompson. In their article "Coming to America: Historical Ontologies and United States Soccer," they write, "By adopting soccer as 'their game' middle-class parents have self-consciously created a counterculture that separates them from the values of "traditional America." Armstrong and Rosbrook-Thompson then make the direct connection, writing that those same middle class parents had gradually "also identified a new adversary: traditional America" (259).

Twice using O'Reilly's exact linguistic and conceptual formulation, Armstrong and Rosbrook-Thompson posit "traditional America" in opposition to those instrumental in driving soccer's growth as a cultural force in the "modern" United States. Progressive-minded middle class parents initially, and eventually the women, Latinos, and Millennials have since also made the game their own. These are precisely the same set of demographic agents who have become pillars of the so-called "Obama Coalition," driving the political realignment behind the United States' recent push into modernity. Interestingly enough, both Foer, and Armstrong and Rosbrook-Thompson use the word "counterculture" to describe soccer's initial push through suburbia, itself a word fraught with the overt and explicit challenges to "tradition" that occurred during America's tumultuous 1960s.

Echoes of this formulation can be connected to and are evident within the shrill protestations of conservative commentators like Glenn Beck who famously fumed in a rant about the 2010 World Cup. He stated that "it doesn't matter how you try to sell it to us, it doesn't matter how many celebrities you get, it doesn't matter how many bars open early, it doesn't matter how many beer commercials they run, we don't want the World Cup, we don't like the World Cup, we don't like soccer, we want nothing to do with it" (Willis). Beck also went on to say that "Barack Obama's policies are the World Cup," articulating their widespread rejection by "traditional" America and overtly blurring the lines between the cultural and political by recognizing soccer as a powerful symbol in the struggle between those seeking to define America in their own image. As Andrew Lindner and Daniel N. Hawkins note, "When media commentators say that soccer is being forced on 'us,' they are quite clearly referring to white Americans and not Hispanics" (75). Dave Zirin also observed that "Beck rejects soccer because his idealized 'real America'—in all its monochromatic glory—rejects it as well." Beck has to attack soccer because he rightly identifies it as a symbol of the rising cultural power of modern America. This is as an overt example of how the forces of "traditional" America try to perpetuate an idea of America that no longer conforms to objective reality, while simultaneously attempting to perpetuate their diminished cultural supremacy at the expense of representatives of an ascendant modern America embodied by Latinos, women, African Americans, and other groups that were long-held from power in "traditional" America.

Comments like those uttered by O'Reilly and Beck reinforce the importance of the symbolic struggle for America's identity being waged by the forces of tradition vs. those of modernity. This theoretical framework was initially formulated in 1991 by sociologist James Davison Hunter in his book *Culture Wars: The Struggle to Define America*. In this book, he argued that Americans "were divided into two broad ideological worldviews: progressivism and orthodoxy" (Lindner and Hawkins 71) and that the two ideologically opposed groups express their differences and try to assert their hegemonic supremacy by contesting what symbols will dominate and ultimately define American culture and thus the American identity (Hunter 135). This work owes a great debt to Hunter's theoretical framework and it will be utilized to demonstrate how baseball and soccer are wielded as such cultural symbols by each side. The accumulation and perpetuation of hegemonic dominance within the context of these symbolic battles is the crucial locus where "the very fabric of national identity is contested," including notions of "masculinity and femininity among the issues being negotiated" (Armstrong and Rosbrook-Thompson 359). Issues of masculinity and femininity do indeed loom large in this negotiation, reflected both in the shifting demographic and economic realities of life in the United States and within the language that frames the symbolic battles themselves. It is no accident that "soccer moms" entered the lexicon and not soccer dads, nor was it that women voters were perhaps the most sought after voting bloc in the 2012 cycle, ultimately yielding President Obama an 18 percent advantage over Mitt Romney (up from the president's 12 percent margin in 2008), signaling a significant rejection of "traditional" America's outdated and problematic gender politics (Bassett). Conversely, part of soccer's initial rise in the suburbs was due to its providing an alternative to the hypermasculine violence of American football. Finally, the language of feminization has often been used by traditionalists to "Other" soccer as something beneath the masculinity of American men.

A struggle to determine the "very fabric of national identity" is being waged in the United States, with the election of President Obama obviously a far more important turning point than the ascendance of soccer in American life, but it is significant that the agents driving both occurrences are largely one and the same. It must be noted, though, that African Americans have yet to embrace soccer on the same scale as other members of the "Obama Coalition" and the question of why is certainly ripe for further exploration. It is clear that the symbolic value and power of soccer, and to perhaps a lesser extent its relationship to baseball, is one of the "battlegrounds" being contested by the "competing worldviews" in Hunter's formulation. Baseball is obviously a cultural symbol "traditional" America values and feels overtly sensitive about and protective of. Objectively, though, there should be no real doubt that baseball is in symbolic decline. Foer accurately described the sport as a "loser" in the high-stakes game of globalization when he noted that "global audiences have shown no hunger for it" (244). But perhaps even more damaging to the game is the fact that American kids are no longer playing it on the same scale as they have in the past. Foer notes that "according to the Sporting Goods Manufacturing Association of America, the number of teens playing baseball fell 47 percent between 1987 and 2000," while, conversely, by 2002 "1.3 million more kids played soccer than Little League" (244). These numbers have continued to grow in both directions as over three million Americans between the ages of five and nineteen were registered participants in U.S. Youth Soccer leagues in 2011 ("U.S. Youth Soccer"). The 2011 Sporting Goods Manufacturing Association of America's shows soccer behind only basketball as a participatory activity engaged in by those seven years and older. That same study shows baseball ranking behind soccer, basketball and tennis, with the sport registering a 1.9 percent decline in participation from 2010 (NSGA). Soccer's initial foothold in the United States can unquestionably be attributed to participation metrics like those. Foer then makes an observation about baseball's demographics which has a stunning political dimension that shows how inextricably linked baseball truly is to the cultural and political axis of "traditional" America, writing "and the demographic profile of baseball has grown ever more lily white" (244). Substitute "baseball" for "Republican Party" or "conservatism" and you have a news story that has run thousands of times over the last few election cycles (Martin), as the demographic agents participating in and consuming baseball are largely the same as those adhering to traditional, conservative values. Many metrics show that both are decline.

Introducing the MLS Coalition: Latinos

Fernando Delgado, a prescient, forecaster of what Armstrong and Rosbrook-Thompson termed the "very fabric of national identity," could look like in the near future, wrote the following of Major League Soccer (MLS) in his article "Major League Soccer, Constitution and [the] Latino Audience[s]":

> Major League Soccer does indicate what is likely to become a more common rhetorical strategy: the appeal to, or construction of, minorities as important economic and social constituents of contemporary U.S. popular culture. It is this projection that will ultimately test the relations between popular culture (sport) and politics (electoral and governmental) in a battle that may pit progressive against reactionary rhetors in the name of political or economic gain [Delgado 41].

This "projection" from the "popular" to the "political" has occurred over the past decade. Just as Armstrong and Rosbrook-Thompson identify that "issues of masculinity and femininity" are being negotiated and contested (359), Delgado views sport "as a cultural site wherein competing visions of democracy, equality and capitalism, among other concepts are articulated and contested" (41). This demonstrates why "reactionary rhetors" like Beck are so relentless in their attacks. Their very power to articulate and define particular (some may say peculiar) notions of democracy and (perhaps more importantly) capitalism is at stake. Part of soccer's ability to "occupy a progressive role in contemporary culture" in the United States was to grant agency to and thus subsequently unleash the latent political, cultural, and economic clout of women, Latinos, and Millennials (Delgado 41). Delgado notes that "Othering Discourses" employed against Latinos had taken a "virulent" turn in the early to mid–1990s, culminating with Pat Buchanan's infamous 1992 Republican National Convention speech. Buchanan urged his listeners to "take back our culture, and take back our country," using essentially the same frame Beck and others use when speaking of the World Cup to exclude Latinos from the political and cultural spaces of "traditional" America (Delgado 43). Delgado demonstrates how from their inception (amidst the aforementioned virulence and toxicity being hurled at Latinos), the MLS identified the dormant socio-economic power of the burgeoning Latino population, helped [create] a Latino audience by affirming their identity" and bestowing an agency upon them as valued, significant cultural and economic actors that was hitherto unprecedented (45). In doing so the MLS successfully used the sport of soccer to establish a "progressive cultural zone" (Delgado 42). In direct contrast to the poisonous rhetoric of Pat Buchanan, the MLS constructed an "affirmative and centralizing constitution of Latinos" that depicted them "not as an Other but as a necessary element of the league's survival" (Delgado 45). Obviously, the MLS, as a corporate entity, was not entirely altruistic in their motives, correctly identifying an underserved demographic that would satisfy demand for their product. But once "fully integrated into the American economy as consumers of mass culture" (Delgado 46) and set into motion as an economic and cultural force, thanks in part to the MLS's vision, Latinos accrued considerable power and began to leverage and "project" that power into the political arena — just as Delgado surmised. This culminated in the 2012 Presidential Election where the President garnered an unbelievable 71 percent of the Latino vote, delivering a severe blow to notions of "traditional" America (Teixeira and Halpin). MLS commissioner Don Garber has often remarked that the "Hispanic market is part of the league's DNA" (Ortiz). Ultimately, the league delivered the game to an emergent Latino population, one of the key constituents representing "the modern face of American national identity—an identity that was being subtly reshaped in terms of its expression through soccer" (Armstrong and Rosbrook-Thompson 354).

How the Symbolic Battle Between Soccer and Baseball Functions: A Case Study

Long an easy target in America, due to the demographic makeup of its fan base and its place outside the margins of America's "hegemonic sports culture" (Markovits and Hellerman 9–13), soccer often functioned as an outsize receptacle of traditionalist vitriol. Its very vehemence is emblematic of the fear and paranoia felt by conservative voices who now target the game for its symbolic role in the cultural decline and dissolution of "traditional" America. This is the only time when the voices of "traditional" America do not actually ignore outright the gradual, dramatic rise of soccer in the landscape of American sports. A rise punctuated emphatically by a Luker on Trends/ESPN study released in March 2012 that saw respondents between the ages of twelve and twenty-four identify "Pro Soccer" as the second most popular sport in the nation, behind only the NFL and narrowly edging out the NBA (Bennett, "MLS Takes in"). Lest you were wondering about the ambiguities attached to the nebulous term "Pro Soccer," MLS chief marketing officer Howard Handler "followed up with pollsters," according to ESPN, "and was relieved to learn that if you pull out MLS alone, it still ranks No. 4, ahead of Major League Baseball and NCAA football/basketball" (Bennett, "MLS Takes in"). This means the orthodox anti-soccer narrative is either stuck helplessly in the past, or operating in deliberate ignorance of evidence such as the Luker on Trends poll. Conversely, Major League Baseball, pillar of "traditional" America, central to many "traditional" American identity narratives, is showing discernible signs of decline in influence and cache, two key hegemonic determinants. And just like distortions either lazily or purposefully utilized to perpetuate the anti-soccer narrative, baseball's decline has a protective doppelganger narrative designed to purposely or lazily obscure the game's cultural erosion. Both narratives are definitively grounded in old modes of thinking.

Baseball and soccer often become diametrically/dialectically opposed in this traditional vs. modern discourse. There are many interesting aspects of this discourse to explore, including similarity intone and the body of narrative tactics and traits employed by each side. Desperate repetition of a few core thesis statements characterizes each narrative inverse. Generally they are:

- Soccer will NEVER be big in the United States or Soccer will disappear.
- What, me worry? Baseball is MORE popular than EVER. No, really, it REALLY is.

Convincing cases can be made that neither of these statements are true yet the narratives pushing them continue to be produced. The similarities shared by these diametrically opposed narratives are profound and instructive. Here are a few of their most distinct tics and traits:

- Vagueness (stridency without assertion);
- willful ignorance of reality based on verifiable facts; and
- sheer volume, belligerence and repetition.

For example, a tireless proponent of the "Soccer will NEVER be big in the United States" meme/narrative is columnist and "self-styled negative humorist" Joe Queenan. Queenan wrote a column for the *Wall Street Journal* on March 30, 2012, titled "A Final Red Card for American Soccer" wherein he gleefully mocks the United States Men's National Team's (USMNT) failure to qualify for the 2012 Summer Olympic Games. First of all, since when did Americans openly celebrate the failure of American athletes in any context related to the Olympic Games — and from the pages of the *Wall Street Journal*, no less? The only correlate to the shameful abnormality of Queenan's column that I can recall is in October 2009 when Glenn Beck, Rush Limbaugh, Matt Drudge and other conservative, "traditional" American media personalities openly rejoiced in the United States' failure to bring the 2016 Olympic Games to Chicago, despite intense personal lobbying by the President and First Lady. Beck in particular, cloaked in the flimsiest garb of uber-patriotism at all other times, was downright giddy over the President's perceived failure, characterizing what in reality *was* America's failure as "sweet," while a group of conservatives at an Americans for Prosperity meeting actually erupted into applause over the news, as did the editors William Kristol's *Weekly Standard* (Slajda). Still another conservative columnist, Tom Piatak, admitted he was a "little disappointed" to hear of the USMNT's electric comeback against Slovenia in the 2010 FIFA Men's World Cup. Yet in a stunning, brazen act of cognitive dissonance Piatak urged his readers to continue to reject soccer, and by extension the very athletes representing them on a global stage, in a "healthy spirit of patriotic defiance" (Piatak). Americans ridiculing American athletes at the international level and openly mocking their failures can only be attributed to the pathologies soccer inspires in these self-appointed guardians of authenticity and tradition in American culture as the tide shifts against them. A similar wish for President Obama — and by extension the entire American enterprise which "traditional" American mouthpieces claim to love unconditionally — to fail was voiced, you will recall by Rush Limbaugh (Limbaugh). Note the striking similarities in tone between the cultural and political rhetoric employed by "traditionalists."

Back to Queenan who notes that the match which determined the USMNT's failure to qualify (a 3–3 draw with El Salvador) was held in "Nashville, Tenn., one of the many states where nobody cares about soccer. There are 49 other states matching this description" (Queenan, "A Final Red").

Queenan's only evidence to back up his bold, broad-stroke assertion that "nobody cares about soccer" is to cite the match's admittedly paltry attendance of 7,889. On the surface this is damning evidence, but if Queenan would have stepped out of the confines of the hidebound, traditionalist narrative concerning soccer's cultural status in America he's so zealously committed to he might have noticed a report in November 2011 from *Slate.com*, announcing that the MLS now has the third highest average attendance (17,872) of all major sports in the United States, ahead of the NBA (17,323) and the NHL (17,132) (Howard "Major League Soccer"). Furthermore, the title of his book, *True Believers: The Tragic Inner Lives of Sports Fans*, would lead you to believe he could/should may have a reasonable grasp of some objective facts related to attendance at sporting events in the United States. Also, anecdotally the USMNT sold out the New Meadowlands stadium to the tune of 78,936 for a friendly against Lionel Messi's Argentina squad in March 2011 (Tenorio). Coincidentally, the aforementioned Luker on Trends/ESPN report discovered that Messi was the sixteenth most popular athlete in America, beating out omnipresent superstars such as the Miami Heat's Dwayne Wade (Bennett, "MLS Takes in"). But it appears that reporting easily verifiable facts like this would damage the outmoded narrative that writers like Queenan are so philosophically and emotionally invested in as guardians of "traditional" America. To acknowledge them would cede precious cultural ground, thus omission becomes convenient, perhaps necessary.

Queenan continues insisting that the setback suffered by the USMNT is the latest in a long line of examples of why soccer cannot and will not gain a foothold in the U.S. He writes "the plant never took root, because the soil wasn't right and never would be. Never. Americans hate things that are boring." No evidence is offered in support of soccer "NEVER" taking root, as if it is so self-evident. But timing and fate appear not to favor Queenan because this column was published in the *Wall Street Journal* the exact same month the Luker on Trends/ESPN report was released, confirming that soccer has indeed taken root in America. The report's findings obliterate Queenan's erroneous (yet vigorously) asserted claims of contempt and indifference towards the game emanating from all fifty states. The reality no longer fits the "traditionalist" narrative, yet people like Queenan remain committed to it. He also dutifully demonstrates another trope/trait common to the anti-soccer narrative, contextualizing the sport alongside of "Kylie Minogue, Mr. Bean and Fascism" as a "European import that Americans do not need" (Queenan, "A Final Red"). Soccer is always posited as the "Other" in these narrative discourses. Insulting and "Othering" Europeans is a convenient refuge for traditionalists tired of using soccer and myriad other discourses to "Other"

Latinos and women. It is also instructive that the sport is linked, not so subtly, to fascism. It seems overtly linking soccer to socialism à la former Congressman (and Buffalo Bills QB) Jack Kemp, who famously said "a distinction should be made that football is democratic, capitalism, whereas soccer is a European socialist sport," is passé now (Foer 241). This is telling because it illuminates the psychology behind conservative commentators reflexively associating soccer with communism, socialism or as overtly "European," not just to "Other" it in a demeaning way but to neutralize it as a progressive force, or, as Delgado put it, "a progressive zone" capable of producing considerable, decisive symbolic and electoral power. Conflating it with overtly horrific symbols (Fascism, socialism) of the twentieth century is a way to drain strength from it. Briefly, though, regarding the frame that soccer embodies socialism, whereas traditional American sports such as baseball and football symbolize unfettered capitalism, journalist Daniel Gross makes an excellent point about the irony of said framing, and indeed the exact inversion of reality contained within that formulation, writing:

> To different degrees, Major League Baseball, the NFL, and the NBA are examples of European-style socialism among billionaires and Fortune 500 companies. They share revenues, tightly regulate admission to the cartel, and bargain collectively with powerful European-style unions, which act as barriers against reform. Losers not only can prosper, but they get first dibs on next year's crop of talent" [Gross].

He continued to state that "in other words, the European system rewards ambition and ruthlessly punishes sloth and incompetence" (Gross). That last sentence ends with a quote that encapsulates how the promotion and relegation structure in major European domestic leagues perfectly resembles the "rags-to-riches" Horatio Alger ethos embedded in American lore which has been internalized by Americans on almost subconscious level for decades. In an almost Orwellian inversion of the moth-eaten tropes that constitute traditionalist narratives of soccer in America, upon closer examination, it is actually "socialist" European soccer leagues in places like England and Italy that more clearly reflect fundamental capitalist principles in the realm of sport.

Queenan's column ends, mercifully, with a strange anecdote involving San Francisco Giants' pitcher and two-time Cy Young Award winner Tim Lincecum's 3–2 triumph over Landon Donavan in a game of *FIFA Soccer 12* that overwhelmingly signifies ... something. Not sure what, Queenan is not clear — but rest assured it *isn't* good for the status of soccer in the United States. So take that, Landon. Seriously, though, the direct symbolic intrusion/imposition of baseball's inherent superiority over soccer at the end of the piece actually serves to highlight the creeping inferiority complex growing in the psyche of traditionalist pundits committed to the anti-soccer narrative and their almost pathological insistence in standing baseball in opposition to the sport. Queenan has truly produced a gem of the genre, illuminating the battered psyche of those committed to baseball's place in the pantheon of the "traditional" American sports hegemony, while simultaneously being reduced to asserting the game's masculine superiority over soccer in what, tellingly, is a symbolic contest played out on a virtual platform.

Alas, Queenan is no stranger to this type of column, the notable difference within the proceeding example being the open ridicule of American athletes failing to qualify for the Olympics. It turns out that he was actually tasked with reviewing *How Soccer Explains the World* for the *New York Times* in 2004. Just as he wrote in 2012 that soccer, like "Mr. Bean and fascism," was a European import, superfluous to American needs, in 2004 he writes, "I suspect most readers will come away from this book relieved that professional soccer, like French pop music, German stand-up comedy and Indian movies, is something profoundly annoying that mercifully stays overseas where it can't do any damage to our fragile republic" (Queenan, "Of Headers"). The structural and rhetorical framework employed in this column are essentially identical to the one he would go on to write for the *Wall Street Journal* nearly a decade later, only the levels of denial and dated references have been changed. The shrill, vague persistence of these columns—separated by an eight year interval that only saw (in every possible metric) soccer's stature increase exponentially—demonstrate that the rigidity of the preset narrative peddled and produced by zealous defenders of orthodoxy like Joe Queenan cannot be altered by facts. "Traditional" rhetors like Queenan adhere to and perpetuate long established tropes that are trotted out with minimal variation to downplay and degrade soccer's symbolic vitality as a cultural touchstone in an emerging, modern America that has shifted radically away from widespread acknowledgement and valuation of many of "traditional" America's symbols and signifiers (like Cy Young Award winners), thus greatly diminishing the cultural potency such symbols once enjoyed. The sheer volume and insistence of Queenan's desire to pretend that soccer is not established in American life is stunning, providing an example of how soccer as cultural signifier threatens to damage, undermine and usurp symbols of tradition (particularly as they relate to baseball) formerly intrinsic to conceptions of American identity.

"Actually, the game is doing just fine"

The flipside of the anti-soccer narrative is one that promotes an idea that baseball is stronger than ever. Although the message and content of this narrative is in direct contrast to the one claiming soccer will never take root in the U.S., the opposing narrative threads contain many of the same traits, specifically: willful ignorance of reality, persistence, repetition and vague shrillness. A textbook example of how the traditionalist baseball narrative works can be glimpsed within an article that Tom Verducci wrote for *Sports Illustrated* in 2008 titled "Phillies Win! Why They Deserve Better" which includes an allusion to an astonishing allegation that *Fox pushes back the start times of their evening World Series games because many of their affiliates do better business at 7:30 P.M. with 15-year-old reruns of Seinfeld.* Obviously, *Seinfeld* is an epochal show that has had a seismic, lingering impact on American popular culture, but reruns of these shows are better revenue generators than the "Crown Jewel" of "America's National Pastime?" (Verducci) Something like that would seem, at least circumstantially, to indicate grave danger for baseball's status as a hegemonic symbol central to the cultural identity of "traditional" America. From the same article Verducci notes:

> More people watched the NBA Finals, according to Nielsen ratings, than the World Series, the first time that had happened since a popular fellow named Michael Jordan was winning the last of his championships in 1998. More people — 29% more — watched a football game between Penn State and Ohio State than the rain-delayed Game 3, which was the least-watched World Series game on record. Overall World Series viewership dropped 17% from the previous worst-rated Series (2006, St. Louis versus Detroit), 21% from last year (Boston versus Colorado) and 47% from the high-water mark of Fox Series telecasts since 2000 (2004, Boston versus St. Louis). The World Series audience has been cut by more than half since the expanded playoff format began in 1995.

Again, all the proceeding empirical data would seem to indicate severe problems for Major League Baseball and its standing within the hegemonic sports culture it once dominated. But instead of interpreting that data as tangible proof of baseball's accelerating descent into cultural irrelevance — Verducci chooses, briefly, to consider the possibility, asking, "Is baseball in trouble?" and then dismiss it out of hand in the very next sentence, writing, "Is baseball in trouble? Not even close. On the contrary." The evidence for which follows ("Local TV ratings, property sales, regional ratings," etc.) is in no way as convincing as the evidence against. But more importantly, note the similarity in Verducci's tone as he stridently, against significant evidence to the contrary, dismisses baseball's diminishing cultural cache as something not even worth seriously considering and how closely it matches Queenan's insistence, against all tangible, quantifiable evidence that Americans *do not* consume and/or care about soccer. Just as Queenan and his ilk willfully (or lazily) ignore the numerical realities of attendance at soccer matches in the United States, along with participation in the sport at all age levels, defenders of baseball's role in traditional conceptions of American identity willfully ignore and deny data such as that cited by Verducci that less and less American's actually watch baseball's "crown jewel, the World Series" (Verducci).

In the intervening years since Verducci wrote that article in November 2008, as the MLS and domestic European leagues such as the English Premier League (EPL) have continued to gain cultural status and currency with Americans, television ratings for the World Series have continued to plummet, bottoming out in 2012 with record lows (Associated Press, "World Series"). In fact, as *Forbes.com* noted, "The seven most recent World Series before 2012 have been the seven lowest-rated World Series all-time" (Badenhausen), continuing a trend which shows World Series "ratings have been slipping for three decades, according to Nielsen Sports Marketing Service via *Reuters*" (Baker and Richwine, "World Series Ratings"). That period of three decades parallels almost exactly soccer's climb to cultural relevance and its accumulation of status as an important symbol of "modern" America's identity. This is a near perfect inverse with the decline in World Series ratings as "traditional" America loses ground in this particular arena of cultural warfare. Yet this stark decline in television ratings, one of America's most influential metrics, is still somehow good for Major League Baseball and a demonstration of its undiminished strength. According to Rosecrans, low ratings do not matter because, this should sound familiar à la Verducci, "actually, the game is doing just fine" (Rosecrans, "World Series Ratings"). Just as eight years separated essentially the same fact-free insistence from Queenan that soccer would never take root or prosper in the United States, four years separate essentially the same fact-free insistence from Verducci, initially, and Rosecrans, presently, that baseball is doing just fine, despite a pronounced, long-term decrease in television viewership of the World Series, a formerly iconic event in "traditional" America. It must be said that Rosecrans makes a better case for the relative strength of MLB than Verducci and the league's solid attendance and revenue numbers should be acknowledged. Nevertheless, there are also eerie parallels here with the conservative punditry establishment's insistent predictions, in the face of mounting evidence to the contrary, that Mitt Romney would trounce President Obama in the 2012 general election, another instance where "traditional" America assembled and propagated a narrative at odds with measurable reality designed to obfuscate the strength of the more powerful signifier of "modern" America. It also resembles how modern political consultants scramble to set, solidify and define narrative frames on familiar and expedient terms, controlling how information is delivered and received. If you look closely you can see that all these "ratings don't matter for baseball" stories/memes began before the 2012 Series even ended, shaping the message before any astute observers could ask legitimate questions about baseball's cultural decline.

The Battle for Identity

In his influential essay "Sport and Ideology in Contemporary Society," R.W. Thompson characterizes as a necessity the need to "examine the characteristics of the dominant ideology of contemporary society to determine whether this ideology is also reflected in the social institution of sport" (82). Thompson's words provide an excellent frame for a discussion of whether the dominant ideology of contemporary American society is more accurately reflected through the cultural organs of baseball or soccer. But his words provide yet another indication of why the battle to define, seek, and secure cultural hegemony through sport is contested so heatedly in the U.S. Speaking of the initial rush of success experienced by the American Soccer League in the early 1920s, Armstrong and Rosbrook-Thompson note that "the increasing power of ASL would challenge the definitions of legitimate citizenship identified with baseball and Gridiron." You can substitute "MLS" for "ASL" and see not only that the discourses surrounding definitions of American citizenship and identity as they pertain to the cultural realm of sport, particularly soccer, have been defined, contested, and refashioned constantly over the last century. But you can also see that the "players and spectators" who in the ASL's time "embraced a position outside of the American body politic" (Armstrong and Rosbrook-Thompson 352) are currently, in the MLS era, asserting political and economic clout that is re-defining rigid, traditional notions of what the "American body politic" is, reimagining it in their own image and according to their own values.

In the long wake of the ASL's dissolution, through the brief flickers of hope embodied by the NASL, the success of the 1994 World Cup, the iconic World Cup victory delivered by Mia Hamm, Brandi Chastain, 1999 United States Women's National Team (USWNT), and, finally, the slow, gradual ascent of the MLS — it appears that "certain values of the game were embraced by a section of the population who represented the modern face of American national identity — an identity that was being subtly reshaped in terms of its expression through soccer" (Armstrong and Rosbrook-Thompson 354). Women, Latinos, and Millennials are among the groups currently constituting the emerging "modern face of American national identity" and "subtly" reshaping the contours of that identity using soccer as a means of expression. These same actors are also reshaping America's political identity along progressive lines — re-electing President Obama in 2012 as well as electing a record shattering 20 female United States senators, including the first openly gay U.S. senator, Wisconsin's Tammy Baldwin — as they acquire more cultural, economic and electoral power.

An example of this new identity being expressed through soccer, an identity that can be characterized as expressing core progressive values, is in the practice of tolerance, particular with regards to LGBT issues. A level of tolerance bravely embodied by the MLS, which not only is the major American sports league least tolerant of homophobia, it also boasts an extremely diverse front office with "minorities holding 40% of all professional positions, and women 42 percent," according to a study released by the University of Central Florida's Institute for Diversity and Ethics in Sports (Associated Press "MLS sets record"). Back to the MLS's emphatic crackdown on homophobia, which saw the league immediately fine, suspend (three matches) and order sensitivity training for Seattle Sounders left back Marc Burch after he uttered a gay slur in a November 2012 playoff match against Real Salt Lake. Due to their youth, not only in America, but in the firmament of global domestic leagues, the MLS seems to be trying to prevent homophobia and anti-gay slurs from ever establishing any sort of foothold in the American game. The league's swift and comparatively severe (the suspension ended his season while the Sounders were contending for the MLS Cup) punishment of Burch provides a stark contrast to similar recent incidents involving homophobic slurs uttered by the NBA's Kobe Bryant (Bryant was fined $100,000 and not suspended) and the NFL's DeSean Jackson (not officially sanctioned at all). Caleb Hannan asked why the MLS is so proactive in punishing the use of homophobic slurs (besides the obvious fact that it is morally the right thing to do) and he came to an interesting conclusion, which is simply demographics. Hannan notes that the league is not only America's youngest, but it generally has the youngest fans going by the Luker on Trends/ESPN poll and other metrics. Hannan also notes that "generally speaking, the younger you are, the more likely you are to have progressive views on homosexuality, and an intolerance for words that seek to demonize it." Hannan quotes an anonymous MLS official who says rather forthrightly, "We're doing what we're doing because it's the right thing to do. But we're also appealing to the Millennial generation. According to ESPN's own numbers, our audience skews younger than anyone but the X Games" (Hannan). This is an explicit confirmation/admission that in this context the popular (i.e., sport as culture) has indeed crossed over into the political (i.e., overwhelming Millennial support of LGBT rights).

As with Dr. Delgado's research regarding Latinos, the MLS explicitly constructing a social space where a constituency, in this instance Millennials, are given a sense of agency where the importance of their burgeoning cultural and economic clout is acknowledged, respected and catered to. We can also make a direct connection to a similar level of clout being exercised by Millennials in the political arena with regards to these very issues of tolerance, sexuality, LGBT rights, and marriage equality, as Hannan correctly pointed out. According to Teixeira and Halpin, young voters amounted to a significant 19 percent of all voters in the 2012 general election, with Millennials in particular increasing to 11 percent of the vote. Their impact can be viewed as providing President Obama a crucial edge, as 60 percent of the entire youth vote broke in his direction. This influence can also be detected in the fact that four states (Maryland, Minnesota, Washington, and Maine) either legalized or rejected initiatives to ban or restrict same-sex marriage. A 2012 report issued by Advocates for Youth says that 63 percent of all Millennials believe that same-sex marriage should be legal, a number essentially identical to the percentage of this age group that broke towards the President ("Millennials: Diverse, Connected"). Millennial views of LGBT issues like marriage equality are a crucial part of their identity as significant authors of the modern American identity and their values are reflected in America's continuing evolution on these issues. Traditionalist symbols and pursuits such as football and basketball apparently offer Millennials no such recognition of or outlet for this expression.

The twin pillars of soccer's dominance as a participatory sport are: the advent of Title IV in 1972, giving American women access to the game which they then used to build the world's best national team, and soccer's much studied dominance of the post-war suburbs where its visibility as a status symbol and cultural signifier was valued by the growing suburban classes. This, as we have seen, created a new battleground for issues of identity as well as new divisions between heretofore relatively homogenous and compatible (read: white) segments of American society. In other words,

> today's custodians of United States soccer have sought succor from the old enemy in entrenching societal divisions that ensure the sport remains the preserve of the (predominantly) white middle classes. However, they have also identified a new adversary: traditional America [Armstrong and Rosbrook-Thompson 359].

We analyzed the final part of that quote in our discussion of the startling linguistic similarities inherent in the political and cultural battles raging between traditionalists and modernists. These authors are essentially characterizing what was a rigid divide between residents of affluent suburbs and the urban poor, mostly Latinos and other immigrants. These divided and disparate communities had virtually nothing in common culturally or economically, except their love for the game of soccer. This divide remained relatively intact up until the formation of the MLS, who decided to rely "on two main sources of customers: The growing number of immigrants from soccer driven South and Central America and the suburbanites (soccer moms and dads) who've migrated to the sport through the rising number of youth leagues" (Minzesheimer). The MLS's marketing instincts were sound and the league now stands as a diverse, tolerant, multicultural expression of its constituent parts. As a core element of the identity of these divergent groups, it seems that the game of soccer has actually managed to unite, both politically and culturally, these disparate and previously unconnected segments of American society, who are now able to communicate and in act concert with one another. Armstrong and Rosbrook-Thompson labeled these groups "the suburban middle class," "young, white middle class and often female" and the "non-white urban poor" (358). Political pundits and sociologists have taken to referring to them collectively as important facets of "the Obama Coalition," but I call them MLS voters, "wholly consonant with the values of 'modern' America" (359).

Gender, Identity, and Soccer

An example of the gender issues being contested can be viewed in "traditional" America's reactions to the dominance of the USWNT, who at times have also actually inspired those same cacophonous Tourette's like outbreaks of anti-patriotism from the voices representing "traditional" America. These are the voices who did their best to instigate a backlash against the USWNT and were designed "to condemn soccer to the periphery of the American sporting landscape as a consequence of its supposed lack of masculinity" (Armstrong and Rosbrook-Thompson 359). Another example of how this "feminization" of the game has typically worked in traditionalist discourse can be glimpsed in sports radio shock-jock Jim Rome's unfortunate remark, "My son is not playing soccer. I will hand him ice skates and a shimmering sequined blouse before I hand him a soccer ball. Soccer is not a sport" (Foer 242). Perhaps Foer highlighted this particular quote, out of many similar ones Rome has uttered through the years, because he knew what a rhetorical goldmine it was, containing a pure, unadulterated strain of this specific anti-soccer trope: soccer is feminine and thus not a sport.

The "soccer is not a sport" meme reared its ugly head again, not surprisingly also within the context of women playing it, during the breathtaking U.S./Brazil quarterfinal match in the 2011 FIFA Women's World Cup, when it was uttered by well-known sports writer John Feinstein in a conversation recounted on the *Washington Post's D.C. Sports Bog*. A quick side note about that match: in his classic *Soccer in Sun and Shadow*, Eduardo Galeano refers to "matches that made your hair stand on end" while writing about the 1986 FIFA Men's World Cup in Mexico. Never was a match more worthy of that description than this astonishing U.S./Brazil instant classic. Feinstein, a man "who writes a lot about people walking around with sticks" was on *Washington Post Live* bragging about watching C.C. Sabathia pitch for the Yankees while the USWNT team were playing (Steinberg). When pushed as to why, Feinstein replied: "Yeah, because it's [baseball] a real sport." To their credit, the incredulous *Post* writers took Feinstein to task, labeling his comment "chauvinist." Feinstein said he felt that way about the men's game too and that soccer was not really a sport to due to some matches being decided on kicks from the mark. "You can't call something a real sport if you don't decide it by playing the sport" (Steinberg). And thus we have another gem of the "traditional" America anti-soccer meme genre. Blatant insertion of baseball as a more worthy and masculine athletic pursuit (which, it has to be said, is hilarious considering he invoked Sabathia of all people) in direct counterpoint to soccer, which is not a real sport anyway because women play it at the same level as men and I, John Feinstein, do not like how it ends, sometimes. The "not-a-sport" meme shows the complete and utter desperation displayed by traditional voices who know they are losing this particular symbolic battle to keep defining America in their image.

The feminization of the sport has a long, sorry history in American discourse, perhaps culminating, surprisingly, in the introduction of the term, "soccer moms." Lisa Swanson argues that the term, far from bestowing power and agency on women, as most assume, can actually be viewed as a tactic devised to perpetuate the patriarchal order of "traditional" America. The term generally used to "refer to white, suburban women" actually "simplifies who they are and homogenizes their experience." Swanson characterizes the "soccer mom" label as being a subtle yet deliberate way of stripping away their "power as women and individuals" (345), ultimately diminishing their hard-won agency. Going into greater detail on this point, Swanson emphasizes that when the label was conceived in the mid-'90s American women were making great strides as political actors. But once the term entered the lexicon "women were suddenly no longer characterized as strong individuals of the verge of making significant inroads as political figures, instead they were undermined by this labeling, which relegated them to merely a specific type of domestic role" (Swanson 345). Swanson views this linguistic sleight-of-hand as being utilized as a tool, securing "the further entrenchment of patriarchal ideology in the United States" (345). What's even more insidious is that the forces of patriarchy and tradition explicitly chose "soccer," a cultural force that had actually given women a modicum of agency and a space to excel, to burden with a label that sought to undermine their burgeoning socio-political agency in the public/political sphere. It is no accident that the forces of "traditional" America chose soccer. The formulation of the "soccer mom" label is perhaps the traditionalists most damaging and subversive gambit yet, as it manages to further "feminize" soccer in American discourse, while simultaneously negating agency and individuality for women politically, even as it outwardly appears to be championing and/or promoting it. Swanson notes that these mothers have the chance to break the traditionalist paradigm, only if they become "cognizant of the hegemonic forces at play on the American, suburban, soccer field" (Swanson 353). Can the recent gains made by women — as legitimately crucial, determinative voting blocs, not to mention the large gains they have made as elected officials at the state and federal level — be read as the first stirrings of this cognizance?

Alt-Metrics

Soccer has definitely asserted itself within American cultural life. The MLS live attendance metric and the Luker on Trends/ESPN report are monumental pieces of quantitative data that show beyond a shadow of a doubt that no matter the wishes of the Becks, Queenans, Feinsteins and O'Reillys of the world: Americans do like, play, and consume soccer. To claim otherwise negates the reality. Other metrics such as television ratings, whether they be for the MLS or the EPL that have room for growth and consistency are often the only remaining ones cited by soccer detractors possessed of enough effort to venture outside the contours of the withered "soccer will never be big here" narrative. Paradoxically, soccer's low ratings are often cited in the very same columns where the significance of diminishing ratings for baseball are vehemently discounted (Hiestand). The television ratings narrative, specifically the game's failure to general high ratings consistently, stands as the last legitimate refuge for traditionalist soccer haters in the United States. Never mind the fact that "ESPN and ABC averaged 80 percent higher ratings per match for the 2010 World Cup than in the 2006 World Cup. Both the U.S.-England and U.S.-Ghana matches drew over 17 million viewers, more than any single game of either the NBA or Stanley Cup Finals" (Lindner and Hawkins 70). Despite tangible, objective evidence like this as well as strong anecdotal evidence such as Fox's decision to rearrange their coverage of a baseball game between the Yankees and Mets in favor of live coverage of the 2010 Champions League final between Inter Milan and Bayern Munich (Saporito). You still encounter the same strange "wish-it-were-so" persistence about the sport's dismal future on American television. Lack of consistently large numbers did not stop NBC for paying $85 million annually to broadcast the EPL in the United States over the next three years starting in the summer of 2013. Granted that figure pales in comparison to the $800 million Fox and Turner invested, rather poorly it seems, in securing post-season baseball (Rosecrans; Hiestand).

Besides the myriad sociopolitical baggage attached to the game thanks to the efforts of people like Queenan and Rome, there is some truth in the notion that soccer is a tough-sell to casual American viewers weaned on "the corporate driven rhythms of the 'Big Three,' in which frequent stoppages in play allow for commercials to be regularly aired" (Armstrong and Rosbrook-Thompson 360). Less time for commercials obviously means less value for advertisers, thus making soccer a less lucrative property to corporate America before issues of demand and popularity even have a chance to influence matters. But the MLS is run by savvy individuals who are seeking ways to circumvent these problems and make their product more attractive. Howard Handler, the league's recently appointed chief marketing officer, immediately honed in on one aspect of the television quandary that he seeks to change, maximizing the league's presence and impact in the last indicator in which it lags. Addressing the television problem with ESPN's Roger Bennett, he remarked that "right now our matches are all over the dial, unlike the Premier League, where you roll right out of bed on a Saturday morning" (Bennett, "MLS Takes in"). Ruing the league's inability able to create a "habitual time slot that spells MLS soccer," like the EPL has established or the NFL has done so expertly, Handler vowed to somehow stake out a uniform, standardized television time to galvanize existing fans while attracting new ones. The MLS has intense, devoted, yet strangely atomized, pockets of fans spread throughout the United States, something Bennett characterized as a "patchwork of localized fan frenzy" which the league has thus far been unable to translate into a national presence that registers significant television ratings.

Overall signs for the league are encouraging though, as 2012 MLS regular season games ratings on NBC and the NBC Sports Network "increased 122 percent overall compared to 2011 telecasts" (Mahoney). That "patchwork localized frenzy" or regional, decentralized segments of soccer fandom can be overcome culturally as a whole, but the strange inability to articulate soccer's importance in a coordinated national manner expressed in regular TV viewing is part of the strained, unbalanced relationship between participation and consumption that the game still struggles with in the United States. Once consumption can regularly be measured to be near or equal to the levels of participation the game enjoys, then not even the most stalwart defenders of "traditional" America will be able to objectively deny soccer's cultural power and place within a reconfigured "hegemonic sports culture" aligned more with the identity of "modern" America. The failure to expand their ratings has denied the MLS an important, traditional means of entering the national narrative because, as Handler notes, "a true supporters movement has emerged here in the United States that has not been covered in the national media because our position has barely changed since kickoff in 1996" (Bennett, "MLS Takes in"). By "position," he can only mean ratings. Substantial MLS (and to a lesser degree EPL) ratings will force the gatekeepers to finally admit, even as they ignore the staggering evidence in every other metric, that soccer is a thriving part of the identity and culture of "modern" America. Since what is being contested is a refashioning of the cultural landscape and identity of America, a tumultuous rebirth, restatement and reconstitution of a "modern" America that by its very newness might call for a reconsideration of hitherto standard metrics and concepts designed to measure cultural importance. In other words, a new, non-traditional American needs new non-traditional measurements.

This point is addressed in an interesting column on *Grantland.com* by Brian Phillips where he discusses the relative health of soccer in the United States despite recent criticism of the MLS, in particular, by FIFA president Sepp Blatter. Writing of the MLS's penetration into American society, Phillips notes that you "can point to a hundred measurables that confirm" the league's steady, yet gradual ascension, but he also concedes "on the other hand, has the league been embraced by *Tonight Show* American society? Obviously not." Phillips chose a fascinating way of defining "traditional" American audiences and metrics, and it positions him to make a cogent point regarding soccer's cultural position in the United States, which is "Blatter looks at America, sees a country where soccer is the most popular youth sport, and calls that 'struggling' because they don't run MLS spots during *How I Met Your Mother*." Phillips excellently frames the same disconnect experienced by MLS marketing execs. like Handler regarding the need to craft a national narrative built on consumption rather than participation, while also underlining how entrenched the tension between the two metrics really is. But Phillips also observes something else, something extremely important which speaks to the notion that as an atomized force reshaping the cultural landscape of America in its own image — maybe the true depth and breadth of soccer's cultural impact cannot be adequately measured in the language and metrics of "traditional" America after all. Phillips notes that "where American soccer has grown the most over the past decade is in the area where *sport* exists outside the business of sport," or in other words, culturally. Its growth lies in those incredibly diffuse, hard to measure areas that fall "outside the traditional benchmarks" of the standardized metrics of big business, including most prominently and importantly, television ratings. Instead of impressive television ratings, soccer's growth can be glimpsed every day in "playgrounds and mall concourses and the jokes people you haven't talked to in 12 years are making on Facebook," not to mention increasing numbers of American soccer fans "painting their faces for MLS games and/or streaming gray-market Blackburn matches and/or hanging out in soccer bars and/or arguing with Spanish fans about Thierry Henry on Barcelona message boards" (Phillips).

Bill Saporito wrote an interesting hybrid of the traditionalist, "Soccer will never be big here" column for *Time* on the eve of the 2010 FIFA World Cup in South Africa, that also contained the initial stirrings of the "how do we measure how much this sport really is a cultural reality in America" meme expanded upon by Phillips. Saporito splits the difference between "traditional" and "modern" ways of understanding soccer in the United States, writing, "And stop asking that question, 'When is soccer ever going to be big in America?' Soccer won't ever be NFL big or Major League Baseball big, but in so many other ways, soccer has become a big and growing sport. An American sport." Note the persistence of the blanket "It'll never be as big as _____." But Saporito is perceptive enough to realize what Phillips articulates so well: i.e., soccer *is* already big here and we need to develop ways to measure and articulate that on its own terms. Saporito unearths another unorthodox data point that shows the spread of soccer culturally, as well as delineating who is spreading it, and that is within the realm of gaming. Saporito writes that EA Sports has seen "startling changes" in who is playing its annually released FIFA soccer games, noting that as of the summer of 2010, on any given day upwards of "750,000 Americans compete online, second only to the British." Saporito interviewed Peter Moore, the President of EA Sports who said, "We see *FIFA* as a game that creeps into every neighborhood in America." Another telling non-traditional metric that shows soccer's cultural ascendance.

It is like a new form of insurgent, asymmetrical symbolic warfare that occurs outside of the existing paradigm, even though successes within the traditional paradigm like the MLS's live attendance numbers can certainly be pointed to. Phillips admits that "there's no real rubric for evaluating the success of that kind of diffuse participation." A true test case of this new type of symbolic warfare that illuminates the disconnect between the guardians of "traditional" America and their tenacious grip on traditional levers of power and influence such as newspapers and magazines can be seen by examining *Sports Illustrated*'s decision to keep the USWNT off their cover in the wake of their victory over Brazil in 2011. The magazine instead chose to commemorate New York Yankee shortstop Derek Jeter for recording his 3,000th Major League hit. Outmoded MLB signifiers such as the Cy Young have been discussed briefly before, but it must be reiterated that these symbols are still reported with an air of import and significance that is substantially overstated and bears little relation to what everyday people are actually talking about, which is an extremely simplified definition of what constitutes "hegemonic sports culture." The prestige of the 3,000 hit milestone lives on largely, almost exclusively, within the bubble of the overwhelmingly white male sports punditocracy, who abide by their function as arbiters and advertisers of "traditional" America, insisting with the sheer belligerence of their repetition that modern America should and must value this diluted cultural symbol in the same manner they do.

Perhaps this inability to measure such buzz in traditional terms is why *SI* decided to stay in their traditionalist bubble and force people to consume something they did not seem to really want or value, denying, thus negating the weight of the cultural cache and symbolism generated by the USWNT's incredible performance. *SI*'s official reason for doing so was that they "were very tempted to go with the women's soccer team, but they could have been eliminated by the time the issue reached subscribers" (Davis). A flimsy rationale in favor of Jeter that Yahoo.com sports writer Brooks Peck noted "made it hard to argue how special it [the hit]was for the whole country and not just fans of one particular club like, say, the Yankees." Peck goes on to wonder if it was ultimately a "business decision" to put a member of the iconic New York Yankees on the magazine's cover (Peck). Perhaps there is some truth to that, but this is also emblematic of the traditionalist's refusal to understand that these "hallowed" MLB milestones just do not resonate, particularly with young people, in ways that they did even a decade ago. Their potency as cultural signifiers has been drained.

Viewing the two events armed with measurable, quantifiable data proves beyond doubt that people in the United States were absolutely transfixed by the USWNT and the conclusion of the 2011 Women's World Cup, with the final match, featuring the United States squaring off against Japan, "generated more tweets per second on Twitter than either the British royal wedding or the capture of Osama Bin Laden" (Lindner and Hawkins 70). Undeniable evidence, which should have been heeded by *SI* that USWNT were, without question, driving the national conversation at that moment far more than Jeter. Again, the level of cultural activity and capital generated by the USWNT is indicative of a sport that can reasonably and legitimately be depicted as "hegemonic" in modern America, to once again use Markovits and Hellerman's construct. Many media observers have remarked that soccer cannot truly succeed on a macro cultural level in the United States until it fashions an entry point into the national narrative, but instances like this generate the question as to whether the traditionalists are determined to prevent that from ever happening. Not to get conspiratorial, but if the USWNT's athletically brilliant, culturally resonant march to the 2011 World Cup finals cannot make enough space for itself in the national narrative/discourse, then what can? Daniel Durbin, director of the Annenberg Institute of Sports, Media and Society at the University of Southern California explicitly told ESPN that "you need persistent coverage in national media that reinforces the message that this is a league of some importance" (Bennett, "MLS Takes in"). You read quotes like these all the time regarding the importance of the MLS's need to truly enter the national conversation. The juxtaposition of the cover of *Sports Illustrated* and the (at the time) recording shattering volume of Tweets provides a concise image of not only the divide between traditional and modern, but also the need for new ways of measuring cultural impact to be devised, legitimized and recognized as such.

As the game is flourishing in non-traditional, non-monetized ways, but as the question of the MLS's need for a national narrative asserts itself, there are two disparate strands of thinking. First, does a non-traditional expression of "modern" American culture need to be validated by "traditional" and in some ways outmoded means of measurement? Or, does a new expression of "modern" American cultural symbols like soccer also require new metrics for measurement and evaluation, measurements that mirror modern values and habits? Second, if the MLS and/or the USWNT heed the advice of the voices of "traditional" America and go all in towards forming a "national" narrative, will they be allowed to do so? What could be the catalyst if not events like the journey of the 2011 USWNT or the Luker on Trends/EPSN poll? Can traditional language, metrics and symbols even properly frame a "national" narrative around soccer on its own terms? More importantly, has the battle between the forces of tradition and modernity over the symbols which will define our identity as Americans and form the structure of our shared national vocabulary actually created two separate, mutually incompatible cultural lexicons completely unable to communicate with one another, making the idea of a truly authentic, cohesive "national" voice and/or identity obsolete?

Perhaps the most remarkable asymmetrical/non-traditional metric that demonstrates the strength of soccer in the United States was articulated by Rich Luker, ironically, the man trying to assemble more traditional, objective forms of data. He said, "My greatest delight is to look out of a plane's window when I am crossing the country and see what people are playing in the parks below" and "If you watch it like that, soccer is the biggest sport in the nation" (Bennett, "Soccer's Big"). Luker characterized it as an "inevitability that soccer will soon be as popular as MLB and NBA" (Bennett, "Soccer's Big"). Just as the traditional political classes are losing control of the means of influencing the younger, more diverse segments of the American populace (President Obama's trailblazing, massively successful social media outreach comes immediately to mind as an inverse), the cultural organs of traditional America (in this case, *SI*) should intuit that there are new ways of communicating and demonstrating what really has significant cultural cache or risk ceding the same level of ground the traditionalists have politically.

Conclusion

If one takes the long view culturally and politically, soccer can be viewed as a catalyst and a core constitutive element of the major groups that comprise "the Obama coalition." Title IX gave women the freedom to play sports in schools and many of them chose soccer, making the game a part of their lives and identities. Some of them went on to build the USWNT, an object of national pride that has inspired millions of American women for three decades now. From another angle, many of these same women were also constituted — ultimately to their detriment as diverse, individualistic agents — as the "soccer mom" constituency. It seems that the label is finally losing its potency to "homogenize" women, as Swanson so eloquently put it (345). Soccer has unquestionably helped elevate women, culturally and politically. The same can also be said of the MLS's decision to essentially build their business model on the projected, yet never tapped, economic and cultural clout of Latinos in the United States, providing them with a positively constituted socioeconomic space which they were free to fashion as their own. Now, following the MLS's example, all serious enterprises (including presidential campaigns) are going out of their way to cultivate and secure the allegiance of the Latino community. Soccer stands inextricably linked to the core of that gift of agency as well. Finally, Millennials with deep participatory *and* consumption-based ties to the game have come of age electorally and cumulatively as voters. They wield power comparable to that of the baby boomers. It is estimated that by 2020 Millennials will account for just under 40 percent of the eligible electorate ("Millennials: Diverse"). Soccer is an intrinsic part of their identity, how they have fashioned and constituted themselves as "modern" American citizens. This was something MLS Chief Marketing Officer Howard Handler was perceptive enough to pick up quickly after his experiences with Seattle Sounders fans, telling ESPN that he "realized their support was an expression of their own identities — a reflection of how they are and what it means to be 20- and 30-year-olds in Seattle" (Bennett, "MLS Takes in"). The Millennial identity is also informed by principles of tolerance and diversity (39 percent are non-white, according to Advocates for Youth) that find expression in their tendency to favor Democratic and/or progressive political causes such as marriage equality and a woman's right to choose.

There is already some initial quantitative evidence from the *National Journal* (Shannon) and a 2010 National Media Research, Planning and Placement poll that "suggests that MLS Cup viewers tend to skew Democratic" (Lindner and Hawkins 72). Both objective and asymmetrical, and modern and traditional evidence demonstrating the commitment of these constituencies to a progressive vision of an America forged in their own image, a modern America, will continue to mount. Hopefully, unlike the "soccer mom" label, the designation "MLS voters" will always embody a sense of recognition and pride regarding the remarkable strides these groups have made in refashioning rigid, outdated, and monochromatic notions of what it means to be an American in the twenty-first century, partially through the cultural bonds forged and expressed through their love for the game of soccer. The battle is not over and the forces representing "traditional" America are nothing if not tireless, but as the narrative and demographic forces of modernity continue to marshal and assert their strength — the gains they have undoubtedly made thus far may prove irrevocable.

Works Cited

Armstrong, Gary, and James Rosbrook-Thompson. "Coming to America: Historical Ontologies and United States Soccer." *Identities: Global Studies in Culture and Power* 17.4 (2010): 348–71. 9 July 2010. Web. 4 Dec. 2012.
Associated Press. "MLS Sets Record in Racial Diversity." *FOX Soccer*. Fox Sports, 8 Nov. 2012. Web. 18 Jan. 2013.
_____. "World Series Has Record-Low Rating." *ESPN*. ESPN Internet Ventures, 30 Oct. 2012. Web. 29 Jan. 2013.
Badenhausen, Kurt. "World Series Sweep Proves Costly for Giants, Tigers and Fox." *Forbes*. Forbes Magazine, 29 Oct. 2012. Web. 25 Jan. 2013.
Baker, Liana B., and Lisa Richwine. "World Series Ratings Facing Likely Slump Without Yankees." *Reuters*. Thomson Reuters, 22 Oct. 2012. Web. 25 Jan. 2013.
Bassett, Laura. "Women in Politics Break Records in 2012 Election." *The Huffington Post*. TheHuffingtonPost.com, 7 Nov. 2012. Web. 27 Jan. 2013.
Bennett, Roger. "MLS Takes in the Big Picture." *ESPN*. ESPN Internet Ventures, 24 July 2012. Web. 18 Jan. 2013.
_____. "Soccer's Big Takeover." *ESPNFC*. ESPN Internet Ventures, 20 Sept. 2013. Web. 18 Jan. 2013.
"Bill O'Reilly: 'The White Establishment Is Now the Minority.'" *Fox Nation*. Fox News Network, 7 Nov. 2012. Web. 1 Feb. 2013.
Buffington, Daniel T. "Us and Them: U.S. Ambivalence Toward the World Cup and American Nationalism." *Journal of Sport & Social Issues* 36.2 (2012): 135–54. Sage Publications, 14 Feb. 2012. Web. 18 Nov. 2012.
Davis, Noah. "Here's Why *Sports Illustrated* Kept the US Women's Soccer Team Off Its Cover." *The Wire*. Business Insider, 12 July 2011. Web. 21 Jan. 2013.

Delgado, Fernando. "Sport and Politics: Major League Soccer, Constitution, and (The) Latino Audience(s)." *Journal of Sport & Social Issues* 23.1 (1999): 41–54. Sage Publications, 1 Feb. 1999. Web. 18 Nov. 2012.

Foer, Franklin. *How Soccer Explains the World: An Unlikely Theory of Globalization*. New York: HarperCollins, 2004. Print.

Ford, Zack. "Millennials Continue to Support Marriage Equality at High Rates." *Think Progress LGBT*. ThinkProgress, 19 Apr. 2012. Web. 26 Jan. 2013.

Galeano, Eduardo. *Soccer in Sun and Shadow*. London: Verso, 1998. Print.

Gross, Daniel. "Why Europe's Favorite Sport Is More American Than Baseball." *Slate Magazine*. Slate, 30 June 2004. Web. 18 Jan. 2013.

Hannan, Caleb. "Why MLS Cracks Down Harder on Homophobia Than Any Other League." *Grantland*. ESPN Internet Ventures, 15 Nov. 2012. Web. 15 Nov. 2012.

Hertzberg, Hendrik. "The Name of the Game." *The New Yorker*. The New Yorker, 12 July 2010. Web. 21 Jan. 2013.

Hiestand, Michael. "World Series No Sweep for Fox in TV Ratings." *USA Today*. Gannett, 28 Oct. 2012. Web. 21 Jan. 2013.

Howard, Greg. "Major League Soccer Now 3rd-Most Attended Sport." *The Slatest*. Slate, 9 Nov. 2011. Web. 18 Jan. 2013.

Hunter, James Davison. *Culture Wars: The Struggle to Define America*. New York: Basic, 1991. Print.

Limbaugh, Rush. "Limbaugh: I Hope Obama Fails." *RushLimbaugh.com*. Premier Radio Networks, 16 Jan. 2009. Web. 1 Feb. 2013.

Lindner, Andrew M., and Daniel N. Hawkins. "Globalization, Culture Wars, and Attitudes Towards Soccer in America: An Empirical Assessment of *How Soccer Explains the World*." *The Sociological Quarterly* 53.1 (2012): 68–91. Wiley Online Library. Web. 4 Dec. 2012.

Mahoney, Ridge, and Paul Kennedy. "NBC Cites Improved Ratings for MLS Coverage." *SoccerAmerica*. SoccerAmerica, 28 Nov. 2012. Web. 21 Jan. 2013.

Markovits, Andrei S., and Steven L. Hellerman. *Offside: Soccer and American Exceptionalism*. Princeton: Princeton University Press, 2001. Print.

Martin, Jonathan. "Election Aftermath: GOP Soul-searching: 'Too Old, Too White, Too Male'?" *POLITICO*. N.p., 7 Nov. 2012. Web. 27 Jan. 2013.

McCormack, John. "Chicago Loses (Update: Rio Wins)." *The Weekly Standard*. TheWeeklyStandard.com, 2 Oct. 2009. Web. 25 Jan. 2013.

"Millennials: Diverse, Connected, and Committed to Sexual Health and Rights." *Millennials: Diverse, Connected, and Committed to Sexual Health and Rights*. Advocates for Youth, n.d. Web. 26 Jan. 2013.

Minzesheimer, Bob. "Game Creates Bridge Linking Diverse Groups." *USA TODAY* [Arlington, VA] 29 May 1996: C3. *ProQuestCentral*. Web. 29 Jan. 2013.

NSGA: "2011 Sports Participation." *2011 Sports Participation*. National Sporting Goods Association, 2012. Web. 10 Feb. 2013.

Ortiz, Maria B. "Hispanic Market Part of DNA of MLS." *ESPNFC*. ESPN Internet Ventures, 14 Oct. 2009. Web. 28 Jan. 2013.

Peck, Brooks. "SI Keeps U.S. Women's Team off Cover Fearing Loss to France." *Dirty Tackle*. Yahoo! Sports, 12 July 2011. Web. 21 Jan. 2013.

Phillips, Brian. "Future Creep." *Grantland*. ESPN Internet Ventures, 3 Jan. 2013. Web. 21 Jan. 2013.

Piatak, Tom. "Still the Metric System in Short Pants." *Chronicles: A Magazine of American Culture*. Chronicles: A Magazine of American Culture, 18 June 2010. Web. 25 Jan. 2013.

Queenan, Joe. "A Final Red Card for American Soccer." *Wall Street Journal* 30 Mar. 2012, U.S. Edition ed., Life & Culture sec.: n.p. *Wall Street Journal*. 30 Mar. 2012. Web.

_____. "Of Headers and Hooligans." *The New York Times* 4 July 2004, Arts sec.: n.p. *New York Times*. Web.

Rosecrans, C. T. "World Series Ratings Might Be Lowest Ever, but Does It Really Matter?" *CBSSports.com*. CBS Interactive, 29 Oct. 2012. Web. 25 Jan. 2013.

Saporito, Bill. "Yes, Soccer Is America's Game." *Time* 14 June 2010: 82–86. *Academic Search Alumni Edition*. Web. 11 Dec. 2012.

Shannon, Mike, and Will Feltus. "Play Ball: What Your Favorite Sports Say About Your Politics." *Hotline on Call*. NationalJournal.com, 26 Oct. 2012. Web. 1 Feb. 2013.

Slajda, Rachel. "Conservatives Revel in America's Olympic Defeat." *TPM LiveWire*. Talking Points Memo, 2 Oct. 2009. Web. 25 Jan. 2013.

Stein, Sam. "Conservatives Revel in Obama's Olympic Bid Failure." *The Huffington Post*. TheHuffingtonPost.com, 2 Oct. 2009. Web. 25 Jan. 2013.

Steinberg, Dan. "John Feinstein on Why Soccer Is Not a Real Sport." *Washington Post D.C. Sports Bog*. The Washington Post, 12 July 2011. Web. 26 Jan. 2013.

Swanson, Lisa. "Complicating the "Soccer Mom:" The Cultural Politics of Forming Class-Based Identity, Distinction, and Necessity." *Research Quarterly for Exercise and Sport* 80.2 (2009): 345–54. *ProQuest Central*. Web. 28 Jan. 2013.

Teixeira, Ruy. "The Obama Coalition in the 2012 Election and Beyond." *Center for American Progress*. Center for American Progress, 4 Dec. 2012. Web. 31 Jan. 2013.

Teixeira, Ruy, and John Halpin. "The Return of the Obama Coalition." *Center for American Progress*. Center for American Progress, 8 Nov. 2012. Web. 19 Jan. 2013.

Tenorio, Paul. "U.S.-Argentina Soccer: Juan Agudelo's Goal Lifts Americans to 1-1 Tie." *Washington Post*. N.p., 26 Mar. 2011. Web. 19 Jan. 2013.

Thompson, Rex W. "Sport and Ideology in Contemporary Society." *International Review for the Sociology of Sport* 13.2 (1978): 81–94. *Sage Premier 2012*. Web. 4 Feb. 2013.

"US Youth Soccer: What Is Youth Soccer." *What Is Youth Soccer*. US Youth Soccer, 2012. Web. 10 Feb. 2013.

Verducci, Tom. "Phillies Win! Why They Deserve Better." *Sports Illustrated* 10 Nov. 2008: n.p. *Sports Illustrated Vault*. Sports Illustrated, 10 Nov. 2008. Web. 18 Jan. 2013.

Willis, Oliver. "As the World Cup Starts, Conservative Media Declare War on Soccer." *Media Matters for America*. Media Matters for America, 11 June 2010. Web. 25 Jan. 2013.

Zirin, Dave. "Glenn Beck's Blues: Why the Far Right Hates the World Cup." *The Notion*. The Nation, 13 June 2010. Web. 19 Jan. 2013.

PART II: AMERICAN SOCCER ECONOMICS

4

It's All Fun and Games Until No One Gets Hurt

European Soccer Leagues, Capitalism and the Movement Towards a Socialist American Model

CLIFF STARKEY

The United States is a country dominated by the "big four" sports: American football, baseball, basketball, and ice hockey. Cable television has brought with it a host of second-tier sports, vying for promotion into the top echelon of American sports as well as the money that comes with it. Extreme sports like skateboarding and snowboarding get their yearly X Games showcase on ESPN, but cannot gain a foothold outside of the months of August and December, and NASCAR's decade-long surge has started to recede (Peltz). In this environment, soccer seems to be one of the very few, if not the only, sport that is making inroads on becoming a sports mainstay in the United States.

The caveat, of course, is that soccer has been on this threshold for decades. In the 1970s and 1980s, the North American Soccer League (NASL) succeeded in bringing in top talent from around the world to play in sold out American football stadiums. A decade after the NASL folded — due to an unsustainable model built upon unlimited spending — Americans were given the gift of hosting the largest sporting event in the world: the 1994 World Cup. To make the country look more receptive to the sport, Major League Soccer was formed just one year earlier. The sport underwent growing pains — two of the league's Florida-based teams had to fold in 2002, bringing the number of teams at the time to ten ("Major League Soccer") — but the league now appears to have stability, and is becoming a viable destination for soccer-loving youths, as well as soccer-loving fans. In 2012, NBC acquired the rights to air games, with a bid of $10 million dollars per year (Bell).

But the MLS, with all of its growth, is still playing second fiddle not only to baseball and hockey, but to its European cousin — *football* — as well. Satellite television has brought world-class level soccer into homes of millions of people, and in true fashion, Americans demand the best. Thus, while MLS continues steady — albeit slow — growth, Fox Soccer Channel, ESPN and NBC are making English teams like Manchester United and Liverpool legitimate brands in this country. Rights to air the World Cup, the European Championships, and various leagues in Europe are hotly contested year after year. FOX even began occasionally airing and promoting English Premier League games before and after Sunday NFL games. While not homegrown, soccer has become big business in the United States — and many wealthy investors here are starting to take note. While American broadcasting companies spend millions to import world-class soccer to the United States, billionaire investors are exporting uniquely American sporting ideals back across the Atlantic. The "soccer-preneurs," with names like *Glazer* and *Kroenke*, are becoming major players in European soccer (primarily, the English Premier League). These investors most likely grew up watching the NBA and the NFL (and probably NOT the NASL or MLS), and are slowly changing the game overseas to mirror the sports model they are used to.

Differences Between American and European League Models

The differences between the sports models of the United States and Europe are all the more striking when one considers the economic structures on which they are based. The United States, despite its strong anti–Communist and anti–Socialist history and leanings, builds its sports leagues around a Socialist model. Europe, and in particular, England, employs a Capitalist, winner-take-all system. This difference is important because it is the driving factor behind all of the key differences between the systems: ownership, acquisition of players, spending limits, and repercussions of on-the-field failure.

To become an owner of your very own English soccer club, all one needs is a dream — and a few hundred million dollars. Teams are run like corporations: complete with stockholders and board members, all influencing the day-to-day decisions of the club. Tensions between managers and the board are often high, as the manager often has very little say in which players are brought in and out of the team's locker room. Decisions best left to a knowledgeable manager are not always made with on-the-field success in mind, in lieu of the overall team profit. In contrast, MLS is a single-entity system. Much (though, admittedly, not all) of the profits of a team are funneled not back to that team, but to the league as a whole. When a player is sold overseas, the deal must be approved by MLS, as the player's contract is owned not by the individual team, but by the league. Though the league has made a few changes to let the teams reap some of the financial benefit of selling a player, the league still takes one-third of the total transfer paid. More than a handful of inquiries from European teams for the likes of MLS stars such as Landon Donovan and Brek Shea have gone nowhere due to the difference in player worth differences not between the two soccer teams (as is common in Europe), but between the selling team and MLS (Straus). Teams in the MLS are owned by individuals, but are at the mercy of the league's decisions. In England, each team is its own corporation. In the United States, the *league* is the corporation (Ayad 421).

The search for on-field talent is also vastly different between these two models. In true capitalist fashion, finding players to wear your club's shirt often comes down to a simple bidding war. Whoever is willing to pay a player the most money will procure the rights to that player's contract. If a player is not under a contract, though, the player has the last say on where he will play next. However, once a player signs a contract, his services are dictated and wholly owned by the team. The team may choose to play him or bench him as they wish, with no possible repercussions. Most importantly, a team may sell the rights to his contract to any other team of their choosing. Bottom-line profit is almost always the deciding factor in who is bought and sold. Because clubs can earn a substantial payday from selling promising young players, they enlist the expertise of scouts, whose sole job is to travel the world seeking youth prodigies to purchase. These promising players play in lower levels of top leagues, growing their talents — and their overall net worth. After two or three years, if the player has panned out, richer, larger clubs will begin bidding wars to the remaining contract of the youth (prime examples include Premier League superstars Wayne Rooney and Gareth Bale). The more success a club has at this aspect of the game, the less likely they will try to hold on to players for on-field success. These "selling clubs" do service not for their fans, but for their investors.

The United States model could not be more different. Because of the profitability of college sports, skilled youths are not tempted with playing professionally until they are in their early twenties. After the player plays at the collegiate level, he can only enter the ranks of the professionals through a league-run draft. The best players have an incredibly small amount of say in where they will play: the team who first drafts the player wins the rights to that player. This is the model by which all major team-based sports are run in the United States, though the MLS has an added unique concept with which to distribute players.

Because the MLS is not one of the top leagues in the world in terms of money or talent, there are many more players leaving the league to play overseas than coming in from abroad. Much like the smaller "selling clubs" in Europe, MLS is indeed a "selling league"—the journey, not necessarily the destination. When a player leaves the MLS, plays for a few years in Europe, and decides that he wants to come back, an allocation draft is held. Even if he is out of contract, rarely will he get to sign with the team of his choosing. The league's interest here is parity: a league in which all teams have a reasonable chance of success in. The U.S. model—for all major sports—is the *desire* for no team to grow substantially larger than the other teams in the league (though dynasties such as the New York Yankees and the New England Patriots have successfully subverted the system). American leagues have many ways with which to keep the league in relative balance.

While English teams are limited in their spending only by their pocket books—and often not even that is a realistic limit as most teams, including juggernauts Arsenal and Manchester United, find themselves in considerable debt (Conn, "Premier League")—the American sports model hamstrings teams financially in the interest of a fair and balanced league. In his essay, Michael Lewis explains that "The fear is that in the absence of salary caps or other regulatory mechanisms, smaller-market teams will be unable to remain competitive" (535). While there is no larger disparity of large and small-market teams than in European soccer leagues, the concept of a salary cap is as of yet unknown in Europe—though that may change soon. For the 2010-11 season, the average total salary paid for a team in England's Premier League was roughly $121 million. The highest two salaries paid that year were Chelsea ($297 million) and Manchester City ($272 million). Blackburn Rovers, who narrowly avoided relegation that year, paid $21 million (Oliver). They were relegated last year.

In contrast, American teams must adhere to the strict salary limits set by the league. In the MLS, no team may have a total salary above $2.81 million ("2012 MLS Roster Rules"). Again, there are some exceptions for "Designated Players," but by and large, this is a constant not only in MLS, but in the NBA and NFL as well. Teams that go over this limit are penalized in future years (by paying a "luxury tax" of sorts to the league). There is little risk involved in the American model: each team will be around next year, and it will have, in theory, the same chance of winning the title as every other team. If a European team wants to spend astronomical amounts of money, it is completely free to do so. If the team fails, it may go bankrupt and completely cease to exist. If it enters administration — an alternative to total liquidation due to unpayable debt — it will be allowed to stay in the league, but suffer a very large point penalty, and almost assuredly finish the year near the bottom of the league. The difference between American and European sports models is not more pronounced in any other area than it is when examining how the teams in the cellar of the leagues are treated.

As you would expect from a Socialist model, the teams that finish at the bottom of the league are given the means by which to survive and be competitive in the future. The order of the draft is inversely proportional to the final standings of teams in the previous seasons. The Super Bowl winners, for example, get the last pick of collegiate talent — they won the league, and theoretically, need the least amount of help to ensure success next year. The team that finishes with the worst record is given the first pick of the collegiate litter. While this might not ensure a successful team next year, it can certainly make a substantial difference. Because of this, the end of the season may often be spent by bottom-tier teams vying for that coveted first draft pick — meaning teams may in fact lose on purpose. The hottest collegiate commodity in the 2012 NFL draft was Stanford's quarterback Andrew Luck — sparking a battle to "Suck for Luck" (Politi). As Lewis says, "[T]he structure also has the potential to create perverse incentives for small-market teams" (537). Short of the mockery of rival teams, there is no consequence of finishing poorly in the American sports model.

In Europe, the penalty for finishing at the bottom of a league is severe, and ensures that teams fight and scrap to the very end. The concept of promotion and relegation has been around in Europe for decades. In the model, teams that finish at the bottom of the league are relegated to the next lowest league in the system, while teams that finish at the top of lower leagues are promoted upward to the next level. The differences in these leagues are substantial: in addition to the staggering financial reward difference — $100 million per team in the Premier League vs. $5 million per team in the English League Championship (the second division of English soccer) (Switzer) — there is no guarantee that the team will easily be able to rise to the top again. To avoid relegation, teams must constantly spend to fight for talent to shore up weaknesses in their on-field product. If the NFL, NBA, or MLS employed this rule, many of the current top teams in these leagues — the San Francisco 49ers, Miami Heat, and Los Angeles Galaxy — may not even be part of the leagues they are now finding so much success in. In the American model, the line between successful and unsuccessful years is blurred, while in Europe, the difference is quite tangible. The teams relegated are cast down to the depths of the lower leagues, where they do not receive the bounty of riches that the top leagues are privy to. These riches are growing yearly, thanks in large part to the popularity of the leagues, and television viewership, which surprisingly, mirrors the American model of shared revenue.

An Expensive Game

Although the United States has been hesitant to embrace it, world soccer is starting to become an important part of sports culture. Thanks to the Internet's ability to swiftly import and export culture — and, to some extent, the MLS keeping the American public at least somewhat aware of soccer throughout the year — soccer is beginning to be a viable financial investment by television networks. When ABC bought the broadcasting rights to the World Cup and European Championship in 1994, the network paid $23 million (Field 4). For the 2006 and 2010 World Cups, ABC paid $100 million ("Briefs: ABC, ESPN"). After these competitions, interest in watching these star players week-in and week-out rose. As such, airing European Club competitions and leagues became more lucrative. A bidding war ensued, and in 2005, Fox created the Fox Soccer Channel to show various European league competitions, including the English Premier League. Fox also recently began showing games outside of its soccer-specific network, including a few marquee matchups on its flagship station. These games aired right before and after a proven American cash cow — the NFL. In addition, FOX sublicensed a few dozen matches to ESPN, who broadcasts those games live on many Saturday and Sunday mornings throughout the season.

In 2012, when Fox's and EPSN's contracts to air the English Premier League were set to expire, another bidding war began. NBC emerged the victor with the rights to air English Premier League soccer through 2015 for a whopping $250 million (Sandomir). Fox, on the other hand, has secured the rights for the 2018 and 2022 World Cup, to a tune of $400 million (Longman). As these numbers increase, so too do the bank accounts of the Premier League teams.

Domestic Premier League broadcast revenue is divided 50:25:25, offering a free-market twist to the American model. This means that 50 percent is divided equally between the clubs, 25 percent is awarded on a merit basis determined by a club's final league position and the final 25 percent is distributed as a facilities fee for the number of matches shown on television involving the club. International broadcast revenue is distributed equally. Again, much as in the United States, this is done to keep smaller-market teams competitive. In 2012, the average domestic payout to each team was around $72 million, in addition to the roughly $30 million given equally per team due to international rights ("Premier League Announces"). This revenue exemplifies why relegation is such a colossal blow to a team — the revenue awarded to each team in the League Championship in 2011 was less than $5 million (Switzer).

The financial allure of the Premier League has brought more suitors than just ESPN and FOX. Billionaires from around the world — notably the United States, Russia, and the Middle East — have begun buying European teams, in the hopes of getting in on the monetary windfall. Since around 2000, many teams in England found themselves under foreign ownership — including Chelsea, Manchester City, Arsenal, Liverpool, and Queens Park Rangers. These purchases, although seemingly benign enough, are causing large and possibly irreversible changes to the makeup of the structure of the league. The American "soccer-preneurs" are using the teams as playthings, and though they are used to the Socialist American sports model, they are buying in wholeheartedly into the Capitalist model that Europe offers: if you have the money, you can have the fun. However, too much American influence is threatening to turn the capitalist European model on its head by coddling and rewarding the richest of the rich.

Financial Influence and the End of Free Market Soccer

With no salary cap or restrictions of any kind, the English Premier League — as with most European soccer leagues — is set up to reward teams that have spent their money most intelligently, and often, most prodigiously. With the sudden interest the rest of the world is taking in the sport, many rich billionaires from America and across the planet are not seeing the purchase of a team as simply a toy, but instead as a low-risk investment. Although many of the have-nots of the English Premier League — teams like Everton, Wigan Athletic, and Fulham — may not like it, it is quite possible, and quite easy, to buy a title. In fact, many of the league's champions over the last ten years have all done so not with hard work and patience, but instead with the stroke of a pen.

In 2003, Russian businessman and billionaire Roman Abramovich gained a majority share in Chelsea Football Club, a team that, with the exception of a third-place finish in 1999, had not had any real success in the league in nearly half a century. After paying nearly $220 million for control, Abramovich continued to use his billions to overhaul the on-field product (Bose). Over the next few years, Abramovich secured the rights to top-level talents such as Arjen Robben, Hernan Crespo, Juan Veron, Didier Drogba, and Andrei Shevchenko — paying a grand total of $500 million in his first few years as owner (Fifield). Abramovich was instantly rewarded for his spending: his team finished second in 2004 before winning back-to-back titles in 2005 and 2006. Since then, the team has finished in the top three in five of the last six seasons, with another league title in 2010, and a Champions League title in 2012.

Similarly, perennial mid-table Manchester City has used a sudden influx of wealth with which to win glory. In 2008 the club was purchased by Abu Dhabi United Group, and almost immediately secured the contracts of some of the biggest names in all of world soccer (Armitstead). Over the next few years, the club spent nearly $760 million on players such as Robinho, Carlos Tevez, Gareth Barry, Emmanuel Adebayor, Sergio Aguero, and Samir Nasri (Scott). Although not as immediately successful as Abramovich's Chelsea, Manchester City finally won the league title in 2012.

American investors are not to be outdone in their attempt at buying success in England's top soccer league. Manchester United, a team owned by the wealthy food service and oil tycoon Glazer family, has won the league in twelve of the last twenty years. Arsenal, another top team, has American Stan Kroenke (married to the heiress of the Walmart billions) as its largest shareholder. The Glazers and Kroenke are not alone. Five of the Premier League's current twenty teams are wholly owned by Americans or have an American as the majority shareholder.

With so many teams in England's top league having virtually unlimited resources to construct modern-day dream teams, the league is in danger of stagnation. Although currently it appears that more and more wealthy billionaires are looking to buy in, at some point, the English Premier League will become a league of six or eight super-rich teams vying for top honors, and the remaining dozen or so teams simply filling roles as cannon fodder. If this continues, wealthy investments may end, as — much the same as the MLS — potential investors do not want to throw cash at something which may very well potentially fail. If someone is not willing to spend upwards of a billion dollars, they may find their team — and themselves — relegated to the wasteland of second-tier soccer. Likewise, those top-flight teams that were not lucky enough to be purchased in the last decade may soon find themselves replaced by some of those teams currently plying their trade in the lower divisions. More and more English League Championship teams are finding themselves becoming potential investment opportunities. Instead of spending hundreds of millions just to buy into the league, crafty businesspeople are looking to the lower leagues for a much cheaper buy-in. After spending considerably less money buying the top talent of the second-tier and guaranteed promotion, they are then free to scrap those players and spend Manchester City–style dollars on a team worthy of fighting for top honors in the Premier League.

In 2011, Malaysian businessman Tony Fernandes did just that, buying a majority share of League Championship side Queens Park Rangers for the comparatively paltry sum of $55 million (Conn, "Tony Fernandes"). After shoring up a squad worthy of winning promotion to the Premier League, the team has spent wildly, paying more than $100 million on players over two years, with the view of becoming yet another mega power in the Premier League (Jackson). As of this writing, Queens Park Rangers are languishing near the bottom of the Premier League. If the team can avoid relegation, more money will assuredly be spent to ensure their tenure in the top flight of English soccer for years to come. If he is successful, Fernandes will establish a model to be copied by other billionaires looking for a cheaper way to the top.

Though the get-titles-quick schemes are proving successful for the ultra-rich, fans and players alike plainly recognize that the competitiveness of the league is in danger. Though the league has had an ardent Capitalist structure for years, the brazen successes of Chelsea and Manchester City in England, as well as Paris Saint-Germain in France, called for a response. In 2009, the Union of European Football Associations (UEFA) designed and began to implement what it called the "Financial Fair Play Regulations." The regulations are meant to curtail exuberant spending, with threatened sanctions—ranging from bans on purchasing players to expulsion from certain competitions—set to be imposed on teams that spent more than they earned ("Financial Fair Play"). However, since the inception of the plan, no action has yet taken place against any of the major teams in Europe. Despite the inability of UEFA to stick to their guns regarding the Financial Fair Play Regulation, the precedent set by creation of this rule (if only in name) has brought with it a host potentially new soon-to-be-implemented changes to the game, all aimed at creating a more American, Socialist-style model.

Perhaps the largest potential change to the structure of the European model is the very real possibility of ending the punishment of relegation. In 2011, several owners put forward a plan that would end relegation — to protect their investments. According to League Managers Association (LMA) chief Richard Bevan, "If you're looking at sport all around the world and you look at sport owners trying to work out how to invest and make money, you'll find the that most of them like the idea of franchises and if you take, in particular, the Americans, they have ... a number of them looking at possibly having more of a franchise situation," and that "If we have four or five more new owners, that could happen" (Gibson and James). For now, the power lies with the Football Association. The popular opinion of fans and managers within the league is that relegation is an important part of European soccer. Manchester United manager, Sir Alex Ferguson, sees the idea of ending relegation as a slippery slope:

> You might as well lock the doors. The only place you can make money and realize your ambitions is in the Premier League and you can't take that away from [traditional powers now in the second division] like Nottingham Forest, Leeds United, Sheffield United and Sheffield Wednesday.

Wigan Athletic chairman Dave Whelan — despite the lure of potentially being locked into a league in which they are currently perennial relegation favorites, also slammed the idea:

> I've never heard anything so stupid, football is about competition and relegation and promotion are obviously vital in that. People might think we have something to gain from it as we are a small club constantly fighting to stay in the Premier League, but if this happened I would resign Wigan Athletic from the Premier League...I'd rather go down to [the fourth division of English soccer]. At least there would be competition [Kelso, Ogden, and Edwards].

The proposed model, while destroying what many people love about the European system, makes sense, at least economically. It solves the problem of a scary investment — your team will always be in the hunt for a title — but it would go a long way toward the Americanization of the European model. The next step to creating the NFL of soccer is, of course, equal distribution of talent via a salary cap — something that is also being discussed (Hare). Even if these changes are not implemented, the final change the European model may see to preserve itself is a truly Capitalist, Ayn Rand–style change. All of the largest and most valuable teams across Europe may leave the leagues they are in to form a European "Super League" while the rest of the teams across Europe are left to rot.

Over the last few years, a handful of Europe's top-performing and top-grossing teams — Bayern Munich, Barcelona, Real Madrid, Arsenal, Chelsea, and Liverpool, to name a few — have been voicing their displeasure with both UEFA and FIFA about a number of items. While the list of grievances is expansive, central to their argument is financial autonomy. The teams with the most influence in Europe are in an ongoing discussion to break away from their respective leagues — as early as in 2014 — to form a league where the best play the best, week in and week out ("Real Madrid's Florentino Perez"). While the prospect may make soccer fans excited, the fact is that it would be an absolute death knell for the thousands of teams across Europe who would not be invited to the money party. Without Manchester United, Manchester City, Arsenal, and Chelsea, the English Premier League does not have the clout to bring in viewers. The proposed change is very unique, as it is at once an ultimate concept of Capitalism, yet Socialist to the core. There is no denying that the teams breaking off to form their own league would find their total income skyrocket. One can only imagine the television and ticket revenue that a super league could generate. The "1%" of the soccer world would see record profits at the expense of the "99%." However, despite this, the structure of the league itself would complete the slow but sure progress of European sports to the Socialist American model. A league in which the number of teams *as well as the teams themselves* are static would, by definition, remove the concepts of promotion and relegation. With a static league, further calls for a level playing field would undoubtedly follow, along with player limits, spending caps, and an equal distribution of television revenue. This league, while certainly appealing to the eyes of soccer fans, would be about as far from the current league model Europeans have enjoyed and perfected for decades.

Conclusion

After threatening to do so for nearly forty years, soccer is starting to build — and maintain — a foothold in American sports culture. Much like with the export of the NFL and NBA, the Internet and satellite television has been instrumental in bringing a sport to a mass of people who have not been receptive to it in the past. With a new interest in the potential profit from the English Premier League, "soccer-preneurs" from around America and across the globe have flocked to England with the hopes of taking advantage of the league's Capitalist system. After a dozen years of foreign ownership buying titles, the league finds itself with a series of decisions to make. How can they keep the league interesting for more than four or five teams? Unless that question is answered soon, drastic changes may soon take shape. The changes, while aimed at saving the league, may destroy not only the Capitalist league structure that English fans have enjoyed for over one hundred years, but the entire league, as well.

Works Cited

Armitstead, Louise. "Sheikh Mansour bin Zayed Al Nahyan Has a Deep Love of Sport and Deeper Pockets." *Telegraph* [London] 2 Sept. 2008, n.p. Web. 6 Feb. 2013.
Ayad, Omar Hafez. "Take the Training Wheels Off the League: Major League Soccer's Dysfunctional Relationship with the International Soccer Transfer System." *Vanderbilt Journal of Entertainment and Tech Law* 10.2 (2008): 413–444. Print.
Bell, Jack. "M.L.S. and NBC Sports Announce New TV Deal." *Goal: The New York Times Soccer Blog*. The New York Times, 10 Aug. 2011. Web. 12 Nov. 2012.
Bose, Mihir. "Bates Sells Off Chelsea to a Russian Billionaire." *Telegraph* [London] 2 July 2003, n.p. Web. 6 Feb. 2013.
"Briefs: ABC, ESPN Secure World Cup TV rights." *Seattle Times* 3 Nov. 2005, n.p. Web. 6 Feb. 2013.
Conn, David. "Premier League Club Accounts: How in Debt Are They?" *Guardian* [London] 23 May 2012, n.p. Web. 6 Feb. 2013.
_____. "Tony Fernandes Announced as New Owner of Queens Park Rangers." *Guardian* [London] 18 Aug. 2011, n.p. Print.
Field, Russel. "Funny ... It Doesn't Look Like Football: America Welcomes the Soccer World." *Origins: Current Events in Historical Perspective* 2.2 (1994): 2–4. Print.
Fifield, Dominic. "Hundreds of Millions Later Chelsea Still Lack the Ultimate Pot of Gold." *Guardian* [London] 5 March 2012, n.p. Web. 7 Feb. 2013.
"Financial fair play." The Official Website for European Football. UEFA. Web. 6 Feb. 2013.
Gibson, Owen, and Stuart James. "Foreign Owners Discuss End to Relegation, Says League Managers Chief." *Guardian* [London] 17 Oct. 2011, n.p. Web. 6 Feb. 2013.
Hare, Joe. "Premier League Clubs Discuss Salary Cap to Curb English Football's Debt, Reveals Dave Whelan." *Telegraph* [London] 6 May 2011, n.p. Web. 6 Feb. 2013.
Jackson, Jamie. "Tony Fernandes's QPR Continue Quest to Spend or Be Damned." *Guardian* [London] 22 Aug. 2012, n.p. Web. 7 Feb. 2013.
Kelso, Paul, Mark Ogden, and Luke Edwards. "Manchester United Sir Alex Ferguson Brands Scrapping Premier League." *Telegraph* [London] 18 Oct. 2011, n.p. Web. 6 Feb. 2013.
Lewis, Michael. "Individual Team Incentives and Managing Competitive Balance in Sports Leagues: An Empirical Analysis of Major League Baseball." *Journal of Marketing Research* 45 (2008): 535–49. Print.
Longman, Jere. "Fox and Telemundo Win U.S. Rights to World Cups." *New York Times* 21 Oct. 2011, n.p. Web. 6 Feb. 2013.
"Major League Soccer Announces Elimination of Tampa Bay Mutiny and Miami Fusion for 2002 Season." U.S. Soccer. N.p., 8 Jan. 2002. Web. 16 Feb. 2013.
Oliver, Mark, and Dan Palmer. *Graphic: Premier League Transfer and Wage Spending from the 2000/01 Season to 2011/12*. Telegraph [London] n.d. Web. 7 Dec. 2012.
Peltz, Jim. "NASCAR Grapples with a Downshift in Popularity." *Los Angeles Times* 21 Mar. 2011, n.p. Web. 6 Feb. 2013.
Politi, Steve. "'Suck for Luck' Could Be Best Hope for NFL's Worst." *CNN.com — Breaking News, U.S., World, Weather, Entertainment & Video News*. CNN, 21 Oct. 2011. Web. 2 Jan. 2013.
"Premier League Announces 2011/12 Broadcast Payments." *The Official Website of the Barclays Premier League*. The Premier League, 15 May 2012. Web. 7 Jan. 2013.
"Real Madrid's Florentino Perez Reveals 'European Super League' Ambition." *Telegraph* [London] 5 July 2009, n.p. Web. 6 Feb. 2013.
Sandomir, Richard. "Deal with Premier League Gives NBC 380 Games." *New York Times* 28 Oct. 2012, n.p. Web. 6 Feb. 2013.
Scott, Matt. "Revealed: Sheikh Mansour's £500m Manchester City Cash Injection." *Guardian* [London] 25 Aug. 2010, n.p. Web. 6 Feb. 2013.

Straus, Brian. "MLS Holding Up Brek Shea Transfer to Stoke City." *Sporting News*. America Online, 22 Jan. 2013. Web. 22 Jan 2013.
Switzer, Alan. "The Cost of Relegation from the Premier League." *Telegraph* [London] 23 May 2011, n.p. Web. 6 Feb. 2013.
"2012 MLS Roster Rules." *Major League Soccer*. Major League Soccer. Web. 1 Feb. 2013.

5

A Resounding Soccer Success ... in the U.S.?

Dwight Branch

The Proof Is in the Average Attendance

General opinion is that soccer is not popular in the United States and that the sport is destined to forever languish, peering up at America's true sports loves: baseball, American football and basketball (sorry hockey). However there has proven to be a considerable appetite for soccer in the U.S. when looking at Americans' interest in international soccer leagues and competitions, particularly the European leagues/teams, as seen through examples including the summer tours in the U.S. and the investment of Premier League powerhouses in the U.S. This also extends to international tournaments, particularly the FIFA World Cup which the U.S. hosted in 1994 and which enjoyed record television viewership in the U.S. in 2010 (Blum). Even despite the geographical and cultural distance, the Euro Cup attained high viewership and also broke the previous U.S. Euro Cup Final viewership record in the U.S. (Tidey).

Until recently, that is where one would stop to submit evidence of soccer's potential in the U.S. Certainly there were no examples from domestic competition that could be cited to show just how popular soccer had in fact become in the U.S., even if only regionally (even the hugely successful National Football League does not have the same level of success in every region). Yet, soccer fans in the U.S. are now watching what may be the start of the golden age of professional soccer in the U.S. Major League Soccer (MLS) attendance figures, which have broken records for the last two years, prove this out at least in those cities with MLS franchises. A cohort of recent additions to the league, the Seattle Sounders FC and their regional rivals the Portland Timbers and the Vancouver Whitecaps, have shown just how strong the appetite for soccer in the U.S. can be, and not only among the expanding Hispanic population that is often cited as the cause of any growth in U.S. soccer interest.

The success of the Seattle Sounders in their first four years in MLS has earned the distinction of being considered one of the great, if not the greatest expansion team launches in history. And that is not a distinction among only MLS teams, but of any expansion sports team globally. A review of the Sounders average game attendance through their first four years in MLS reveals exactly why the team is held in such high esteem for its successful launch.

Table 1. Seattle Sounders Average Game Attendance

2009	30,897 (MLS record)	–
2010	36,173 (MLS record)	+17%
2011	38,498 (MLS record)	+6%
2012	43,144 (MLS record)	+8%

Sources: Oshan, Sounders FC Public Relations

Need perspective on those figures? The Sounders' 2012 average game attendance would have put them in the upper echelon of Europe's top leagues. If the Sounders played in Italy's Serie A in the 2011–2012 season, their average attendance would have been bested by only three teams. If they played in Spain's La Liga, their average would have been bested by only five teams. If they played in England's Barclays Premier League (EPL), their average would have been bested by only six teams. Looking at just the top two teams from each of those leagues, the Seattle Sounders have their work cut out for them to reach the highest levels of fan support and game attendance, but to be currently knocking on the door of two of Italy's giants is quite a marker in its own right. Still not convinced? Then consider that more than 66,000 attendees were on-site to take in a game at CenturyLink Field between the Sounders and their regional rival Portland Timbers. The single-game attendance figure represents the second highest ever for an MLS, bested only by the league's inaugural game between New York and LA in 1996 (Associated Press).

Table 2. Average Game Attendance Figures Comparison

Barcelona	84,119
Manchester United	75,387
Real Madrid	74,678
Arsenal	60,000
A.C. Milan	51,442
Inter Milan	47,913
Seattle Sounders	43,144

Sources: Oshan; "Barclays"; "Italian"; "Spanish"

If you are not yet convinced, consider that Seattle Sounders FC's 2012 average game attendance was above such globally-recognized teams as Chelsea (41,380) and Tottenham Hotspur (35,986) of the EPL, and AS Roma (35,420) and Juventus (32,610) of Serie A (ESPN FC respective teams).

Several factors have contributed to Seattle's success. Certainly the long delayed selection of Seattle to receive an MLS franchise, Seattle had applications for an MLS franchise rejected several times dating back to the league's inaugural season, may have been the single most important choice. The city and surrounding region gifted team management the resources of a countercultural vain, the founding place of such cultural movements as grunge music and coffeehouse culture. Another benefit of Seattle culture was the strong appetite for sport in the city that is currently home to the Seahawks of the National Football League (NFL) and the Mariners of Major League Baseball (MLB), was previously the home of the SuperSonics of the National Basketball Association (NBA), and is often considered to have strong potential for a National Hockey League (NHL) team. And beyond these broader cultural factors, Seattle and the Pacific Northwest, have enjoyed a considerable history of soccer complete with an English derby-style rivalry providing a rich tapestry from which to draw relevance and authenticity. Seattle Sounders FC has taken this ripe opportunity and made shrewd business decisions to convert the reasonable potential of the market into resounding sports success. Their decisions that have drawn the supporting community into the narrative of the club and its commitment to product quality have transformed what could have been a simple fan base into an engaged constituency of secondary team managers.

Consumer engagement is a concept that has become a core pillar of the marketing of many of the most successful businesses and brands, regardless of category, and can be accomplished through a mix of methods from input into product development, social media, staff and customer interactions, product quality, the authenticity and relevance of a brand to customers' lives and more. Businesses' heavy use of social media channels like Facebook and Twitter is geared towards engaging customers in a two-way conversation that can build real connection and relationships and giving customers (at least the appearance of) input into the direction of a brand. Social media also give customers a convenient forum in which to become digital brand advocates within their own social spheres, multiplying the reach and impact of the company's presence in social media. Customer interaction with both staff and other customers can represent a significant part of brand experience, driving engagement as well. Of course, the engagement engendered by simply having an outstanding product that delivers appealing value may be the most important pillar in a program to drive brand engagement. Sounders' leadership has fully embraced fan engagement, drawing the local market into developing the culture and story of the club. The club's management is committed to the idea that fans should have a voice in the direction of both the management and culture of the club, and in doing so, has drawn the ever-growing and record-breaking fan base into a robust, engaging relationship that has led to business success for the club. In addition, the club's leadership invested considerable resources and energy into fostering a vibrant, exciting game experience and high quality product, evidenced by the team's considerable competitive success in its first four years.

Seattle and the Pacific Northwest's Soccer History

As previously stated, selecting the city of Seattle as a market for MLS soccer was perhaps the most important decision team and league management made. The Seattle Sounders may only have four years of history as an MLS club, but their legacy goes back many more years. The team was originally ascribed to a North American Soccer League (NASL) expansion team in 1974 that competed in that league until 1982. In the pursuing years, the team competed in several leagues and ultimately ended up in the top division of the United Soccer Leagues (USL) in 1994 where they won four League Championships and reached the U.S. Open Cup Semifinals three times. It was courtesy of the USL-Sounders owner and MLS-Sounders minority owner/general manager Adrian Hanauer that the name Seattle Sounders was applied to the MLS outfit (Kumming).

With that team history comes a rich regional history as well. The Pacific Northwest has enjoyed a long, deep soccer tradition and rich rivalry between the cities of Seattle and Portland (and Vancouver) that has only helped to invigorate the fan base of both the Sounders and Portland Timbers. In fact the Timbers own history closes matches that of the Sounders in that Timbers too were an NASL expansion team, joining one year after Seattle did, and later joined the USL's top division. Not only did the Sounders hold the number one average attendance with 43,144 per game, in only their second seasons Portland was fifth with an average attendance of 20,438 and the nearby Vancouver Whitecaps were sixth with 19,475 (Oshan). The Cascadia Cup, an award developed and funded by each of these three teams' biggest fan groups, is an example of the great passion held in the region for soccer and the local teams. Since its formal start in 2004, the trophy has been awarded to whichever of the Seattle Sounders, Portland Timbers and Vancouver Whitecaps amassed the most points through the season against the other two teams. This three-team competition has its genesis in the teams' days competing against each other in the USL, was reduced to a two-team competition when the Sounders left the USL for MLS, and now continues with all three teams in MLS ("About"). The MLS league office's attempt to secure the rights of the Cascadia Cup by filing a trademark in Canada, they claim to protect it from third parties, represents a significant departure from the approach of the Sounders to allow fans into the process of driving Sounders FC's narrative, and one that should be monitored intently by Sounders FC management (they have generally remained silent thus far). Leveraging all this history means the club enjoys the highest level of authenticity and relevancy for soccer fans in the region and any others who feel connected to the rivalry the city of Seattle shares with its regional neighbors.

Democratization of Decision-Making

It was the team's history that gave team management their first opportunity to engage potential fans through an ongoing process of democratizing the brand and drawing fans into the club's decision-making. This was in the form of a vote that was held to decide the name of the franchise. Originally "Sounders" was not even one of the options, but after significant feedback from fans, a write-in option was included and the name "Sounders" was noticeably present in those submissions. Following the team's launch, fan involvement continues with the European-style membership group, the Sounders Alliance, modeled after similar membership groups at clubs like Barcelona. The Alliances gives season ticket holders and paying members input into key elements of the fan experience and management of the club. Per the Alliance section of the Sounders' website, the goals of the group are:

> Provide Alliance members with a voice in the overall direction of the organization, including but not limited to the following:
> - A vote on retention or lack of confidence in the Club's General Manager every four years
> - The right to decide on two of the Club's charitable partners
> - The right to advise on matters regarding game-day experience
> - The right to decide matters that primarily affect fan experience ("About the Alliance")

Another way Sounders FC has democratized management of the club and incorporated fans into key decisions is in the vote on retention or lack of confidence in the general manager. The Sounders' first four years in Major League Soccer recently culminated in the first of what will be four year cycles where fans vote to remove or retain the general manager. It is not surprising that with the incredible success Seattle has enjoyed over its first years in the league that season-ticket holders voted overwhelmingly to retain Adrian Hanauer as Sounders FC general manager.

Fan management is not a new concept in sports, certainly not in soccer, but it is a new approach that had not previously been part of the strategy of an MLS team. A look across the Atlantic to some of Europe's top leagues and teams shows how powerful democratization of management decisions can be at strengthening engagement with a soccer team. In England, trusts, conglomerations of fans, own some teams outright while other teams integrate fan clubs into their decision-making process. Ask the Glazer family, majority owners of Manchester United, how engaged and impactful fan clubs can be. In the German Bundesliga, regulations require that at least 51 percent of a team be owned by club members (Duffelen). Not coincidentally, Germany and the UK ranked first and second for game attendance of top tier soccer leagues in 2012 ("Barclays"; "Italian"; "Spanish"). Global powerhouses Barcelona and Real Madrid have had a process in place for years through which fans vote on the retention or removal of the general manager. Seattle's approach is a far cry from the structure of the NFL's Green Bay Packers who are a publicly held company owned completely by fans, with no individual holding more than 200,000 shares. All key management decisions affecting the future of the franchise are made through stock-holder votes ensuring fans, ticket-holders or not, are completely engaged in the team's decision-making process ("Shareholders"). Nonetheless, Seattle's approach is a powerful way to engender a deeper connection with fans (and a masterstroke to time the cycle with the U.S. Presidential election cycles, capitalizing on election fever). That is not to say that democratization of decision-making equals business success. Clearly the Barcelonas, Bayern Munichs, Green Bays and Sounder FCs of the sports world have done a multitude of other things right to achieve the fan success that they have. Clearly only an engaged fan base will care enough to be drawn into the democratization process. That said, it is one effective way to engage a team's fan base with a club and deepen their connection to it.

Socializing the Experience

Another aspect that has added to Sounder FC's success has been the way management allowed fans to socialize their experience of the game. One of the benefits fans enjoyed for purchasing season tickets was the gift of a free team scarf. While branded appreciation gifts are nothing new in sports or business, the selection of a free scarf allowed fans to broadcast their support for the team to fans and non-fans with an apparel item far more versatile than a team jersey or shirt.

The visual and social effects of these scarves were only heightened by the geographic location of the Sounders home turf, CenturyLink Field. Much attention has been paid, including in this book, about the benefits of soccer specific stadiums, but it is interesting to note that MLS's most successful (from an attendance standpoint) club plays in a stadium built for a football team, the Seattle Seahawks. Its design aside, the central location of the stadium ensures that fans represent a powerful marketing tool, showcasing their support of the team to non-fans through their colors, apparel and energy. Evidence of this socialization phenomenon benefiting teams located within city limits may be found in the fact that the top five teams for average game attendance in 2012 all play in stadiums near or within their home cities — Seattle Sounders, LA Galaxy, Montreal Impact, Houston Dynamo and Portland Timbers. Compare this with my own "home" team, the New England Revolution, who enjoy beautiful environs at Gillette Stadium, but find themselves in "distant" Foxborough, Massachusetts, thirty to forty minutes from downtown Boston. Not surprisingly, the Revolution also found themselves in the bottom five teams on the average attendance table in 2012, though the poor attendance may also be connected to their bottom five finish in the league table (Oshan).

Table 3. Top MLS Average Game Attendance for 2012

Seattle Sounders	43,144
LA Galaxy	23,136
Montreal Impact	22,772
Houston Dynamo	21,015
Portland Timbers	20,438

Source: Oshan

Of course, no modern sporting experience would be complete without the splash and dash of the bright lights, loud music, and larger-than-life personalities. Sounders FC was the first MLS club to feature a marching band as part of the game day experience, intended by co-owner Drew Carey, to add some vitality and fun to stadium. And this fun extends to the streets outside the game before the game starts, as the marching band are part of the parade of supports that march down the streets of Seattle before each home game. One struggles to think of what could be more socializing (or attention-grabbing) than the specter of a blaring, blasting marching band announcing the excitement of the Seattle Sounders game experience to game attendees and non-attendees alike. This cacophony is coupled with the thousands of free Seattle Sounders scarves that the team distributed when the team launched and that they continue to distribute to season ticket holders in an effort paint the city green and drive city-wide buzz and attachment to the club.

The Power of a Quality Product

Of course, the importance of delivering a quality product has a huge impact on the overall success of any business organization, and sport organizations are no exception. Sounders FC has shown an immediate strong commitment, a commitment backed by the club's wallet, to deliver a quality product for its exploding fan base. Though not armed with global icons like LA Galaxy's David Beckham or New York Red Bull's Thierry Henry, the Sounders still had 2012's third-highest payroll showing the club's willingness to invest in the players needed to deliver a quality product on the pitch (McIntyre). This partially contributed to the Sounders having the second best goal differential in the league in 2012, and finishing in the top three of the Western Conference earning them automatic qualification for the Conference Semifinals. There they defeated Real Salt Lake, but went lost on aggregate to perennial powerhouse LA Galaxy in the Conference Championships, though managing to win one game of the two-legged series. In its first four years in the MLS, the Sounders have continually delivered impressive results to their loyal fan base.

Table 4. Seattle Sounders Season Results

2009 (inaugural season)	U.S. Open winners Third-place finish — MLS Western Conference MLS Cup Western Conference Semifinals
2010	U.S. Open winners (first repeat winner since 1983) Fourth-place finish — MLS Western Conference MLS Cup Western Conference Semifinals CONCACAF Champions League Group Stages
2011	U.S. Open winners (first three-peat winner in 42 years) Second-place finish — MLS Western Conference MLS Cup Western Conference Semifinals CONCACAF Champions League Quarterfinals
2012	U.S. Open finalist (lost on penalty kicks) Third-place finish — MLS Western Conference MLS Cup Western Conference Finals

Source: Soccerway.com

So committed is Sounders FC's management in delivering a compelling, quality product that the team has taken the unusual step of refunding their loyal fans, season ticket holders, after particularly poor performances. Following a 4–0 loss at the hands of the LA Galaxy in 2010, a game in which General Manager Adrian Hanauer felt the team grossly underperformed, the club offered season ticket holders a refund on that game's cost to be credited on season ticket purchases the following season, likely an attempt to ensure repeat season ticket purchases (Farley). With all this, Seattle has done a commendable job of allowing fans into the process of furthering the narrative of the brand while delivering an engaging, quality product with which Seattle fans connect and for which they return in ever increasing number.

Extending the Approach

The LA Galaxy has shown that other clubs can have notable success with a similar approach that matches a soccer team's narrative to the cultural identity of its local fan base. The LA Galaxy have put together a team with star power, matching the culture of star-heavy Los Angeles, that likely makes the team more relevant to the cultural narrative of their home market. From a global perspective, the LA Galaxy are hardly the "Galacticos" of Real Madrid which featured global soccer icons Luis Figo, Zinedine Zidane, "Ronaldo" Luís Nazário de Lima, and (not ironically) David Beckham. Modest by global standards, but MLS's best version of amassing a star-studded team, has recently featured the aforementioned David Beckham, U.S soccer's best field player of the past decade in Landon Donovan, and Ireland national team captain Robbie Keane. Of course with David Beckham's run with the Galaxy coming to an end in December of 2012, in January of 2013 he signed a short-term contract with Paris Saint Germain (PSG) of the French league's first tier, Ligue Un, attendance trends for the Los Angeles will be heavily scrutinized to see if Beckham was successful in helping bring long-term interest in the club, or if he simply was a short-term draw.

Seattle Sounders FC has delivered a roadmap for driving soccer engagement in a local market (some would argue with a perfectly manicured live game day experience) as have several other MLS clubs, but the true business imperative for the Sounders and the rest of MLS is to find the Holy Grail of the sports entertainment business, high television ratings. Lucrative broadcast and sponsorship contracts from brands looking to spend national budgets to reach national audiences follow high television ratings. And with those lucrative contracts come the financial resources to develop, retain and pursue the kind of player talent that would make the broader product of MLS soccer more competitive for consumer mindshare.

According to Nielsen's television ratings, Super Bowl XLVII achieved a rating of 46.4 (meaning the broadcast reached 46 percent of TV homes in the U.S.) with 108,693 viewers (Nielsen). The MLS Cup's 0.7 rating in 2012 is anemic by comparison (The Gaffer). Despite its regional success stories like the Seattle Sounders, Portland Timbers and LA Galaxy, only when Major League Soccer is able to achieve consistent, considerable TV ratings will the league have proven it has earned mainstream popularity and thus achieve business success. The MLB has presented baseball as America's favorite pastime, part of the fabric of mainstream American culture. The NFL has created a nation-wide cultural experience around football on Sundays and Monday nights. How MLS can achieve this level of acceptance is something that concerned minds at the league offices and at each MLS team likely discuss and debate on a weekly if not daily basis.

Partnerships like 2012's three-year broadcast deal with NBC and NBC Sports Network certainly represent positive signs for the MLS (MLS Communications). However, much like the Seattle Sounders had to turn regional opportunity into success, MLS will need to figure out how to turn the opportunity before them into broadcast and rating success. The greatest perception gap for MLS to hurdle has always been that the quality of play does not match that of its European counterparts, at least not the top flight leagues. The league and its teams have been trying to address this perception with ever heavier sprinkles of top tier (though slightly aged) talent from Europe's most competitive leagues. In recent years this has included the likes of David Beckham, Thierry Henry, Juan Pablo Angel, Freddie Ljundberg, Torsten Frings, Robbie Keane, Tim Cahill, Rafael Marquez and others. Yet this influx of foreign talent has seen a simultaneous export of much of the United States' best soccer talent. Of the twenty-three players on the United States squad for a World Cup qualifier against Honduras on February 6, 2013, only six play domestically in Major League Soccer: Matt Besler, Brad Davis, Brad Evans, Omar Gonzalez, Sean Johnson and Graham Zusi. So while the league continues to look for ways to create an identity and positioning that can draw national attention and interest, it will have to do so without representation of the nation's most familiar, home-grown faces. What product does that leave league officials to package-up for the masses that will compel them to tune in and experience on screens big and small? It is a question this author cannot answer, but it is the business imperative that Major League Soccer must achieve.

Works Cited

"About." *The Cascadia Cup.com*. The Cascadia Cup.com. n.d. Web. 9 Feb. 2013.
"About the Alliance." *Seattle Sounders FC*. Seattle Sounders FC. n.d. Web. 9 Feb. 2013.
Associated Press. "Eddie Johnson, Sounders Pound Timbers." *ESPN FC*. ESPN Internet Ventures. 7 Oct. 2012. Web. 9 Feb. 2013.
"Barclays Premier League." *ESPNFC*. ESPN Internet Ventures. n.d. Web. 9 Feb. 2013.
Blum, Ronald. "World Cup Final Ratings: 24.3 Million Viewers in US for Record." *The Huffington Post*. TheHuffingtonPost.com. 12 July 2010. Web. 9 Feb. 2013.
Duffelen, Terry. "Fan Ownership: The Bundesliga Model." *Pitch Invasion*. Pitch Invasion. 11 Mar. 2010. Web. 9 Feb. 2013.
Farley, Richard. "Seattle Sounders FC to Refund Season Ticket Holders for Performance

against Galaxy." *Major League Soccer Talk.* MLS News from Major League Soccer Talk. 9 May 2010. Web. 9 Feb. 2013.
The Gaffer. "MLS Cup 2012 TV Ratings Worse Than One Year Ago: 3 Ways That MLS Can Reverse the Trend." *Major League Soccer Talk.* MLS News from Major League Soccer Talk. 3 Dec. 2012. Web. 9 Feb. 2013.
"Italian Serie A." *ESPNFC.* ESPN Internet Ventures. n.d. Web. 9 Feb. 2013.
Kumming, Benjamin. "DIY or Prefab? Portland, Seattle and Success in American Soccer Culture." *Pitch Invasion.* Pitch Invasion. 9 Aug. 2009. Web. 9 Feb. 2013.
Mayers, Joshua. "Sounders FC's Success Resonates Globally." *seattletimes.com.* The Seattle Times Company. 24 Oct. 2010. Web. 9 Feb. 2013.
McIntyre, Doug. "Reigning in Seattle. Yes, world, MLS Can Put Fans in the Seats." *ESPN The Magazine.* ESPN Internet Ventures. 16 May 2012. Web. 9 Feb. 2013.
MLS Communications. "MLS, NBC Announce Three-year Broadcast Deal." *Major League Soccer.* Major League Soccer. 10 Aug. 2011. Web. 9 Feb. 2013.
Nielsen.com. "Prime Broadcast Network TV — United States, Week of January 28, 2013." *Nielsen.* The Nielsen Company. n.d. Web. 9 Feb. 2013.
Oshan, Jeremiah. "MLS Attendance Up 5 Percent Over Last Year's Record, Ranks Seventh in the World." *SB Nation.* Vox Media. 30 Oct. 2012. Web. 9 Feb. 2013.
Peterson, Anne. "Supporters, MLS Clash over 'Cascadia Cup.'" *Yahoo! Sports.* Yahoo! Inc. 25 Jan. 2013. Web. 9 Feb. 2013.
"Shareholders" *Packers.com.* NFL. n.d. Web. 9 Feb. 2013.
Sidereal. "2013 Season Ticket Holder Scarf Voting." *Sounder at Heart.* Vox Media. 24 Sept. 2012. Web. 9 Feb. 2013.
Soccerway.com. Global Sports Media. n.d. Web. 9 Feb. 2013.
Sounders FC Public Relations. "Sounders FC Hires CAA Sports." *Seattle Sounders FC.* Seattle Sounders FC. 15 Aug. 2012. Web. 9 Feb. 2013.
"Spanish La Liga." *ESPNFC.* ESPN Internet Ventures. n.d. Web. 9 Feb. 2013.
Tidey, Will. "ESPN Ratings for Euro 2012 Demonstrate Soccer's Growing Reach in America." *Bleacher Report.* Turner Broadcasting System. 3 July 2012. Web. 9 Feb. 2013.

6

"Fast-Kicking, Low-Scoring and Ties"

How Popular Culture Can Help the Global Game Become America's Game

BENJAMIN JAMES DETTMAR

Why Isn't Soccer Popular in the U.S.?
Is Soccer Popular in the U.S.?

The reason for soccer's perceived inability to crack the U.S. market is a hotly debated topic from academics, to soccer pundits, to the average fan around the world, there are many schools of thought. The sport space theory of Andrei Markovits and Steven Hellerman asserts that soccer lost its chance at being accepted when it failed to become ingrained in U.S. society in the early decades of the twentieth century, a time when the authors claim the United States' cultural identity was being shaped. Dolores P. Martinez believes that U.S. soccer is holding out for a hero:

> [A]n American soccer hero in this mould [Santiago Muñez from the film franchise *Goal*], a home-grown talent who achieves international fame, could change the face of the game in the USA. This is the hero that U.S. soccer is holding out for [240].

There is the notion that the game is too long and too low-scoring,[1] does not have enough breaks for commercials,[2] or is too feminine.[3] The sport is even seen as too European, as Franklin Foer notes in his 2005 book *How Soccer*

Explains the World: An Unlikely Theory of Globalization. U.S. soccer fans are as likely to root for a European team and wear an Arsenal or Barcelona jersey as they are to root for a Major League Soccer (MLS) team and wear a DC United or Chicago Fire jersey (Foer 247–248). David Wangerin's *Soccer in a Football World: The Story of America's Forgotten Game* explains how early in the twentieth century the sport's European roots harmed its growth in the United States.

> Not until 1928 did it [the United States Football Association] elect an American-born president, and well into the latter part of the century its chieftains were largely men who spoke with conspicuously foreign accents (mostly British and Irish at first). In a country whose national motto, *e pluribus unum* (out of many, one), articulated a desire for assimilation, leaving soccer in the hands of what Roosevelt, Lodge and their ilk disparagingly referred to as 'hyphenated–Americans' was tantamount to marginalizing it for good. The migrants may have helped to keep soccer alive during its bleakest decades, but the establishment of ethnic clubs and leagues was poison to the game's chances of breaking through into the mainstream of American sports [33–34].

All of these theories have some virtue but none fully explains a definite reason for soccer's relatively low position in the hierarchy of U.S. sport. In fact to argue that soccer is not popular in the U.S. is in many ways a moot point. The women's national team is the most successful in the world with the U.S. boasting one of the only women's professional leagues.[4] The men's national team has qualified for seven consecutive World Cups as of 2014, and has a flourishing domestic league with many of its best players playing in the top divisions around the world. Furthermore, American youth participation in the sport is greater than that of any other country and many of the game's biggest sponsors around the world are U.S. companies. However, even the most ardent believer cannot deny that the game lags behind American football, baseball, basketball, and hockey when it comes to cultural resonance and, importantly for this analysis, TV viewers.

It is perhaps not necessary to explain the benefits of understanding why it matters that "Americans don't get soccer" or some similar cliché to an audience that appreciates the importance of studying a nation's culture. For many people it is just one of those anomalies that makes America different — another form of exceptionalism, as Markovits puts it. There is more to it than that, though. Sport historian Doug Noverr eloquently explains, "Throughout history sports have been so much a part of cultures that they can serve as reflections of culture at any time" (Noverr 167). Similarly, as Stuart Hall has pointed out, it is impossible to study culture, especially contemporary culture, without studying media (Green 28).

How TV Popularized American Football and Basketball

Is it fanciful to suggest that all soccer needs in order to take off in the U.S. is an extensive TV deal? Sociologist Carlos Sandvoss has suggested that "to many fans football on television has replaced the actual game as the point of reference" (173). Furthermore, if we examine the other major team sports in the U.S. we see quite clearly the effect that TV coverage, and other forms of mass communication, has had on their popularity. In their essay "Mass Media and the Experience of Sport," Lever and Wheeler demonstrate how sport in the U.S. reached a new audience in the mid to late nineteenth century due to increased mass communication.

> One catalyst for changing cultural values was the emerging system of mass communications. Along with the technology of the industrial revolution that produced the steamboats, railroads, and mass transit that moved people to leisure events, the rapidly evolving technology of mass media brought the drama and excitement of sporting events to the people.... [M]ass media, more than anything else, were responsible for promoting organized sport from a relatively minor element of culture into a full-blown social institution [126].

Professional American football has by far the most lucrative TV sport deal, and it was TV that unarguably helped create the juggernaut that is the National Football League (NFL). Stations were paying more in the 1960s for football games than ESPN is paying now for soccer games. Coverage of American football saw many innovative production techniques, instant replays, pre-game/post-game interviews, studio style analysis, scheduling for games, etc.— things we take for granted today—that helped to popularize the sport. Football went from being a popular sport to one that is now undoubtedly the biggest in the U.S.

Interestingly, the 1960s was also the decade that saw TV coverage of soccer escalate in Europe. In 1964 the English football league agreed to a one year deal with the BBC that allowed the station to show exclusive highlights of games, and by 1966, the year England won the World Cup, twenty-six million people in the UK were watching England's triumph. The Spanish football league typically had one game per week broadcast live in the 1960s. In Italy and Germany, the successful national teams meant that from the 1960s onwards soccer became increasingly popular on the small screen. Football in the U.S. and soccer in much of Europe were already popular sports, and the increased TV coverage that began in the 1960s strengthened their respective positions as the dominant national sport (Szymanski and Zimbalist 155–157).

America's biggest sport also stages the country's biggest annual event. The Super Bowl has been played annually since 1967 between the winners of what is now the AFC and the NFC. It is watched by upward of 100 million people worldwide and is renowned for its halftime music shows — recent years have featured artists such as Paul McCartney, The Black Eyed Peas, Beyoncé, and The Who; as well as for the commercials that are broadcast during the game — often costing as much as two million dollars for a thirty second spot. The game is heavily commercialized; the 2008 Super Bowl took place in a sponsored stadium (University of Phoenix), with an official beer (Coors), soft drink (Pepsi), camera (Canon), airline (Southwest), and even tire (Bridgestone); furthermore the MVP of the Super Bowl famously stated, "I'm going to Disney World!" With all the distractions it is easy to forget that at its heart the Super Bowl is a football game between the two best teams in the U.S. Yet this was not always the case. The Super Bowl came about quite simply to decide which team was better, the winners of the American Football League (AFL) or the NFL, and in its early years the razzmatazz was noticeably missing — early Super Bowls can be recognized by the empty seats in the stadiums and the relative lack of coverage from TV companies — indeed coverage of some of the earlier Super Bowls was wiped by the broadcasting station (Roth and Diamond).

The Super Bowl has taken on a Gramscian form of hegemony. Gramsci's notion of hegemony states that

> [T]he combination of force and consent ... balance each other reciprocally, without force predominating excessively over consent. Indeed the attempt is always made to ensure that force will appear to be based on the consent of the majority [Gramsci 85].

The Super Bowl gets an incredible amount of exposure in the U.S., but this is not questioned as so many people have a vested interest in the game. Gramsci goes on to opine that "though hegemony is ethical-political, it must also be economic, must necessarily be based on the decisive nucleus of economic activity" (86). When we have fans paying $75 for a replica jersey, children adorning their rooms with memorabilia of their favorite teams, and corporations paying millions of dollars for a few seconds of exposure, the economic consent that allows the Super Bowl to become a hegemonic event has been realized. The evolution of the Super Bowl from championship sport game to hegemonic force has similarities with how Gramsci suggests the bourgeois class separated themselves from the traditional ruling classes in Europe.

> The previous ruling classes were essentially conservative in the sense that they did not tend to construct an organic passage from other classes into their own....

> The bourgeois class poses itself as an organism in continuous movement, capable of absorbing the entire society, assimilating it to its own cultural and economic level [90].

Before 1967, the game of football was a traditional one — with familiar teams playing before a largely male, sport-loving audience. There was little attempt, and little will, to expand the game. With the advent of the Super Bowl and the new ideas that came with the merger of the two professional leagues, football, especially its centerpiece game, became an organism that was capable of commanding the attention of an entire society.

Watching the Super Bowl, whether for the sport, the commercials, the music, or just the sense of occasion, has become an established cultural practice in the U.S.— a practice that transcends categories of sex, class, and race. If, as Pierre Bourdieu famously stated, "taste classifies and it classifies the classifier," then the Super Bowl is one of those rare occasions where the habitus, the systems of disposition that define individuals, are in sync across society — making the Super Bowl a most American of events. Using Bourdieu's theory, we can ascertain that Americans were not born to revere the Super Bowl but do so because of continual exposure; they have developed what Bourdieu calls a "naïve" gaze that encodes them to enjoy a highly choreographed and mimed half-time show, a series of commercials that acquire value simply through the time that they are shown, and a game that many of the viewers understand but do not really care about. In short, they enjoy the Super Bowl because it is the "Super Bowl" and it is expected of them as Americans. The record TV viewership figures for Super Bowl XLV shows that sport, especially the Super Bowl, is still at the vanguard of U.S. cultural economy.[5]

Basketball also benefited greatly from increased TV exposure. By the late 1970s and early 1980s the National Basketball Association (NBA) was lagging far behind Major League Baseball (MLB) and the NFL in terms of viewers and also in terms of how the league resonated within the popular culture of the U.S. In 1981 four of the six games in the NBA finals were shown on tape delay, despite featuring future Hall of Famers Larry Bird and Moses Malone, and the whole series received a paltry (by contemporary standards) 6.7 Nielsen rating. Thankfully for sport fans this was the last year that the NBA Finals would be shown on tape delay, and as TV coverage improved and more channels such as ESPN and USA began to show games, audience numbers increased. This coincided with the Magic Johnson/Larry Bird rivalry and later the Michael Jordan years of the NBA. Jordan could be seen dunking a basketball, advertising Nike, or appearing in Hollywood movies, and was rarely off the viewers' screen. If basketball had experienced this growth in TV coverage twenty years earlier, it could perhaps have avoided the years of tape delay and relatively low viewing figures. The importance of TV coverage in relation to a sport's popularity is evident.

An Overview of the United States' Role in the Globalization of Soccer

Outside of the United States the ubiquity of soccer on television and the popularity of the sport often rivals that of football and basketball in the U.S. The past twenty years in particular have seen soccer's leading clubs attempt to increase their presence across the globe and into the globalized world market that includes the U.S. Major European club teams now tour Asia or the Americas during their pre-season; teams in England's premiership are sponsored by international companies such as Emirates (Arsenal), Samsung (Chelsea), Chang (Everton), and Aon (Manchester United), and each weekend some games in the premiership kick off at 12:45 P.M., much to the chagrin of the traditional football fan, in order to cater to Asian TV audiences. Manchester United even famously signed Chinese player Dong Fangzhuo in 2004 in a bid to increase the club's fan base in China. Fangzhuo made his debut for United in a pre-season "friendly" in Hong Kong in 2005 but did not play a premiership game for the Red Devils until 2007. He eventually left the club playing only three games in four years for the first team. His job was done; Manchester United's profile in China had risen. The World Cup, football's premier event, has in recent years taken place outside of Europe and South America with such hosts as the USA (1994), South Korea and Japan (2002), South Africa (2010), and will be in Qatar in 2022.

To be a globalized sport, indeed to be *the* undoubted leader in globalized sport, soccer has to crack the "sport space" of the U.S. There are many theories given as to why soccer's global march has faltered when it comes to the United States; one of these theories, given by Andrei Markovits and Steven Hellerman in *Offside: Soccer and American Exceptionalism*, is that of "sport space": the notion that historically soccer failed to capitalize on any chance it had to get into the U.S. psyche during *fin de siècle* America.

> Whichever sport entered a country's sport space first and managed to do so in the key period between 1870 and 1930, the crucial decades of industrial proliferation and the establishment of modern mass societies, continues to possess a major advantage to this day.... Once the occupants have settled in, they are virtually impossible to dislodge [15].

This is a neat theory, and indeed basketball, American football, baseball, and hockey, which Markovits terms "the big three and a half" of American sports, all came to varying degrees of prominence during this period. The theory is however almost too neat and has been largely debunked by subsequent scholars. Markovits makes some excellent points regarding the mis-management of soccer leagues and federations during this era, mistakes that opened the door for other sports to overtake soccer in popularity.[6] But to suggest that any aspect of society, let alone sport, has a finite amount of "space" available is to overlook the complex relations that link culture and society. If we look at the music industry, we see that hip-hop music is now the dominant genre, Tex-Mex restaurants are ubiquitous in many U.S. cities, and major international news is broken by bloggers or on Twitter before it is released by Reuters or the Associated Press. Hip-hop, Tex-Mex, and Twitter were not prevalent thirty years ago. Society is organic and a nation's cultural space is always evolving.

Furthermore, approaches like Markovits and Hellerman's, which focus on why soccer is (arguably) not popular in America, also negate the rich history that soccer has within the U.S. The Midwest city of St. Louis, for example, can stake a claim to be the capital of soccer in the U.S., and it comes as no surprise to learn that half of the team that famously played "The Game of Their Lives"[7] when they defeated England 1:0 in a group match during the 1950 World Cup, in what is still regarded as the biggest upset ever in the tournament, were from the Gateway City. Subsequent studies of U.S. soccer such as David Trouille's "Association football to fútbol: ethnic succession and the history of Chicago-area soccer, 1890–1920," which shows how soccer in *fin de siècle* America enhances our understanding of urban and suburban communities, rightly criticize Markovits for his negative approach in marginalizing these early success stories of U.S. soccer (Trouille 456).

One cannot discuss the history of soccer in the U.S., and indeed the history of soccer as a global sport, without mention of the North American Soccer League (NASL) and in particular the New York Cosmos. For a time in the 1970s and 1980s some of the world's greatest players, albeit at the tail end of their careers, played for club teams in the USA. Pelé, Franz Beckenbauer, George Best, and Johan Cruyff all graced the fields of North America, and although the league ultimately failed — due in no small part to its reliance on these aging stars — the U.S. was for a time a major force in the globalization of soccer.

The most recent incarnation of the NASL is Major League Soccer (MLS), and it would appear that the soccer authorities have learned from the mistakes of the NASL. Despite the press fanfare given to international stars such as Lothar Matthäus, Carlos Valderrama, and in particular David Beckham, there is an emphasis on grooming young players in the MLS and every team is required to have a substantial youth development program. The MLS built on the success of the World Cup that was staged by the U.S. in 1994.[8] Soccer-specific stadiums have been built in many cities that host MLS teams and attendances have averaged out to around a very respectable 16,000 (ESPN).

U.S. soccer has tried to embrace supporters from all walks of life and has had reasonable success in gaining the attention of fans from outside of the white suburban demographic that is synonymous with U.S. soccer. Clubs such as the Columbus Crew, from Columbus, Ohio, the city with the smallest Latin American population of any American MLS team, have a visible fan base from Latin America and even have an extremely vocal supporters' group, *La Turbina Amarilla*, who can be seen and heard at all home, and many away, Crew games.

In their article, Rik Jensen and Jason Sosa discuss how no professional sport league in the U.S. has successfully captured the country's growing Hispanic market (480). MLS would appear to be in a great position to tap into a captive and ever-increasing audience. Jensen and Sosa detail how the Houston Dynamo, an expansion team in 2005, tried to tap into the city's huge Hispanic market. The Dynamo did this by having popular Chicano boxer Oscar De La Hoya as a part owner and by playing early exhibition games against FC Barcelona from Spain and Mexican team Club América. However, the club undid much of this good early work by choosing the name Houston 1836, in homage to Mexico's defeat at the hands of General Sam Houston's Texas Patriots in 1836 (482). The club's crest was also to feature a silhouette of Sam Houston. Fortunately for the city of Houston and the MLS, common sense prevailed and after much protest the club instead chose the name Houston Dynamo.[9] The Dynamo and the MLS have improved their attempts at wooing Hispanic fans, and there is TV and radio coverage of all Houston's games on Spanish language TV and radio. There is also a largely Hispanic supporters' group, *El Batallón*; this is tempered somewhat by Houston's other large supporters' group, the *Texian Army*, who take their name from a volunteer military organization that fought against the Mexican army in 1836. Despite the issues discussed here the MLS is trying to tap into its Hispanic audience and Houston's on-field success — that they won the MLS title in 2006 and 2007 — is undoubtedly helping.

U.S. soccer players have also begun to ply their trade in the top leagues around the world. U.S. stars Landon Donovan, Brad Friedel, Stuart Holden, and Jozy Altidore have all played in the English Premiership, and other U.S. stars such as former wunderkind Freddy Adu,[10] Charlie Davies, and Oguchi Onyewu have all played in Europe. The U.S. is playing an active two-way part in soccer's globalization; however, this was not always the case.

Soccer in the U.S.: The First Phase— Until 1900

U.S. soccer history can be loosely categorized into six eras. There is however conjecture over which of these eras, if indeed any of them, were successful. The following section of the chapter will be a brief synopsis of these eras with an emphasis on the TV coverage that was, or was not, apparent.

The first of these eras comes in the late nineteenth century when many nations were beginning to embrace soccer as it spread around the globe. The U.S. remained indifferent to the game. Soccer was spreading through colonial missionaries who were expanding the British Empire; the U.S., while still influenced by immigration from Britain, managed to invent its own national pastimes. David Wangerin, in an interview with CNN's James Montague, suggests that

> soccer was pushed out by the rugby variation [of the ball game], Americans thought it was their destiny to devise games on their own without relying on the old country. There was no interest in games that were seen as un–American [Montague].

This meant that when the newly codified version of association football, or soccer, arrived on America's shores, a different type of football was already evolving. The U.S. universities of Princeton, Yale, Harvard and Columbia each played their own versions of the game, some using their hands, others using their feet (Montague). It was Harvard's rugby-based rules that largely won out. An historic meeting between Harvard and Yale in 1876 was played under the rules which would eventually lead to the game's distinctly "American" character — with touchdowns, snaps, and lines of scrimmage. Wangerin suggests that this was

> a desire amongst immigrants to fit in, [as] multiculturalism wasn't high up on the American agenda back then. [The immigrants] wanted to fit in so [they] played American football [Montague].

Soccer in the U.S.: The Second Phase— 1900–1930

The second era of U.S. soccer began around the turn of the twentieth century and lasted until around the 1930s during which period U.S. soccer had many burgeoning local leagues, hosted a succession of popular tours by leading European clubs, and had a relatively successful national team. Soccer was becoming increasingly popular in some immigrant communities along the east coast — especially in cities like New York, Baltimore, Pittsburgh, and Philadelphia. Teams were often attached to large factories, for example the famous Bethlehem Steel Football Club from Bethlehem, Pennsylvania. As early as 1905 a tour by a collection of leading English players who, with a wry nod to history, called themselves "The Pilgrim Club," saw crowds of up to 28,000 watch them play a game in one of the hotbeds of U.S. soccer, the Midwestern city of St. Louis (Wangerin 25). By 1921 a small professional league, the American Soccer League, had been set up and tours by British and particularly Scottish teams were a huge draw. When Glasgow Celtic toured the north-east of the country in 1931, a crowd of 31,000 watched them in one game at the Polo Grounds (65). Somewhat incredibly, for a country that is derided for its soccer history, 46,000 — again at the Polo Grounds in New York — saw the Austrian team Hakoah Vienna get beaten 3:0 by a U.S. select team in 1926, a record attendance that would stand until the formation of the North American Soccer League (64).

The first FIFA World Cup, in 1930, saw a huge shock as the U.S. national team — nicknamed the "shot-putters" by some of the other squads — beat Belgium and Paraguay on their way to finishing third in the competition. Success for the national team however soon dried up, as did attendances for games in the U.S. domestic leagues — which, in a story that would come to define U.S. soccer, imploded in political squabbling.

Soccer in the U.S.: The Third Phase — 1930–1968

The third incarnation of soccer in the U.S. saw the domestic game fall into perhaps its most barren era. From the onset of the Great Depression until the formation of the NASL in 1968 there was very little in the way of domestic soccer in the U.S. Teams such as Liverpool from England and Hapoel Tel-Aviv from Israel (who participated in the first televised game in the U.S. in 1946) played in front of impressive crowds when they toured the country, but U.S. soccer did not capitalize on this and league structures that had previously been in place were not replicated (105). College soccer was barely non-existent at this time — the first NCAA tournament was in 1959 — and seeing a game on TV was an incredibly rare experience.

This era did, of course, see the famous 1:0 victory by the U.S. over the much vaunted England team at the 1950 World Cup in Brazil. This result went virtually unnoticed in the U.S., there was certainly no TV coverage, and very few newspapers reported on the game. The heroes of the game received little recognition from the U.S. public — goal-scorer Joe Gaetjens moved to France for a brief time to play football and never again played for the U.S. national team (although he did play a national team game for his birth country of Haiti in 1953). Center-back Walter Bahr, widely regarded as one of America's best ever players, claims he did not conduct an interview about the game for twenty-five years and could not make a living playing professionally in the U.S. so he became a high-school gym teacher upon his return (Montague). Interestingly, especially given the current popularity of English soccer in the U.S., the 1961 FA Cup Final between Tottenham Hotspur and Leicester City was broadcast across the U.S. by the ABC network; unfortunately the showpiece event of English soccer did not pique the interest of fans in the U.S. (Wangerin 120).

Soccer in the U.S.: The Fourth Phase — The NASL

If the middle decades of the twentieth century are viewed as the doldrums for U.S. soccer, then the NASL years (1968–1984) saw the sport become highly Americanized, for a short while very popular, and also, essentially for this study, highly indebted to TV coverage.

Much has been written about the NASL years and whether or not they were positive or negative for soccer in the U.S. One positive development was that one of the major networks, CBS, began televising domestic U.S. games — although their coverage was somewhat haphazard and not particularly well organized. When 20,000 paying spectators filled Madison Square Garden in New York City to watch television coverage of the 1970 World Cup final between Brazil and Italy, played in Mexico City, they were mainly there to watch the performance of one man, Pelé. It is no coincidence that when, five years later, Pelé debuted for the New York Cosmos there was high hope for the popularity of soccer in the U.S. CBS covered the game live and an audience of ten million people saw the Brazilian get one goal and provide the assist for another. In actual fact they missed the first goal as CBS was at a commercial break and missed the assist as CBS was showing a replay, thus increasing the doubts of many naysayers of U.S. soccer (Tomasch). Cosmos games aside, there was little interest in the NASL from the U.S. TV audience and even Pelé could not alter the scattered coverage provided by CBS. The NASL was getting the sort of TV money that bigger leagues such as the NFL were getting in the 1950s but even the relative affordability of soccer was not enough to keep CBS enthused about the sport.

With CBS losing interest, TVS, a small network of syndicated stations, took over NASL coverage. As we will see when we discuss the problems that soccer has with its current coverage, being on such a marginal channel served only to marginalize the sport further. TVS was not available in many areas, and when the big stations did carry the coverage, it would be aired in the early hours of the morning. Despite the big names of Pelé, George Best, Johan Cryuff, and Franz Beckenbauer, the NASL and TV coverage of soccer were not yet in the big time.

This would change, somewhat, when ABC took a chance on soccer — what they dubbed the "sport of the '80s" — in the 1979 season. Soccer averaged around a 10 percent audience share and a 2.6 rating during the ABC years, figures which dwarf those of the MLS today but that were ultimately disappointing for ABC.[11] ABC eventually gave up on its soccer contract — showing only the "Soccer Bowl" in 1980 and 1981, with the 1981 game being shown on what is the bane of many U.S. sport enthusiasts — tape delay. The dying years of the NASL would occasionally see a game shown live on the fledgling ESPN station but coverage was sporadic at best and when in 1983, the 1986 World Cup was awarded to Mexico rather than the U.S. and when Time Warner pulled out as a major NASL sponsor, the failure of soccer to attract a large TV audience had led to the demise of soccer in the U.S. (Goldblatt 782).

Soccer in the U.S.: The Fifth Phase — Post-NASL and the World Cup 1994

After the departure of the NASL the fifth incarnation of soccer in the U.S. is evident. Between 1984 and the World Cup staged in the U.S. in 1994, soccer, in many ways, reverted back to its pre–NASL days. Soccer was regionalized and the biggest attraction was another form of the game, unique in the exposure and respect it garners in the U.S., indoor soccer. TV coverage at this time was non-existent but the numbers of people playing the game was up — way up. The NASL, for all its deficiencies, had created an interest in the game:

> It was the NASL that planted the seeds for soccer's subsequent emergence as a recreational activity in the United States by attaining a high profile and a concurrently respectable level of media coverage in the 1970s. This provided a sort of legitimization for the game among the American professional and commercial managerial classes [Markovits 171].

The end of this era saw the biggest soccer event in the world come to the U.S. Despite the increased participation levels the 1994 World Cup was not a guaranteed success. From a TV perspective it was interesting. Many of the games were played in the sweltering mid-day heat of summer — to suit European television audiences. Despite a multitude of sold-out stadia, the event remains the highest-attended World Cup, TV audiences in the U.S. were relatively low.[12] On the first day of the tournament, the TV event of the year was not the opening ceremony, where singer Diana Ross missed a choreographed penalty kick from five yards in front of the goal, but O.J. Simpson's fifty mile police chase in Los Angeles — shown live on TV for an audience of over ninety-five million — far more people than watched any single World Cup game. Twenty-eight million viewers did tune in to watch the U.S. lose 1:0 to Brazil in the tournament's second round; however, the loss and elimination of the U.S. team, coupled with a dull goal-less final that was decided on kicks from the mark, ensured that many who watched were not converted to the global game. Overall, however, the World Cup was a success with corporate America and the average sport fan in the U.S. undoubtedly gained greater exposure to the game. This led to the sixth incarnation of soccer in the U.S. — the MLS era — an era in which the standard and coverage of soccer has arguably grown exponentially.

Soccer in the U.S.: The Sixth Phase — The MLS Years

The MLS years have seen great advances in the standard of the domestic game in the U.S. and, not coincidentally, have also seen great advances in the amount of, and the standard of, TV coverage of the sport. But the situation is still not ideal, and for the game to break through the barrier of the big four sports much needs to be done.

The MLS has grown from an initial league of ten teams to a league that now has nineteen teams. Coverage of the game has increased. From the outset MLS games were covered by ESPN and ABC and also in Spanish by various local TV outlets. From 2003 the Fox Soccer Channel (FSC), the savior of many soccer fans in the U.S., started to broadcast MLS games. Fans who want to watch every game can subscribe to MLS Direct Kick, which screens every game live, and can also pay a small fee to stream games over the internet. MLS has even been sold to international markets — heady days indeed compared to yesteryear.

Yet soccer is still very much the fifth national sport in the U.S., and although the TV coverage has improved, it is by no means perfect. The coverage on ESPN is not frequently advertised and footage of games is often supplanted by other sporting events. And, while the games shown on FSC are a welcome addition for MLS fans, the channel is only available to those who subscribe to it; it is in effect a minority channel for a minority sport. When we look beyond the amount of hours shown, we also see some alarming trends. The first ten years of the league saw MLS actually paying channels to screen games; it is only since 2007 that MLS has managed to sell coverage of its league for a profit — with that profit only being around $4–5 million a year — a paltry sum compared to other professional sport leagues in the U.S. and other soccer leagues around the world.

The actual coverage itself is also routinely criticized. ESPN's stalwart soccer commentator Tommy Smyth is roundly criticized by most viewers who are fans of the game and the channel seems unsure as to whether it is providing coverage for dedicated supporters or casual viewers. But it is the opinions of the non-soccer "experts" on ESPN that really hurt the game. As ESPN slowly acquires more soccer coverage, for instance its serendipitous acquisition of England's Premier League, its hosts are forced to interact with the game. This can lead to embarrassing segments where hosts who know nothing about the game are forced to try and explain why a goal has made it into ESPN's Sports-Center's Top Ten Plays of the day. ESPN analysts on programs like *Round the Horn* and *Pardon the Interruption* can wax lyrical and pull out innumerable statistics on the big four sports, but when it comes discussing the finer elements of soccer, the level of discussion deteriorates noticeably. Even worse for the sport is when some of the network's top sport journalists, such as Jay Mariotti and Jim Rome, show outright disdain for the sport. Quotes from the American media berating soccer and soccer fans are commonplace, but when they come from some of the highest paid stars on the country's biggest sport network, they inevitably have a negative effect. On his ESPN show Jim Rome announced, with typical bombast, "[M]y son is not playing soccer. I will hand him ice-skates and a shimmering sequined blouse before I hand him a soccer ball. Soccer is not a sport, does not need to be on my TV, and my son will not be playing it" (Foer 242). Language such as this, from influential media personalities, does not help the future of soccer in the U.S. The rest of this essay will go on to analyze contemporary U.S. soccer.

The World Series versus the Champions League, World Baseball Classic versus the World Cup

The final game of soccer's Champions League competition, which pits Europe's best club teams in a season-long league format followed by a knockout stage competition, rivals the jewel in North America's sporting calendar, the NFL's Super Bowl, as the most-watched annual sport event, according to a survey by Initiative Futures Sports and Entertainment (BBC, "Champions League"). One hundred nine million viewers around the world watched Manchester United take on Barcelona in May 2009, compared to around 106 million who watched the New Orleans Saints take on the Indianapolis Colts in Super Bowl XLIV (BBC, "Super Bowl XLIV"). Super Bowl XLV did of course break this record again in 2011; it will be interesting to see which event garners the greater audience in the next decade. Baseball's World Series, the culmination of the MLB season, has far lower viewing figures. The respected website *bizofbaseball.com* reports that TV figures for the 2009 World Series featuring the New York Yankees and the Philadelphia Phillies (two big market teams) averaged 19.4 million viewers, up 42 percent from 2008. These figures are even more telling when one discovers that an estimated 98 percent of the audience for the Super Bowl resides within the U.S. (Rushin). Compared to both the World Series and the Super Bowl, the audience for the Champions League final is far more global. Not only are the two teams competing from different countries (as is usually but not always the case) but the players involved come from a much wider array of locales than those involved in the World Series. Kevin Alavay, a director from Initiative Futures Sports and Entertainment, confirmed that

> the Champions League has been better able to exploit the large burgeoning populations of the Asia-Pacific region. While the Super Bowl has secured free-to-air broadcasting deals in a number of important European markets such as the UK, France and Germany, its distribution and popularity in the key Asia-Pacific region lags far behind the Champions League [BBC, "Champions League"].

In a similar fashion it does not take a great deal of research to discover that soccer's World Cup is a far larger global event than baseball's newly formed World Baseball Classic (WBC). As of 2011, soccer's world organizing body Fédération Internationale de Football Association (FIFA) has 208 members, three more than the International Olympic Committee (IOC), sixteen more than the United Nations, and ninety-six more than the International Baseball Federation. The World Cup final is the single most watched sport event in the world, with FIFA claiming that the 2006 final between France and Italy had a cumulative worldwide audience of 715 million viewers (FIFA). Figures for the World Baseball Classic are harder to find but by the best estimation, the 2009 final between Japan and South Korea had a maximum worldwide audience of eighty-two million — a respectable figure but one that pales in comparison to soccer's World Cup.[13]

ESPN's coverage of the 2010 World Cup was noticeably more extensive than in previous years. ESPN aired many more commercials advertising their coverage of the tournament than they did during the 2009 WBC, and American corporations such as Budweiser, McDonald's, Coca-Cola, and Visa poured millions of dollars into sponsorship as FIFA attempted to top the $700 million dollars they made in commercial deals in 2006. This glut of coverage made for four weeks of excellent soccer viewing for fans in the U.S. Subsequent soccer coverage by ESPN has fallen back to that of previous seasons. It is interesting that in terms of viewing figures, global exposure, revenue spent, and revenue generated America's pastime, baseball, simply cannot compete (even within the U.S.) with the behemoth of soccer on a global scale.

An interesting coda to the discussion of the globalizing of baseball and soccer is the Olympic Games. The men's Olympic soccer tournament and the men's Olympic baseball tournament are both held in relatively low esteem by the sports' hierarchies. Olympic soccer is effectively an Under-23 tournament with qualifying countries having to select a squad of players who are twenty-three or under (with the exception of three over-age players). Many of the world's most prestigious soccer nations choose not to compete or take the contest very lightly. Similarly, baseball in the Olympics was for many years an exhibition sport, finally gaining full-medal status at the 1992 Barcelona games only to lose it again after the 2008 Beijing games. The sport was only open to amateur players until the 2000 Sydney games, and even then MLB was reluctant to suspend its season or release its players. The lack of a fairytale story such as the "Miracle on Ice" that Olympic hockey has from the 1980 Lake Placid Winter Olympics, or Michael Jordan's basketball "Dream Team" from the Barcelona Olympics in 1992, along with MLB's refusal to embrace Olympic baseball, their failure to adhere to the much stricter drug-testing regulations of the IOC, and the sheer number of competitors that are needed for a baseball tournament (at a time when the IOC is trying to downsize the games) are all reasons for baseball's failure to succeed as an Olympic sport. It would seem however that if baseball wants to match or even surpass soccer on a global level it could be a wise decision to use soccer's apathy toward the Olympics to their advantage and stage a world-class tournament in the vein of the WBC albeit on a bigger stage — one of the biggest sporting and TV stages of all — the Summer Olympics.

Raging Bull *and* Field of Dreams
Versus the Olsen Twins

A quick examination of how soccer has been treated in TV and film in the U.S. also points to a real reason why soccer is always fighting an uphill battle for respect and popularity. Films based around sport such as *The Blind Side*, *Million Dollar Baby*, *Field of Dreams*, and *Raging Bull* have been critically acclaimed, and many other sport movies, particularly those involving baseball, football, and boxing have gone on to do very well at the box office. Interestingly, the only sport movies to make the prestigious AFI list of the top 100 movies are *Raging Bull* and *Rocky*. U.S. soccer movies have been few and far between. Those that have come out, such as *Switching Goals* and *She's the Man* are often made for a younger audience and feature such stars as Mary-Kate and Ashley Olsen — a far cry from Robert De Niro and Clint Eastwood!

Successful U.S. comedy movies will use soccer as a way to get a cheap laugh from the audience. The 2007 movie *Superbad* features a scene in which one of the main characters, Seth, is trying to convince his friend, Evan, to buy alcohol and attend a party. The scene plays on some of the most common rites of passage for a U.S. teenage boy: buying alcohol, attending a party, losing one's virginity, starting college, and, I would argue, hating soccer. The fact that *Superbad* plays on the idea that insecure teenage males need to shore up their masculinity by joking, alarmingly, about non-consensual sex and by making fun of soccer is extremely telling. Evan is visibly nonplussed about being made to play soccer and Seth's derision of the game is obvious. Greg the soccer player is the only character to show an interest in the game, and the comeback to his request that Evan take the game seriously is telling: "[F]uckin' calm down Greg, it's soccer, it's soccer." This is of course immediately before we find out that Greg was also a bed-wetter. There is no reason for this scene to take place on a soccer field; that it does it just a vehicle to ridicule Greg and get cheap laughs at the expense of soccer.

Outside of the U.S., soccer has fared a little better on the big screen. The 1939 British film *The Arsenal Stadium Mystery* was one of the first films to have soccer integral to its plot and featured some of the most popular British movie stars of the era. Professor of Russian history Bob Edelman cites the 1936 Russian film *The Goalkeeper*, directed by S. Timoshenko, as a "Stalinist *Roy of the Rovers*; a Soviet *Pride of the Yankees*" (Edelman 42). The topic of soccer helped provide a mediocre film with agency in the areas of social and cultural history due to its focus on the sport (Woodward & Goldblatt 2–3). *Zidane: A 21st Century Portrait* followed French superstar Zinedine Zidane over a full ninety minutes as he played for Real Madrid against Villarreal in 2005. The French film *Substitute*, released after the 2006 World Cup, was directed by former French national team player Vikash Dhorasoo, and features the player explaining how it feels to be sitting on the bench as his team successfully navigates its way through the tournament. Both French films were critically acclaimed. The British film *Bend It Like Beckham*, released in 2002, is more in the ilk of the aforementioned U.S. movies on soccer but far more successful in terms of critical and box-office success and watchability. It helped launch the careers of Keira Knightley and Jonathan Rhys Meyers and also increased David Beckham's profile in the U.S.

There is no guarantee that a flood of successful soccer movies would help the sport break into the big four in the U.S., but logic would indicate that success on the big screen could only help the sports growth on the playground. Although a major Hollywood blockbuster focusing on soccer is not on the horizon, the U.S. film industry does seem to be starting to treat soccer with more respect. In 2010 ESPN produced the documentary *The Two Escobars* as part of its *30 for 30* series. The documentary, by Jeff and Michael Zimbalist, follows the intertwined lives of Pablo Escobar, a Colombian drug baron, and Andreas Escobar, a Colombian national team soccer player. The documentary was very well-received and had its world premiere at the Tribeca Film Festival and its international premiere at the Cannes Film Festival. Time will tell if the future of U.S. soccer movies lies in the hands of actors such as the Olsen twins or directors such as the Zimbalists.

Soccer on the small screen has fared little better. *The Simpsons* have regularly lampooned the sport with numerous episodes making fun of low scoring games and rioting fans. The season nine episode "The Cartridge Family" begins with the Simpson family attending a soccer match after viewing a TV commercial promoting an upcoming game:

> The Continental Soccer Association is coming to Springfield!
> It's all here — fast-kicking, low-scoring, and ties? You bet!
> ...You'll see all your favorite soccer stars. Like Adiaga! Adiaga two! Badiaga! Aruglia! And Pizzoza!
> ...This match will determine once and for all which nation is the greatest on earth — Mexico or Portugal!

Predictably the match turns out to be "boring" and the fans erupt in a riot, led by Scottish character Groundskeeper Willy. As a consequence of the riot Homer buys a gun to protect his family and joins the National Rifle Association — an organization which, like soccer, polarizes the U.S. and which is the antithesis of the weedy male soccer player (although not necessarily the soccer fan) that is often depicted. In the episode "Marge Gamer" from season eighteen the writers of *The Simpsons* go even further in their satire of soccer. The episode juxtaposes soccer, and one of its biggest stars Ronaldo, who makes a guest appearance, alongside a storyline that ridicules another social pariah in the U.S., "the gamer"—a figure, similar to the high-school soccer player seen in *Superbad*, that is usually portrayed as not being masculine, unable to get a girl, and a figure of scorn. In the episode Marge becomes addicted to a *World of Warcraft* style game. Lisa and her friends are inspired to play soccer after watching *Bend it Like Beckham*; in an effort to become closer to his daughter Homer volunteers to be a referee. The depiction of soccer in the episode focuses on diving by players, Homer ripping off his referee jersey à la Brandi Chastain and head-butting a linesman while shouting "Zidane," as well as Ronaldo being referred to as Geraldo!

The Simpsons is of course a comedy program and there are some genuinely funny moments in these episodes. The program has also featured sports such as baseball as its focus, and again these episodes are humorous. Season three episode *Homer at the Bat* features major league baseball stars such as Roger Clemens, José Canseco, and Darryl Strawberry playing for the Springfield Nuclear Power Plant as Mr. Burns attempts to assemble a softball team that will win the championship game against its arch-rival Shelbyville. The humor in the episode is noticeably different to those that focus on soccer. It focuses on the absurd — Roger Clemons getting hypnotized and acting like a chicken, Wade Boggs getting knocked out in a bar-room fight over the virtues of British Prime Ministers Pitt the Elder and Lord Palmerston, and Ken Griffey, Jr. contracting a form of gigantism — rather than on specific aspects of the game as was the case with the episodes on soccer.

Other U.S. sitcoms such as *Roseanne*, *The Wonder Years*, and *Friday Night Lights*, to name a few, have also regularly featured episodes involving soccer, and these invariably involve a child taking up the sport much to the chagrin of the child's father who thinks their son or daughter should be playing football or baseball. Few U.S. TV series have featured storylines that focus positively on soccer and certainly none have achieved the critical and commercial success of NBC's American football series *Friday Night Lights*. The first series of *Friday Night Lights* was successful enough for NBC to commission four more series (that were not linked to the original book by H.G. Bissinger); it is difficult to envisage a series focusing on soccer getting such treatment. When we consider the influence that TV has on a culture, it is inevitable that to constantly be the marginalized sport, as soccer is on TV and film, has a negative effect on the popularity and prestige of the sport in the U.S. As soccer slowly gains a greater foothold in U.S. society, it is possible that the types of films and TV shows mentioned above will evolve into featuring more positive storylines; if they do, this might finally be evidence that soccer is becoming an accepted part of U.S. culture.

The U.S. Women's National Team: Too Dominant for Their Own Good?

The U.S. women's national team has constantly been atop of the world ranking for soccer. They have supplied as many household names as their male counterparts and the final of the 1999 World Cup, during which the U.S. beat China on kicks from the mark, was a pivotal moment in U.S. sporting history. In 2011 the U.S. women's team again made the World Cup final. On this occasion 13.5 million viewers in the U.S., more people than watched any men's game from the 2010 World Cup, saw the U.S. lose to Japan on kicks from the mark.

Women's sport in the U.S. has come a long way. In 1928 the *New York Times* suggested that the 800 meter race that women were running at the 1928 Amsterdam Olympics was too long for women to endure — indeed the 800 meter race for women was discontinued after these Olympics and until the 1960 Rome Olympics women would run no further than 200 meters (Longman 95). Title IX, which was enacted in 1972, began the process of equaling the playing field for female athletes in the U.S.; however, things are not now and in all reality probably never will be equal. Women's sport is a hard sell: the Women's National Basketball Association (WNBA) makes a consistent financial loss, the Women's United Soccer Association folded in 2003, it was replaced with the now defunct WPS which in turn has been replaced with the NWSL. The best female athletes and teams are typically not held in the same esteem as their male counterparts.[14]

The success of the 1999 women's World Cup winning team would seem then to be a huge stride for women's sport — but not everyone is convinced. Mary Jo Kane, a sport sociologist at the University of Minnesota, has stated that "there is a cultural expectation that sport is the inherent birthright of males, that by being born male you own sport" (98). Does the success of the women's soccer team and their fleeting fame change this? Harry Edwards, a sociologist at the University of California at Berkeley, suggests that the women's team was simply "marching up the down escalator" and that the fact that Mia Hamm had endorsed a Mia Hamm soccer Barbie was indication that women were still not taken seriously as athletes (98). Of course male athletes also have their product lines, for example the Bobbleheads of many famous baseball and basketball stars and the Fathead wall graphics of many football players. These items are however centered on the sport first, and although they are undoubtedly fun, they are not focused on beauty or style (Mia Hamm Barbie comes with a hairbrush) and the difference is typical of how male and female athletes are treated.

This question leads us to the most iconic image of the 1999 World Cup, Brandi Chastain celebrating winning the game with her shirt held above her head revealing just her athletic body and Nike sport bra. There is little doubt that this image helped to accentuate the fame of the women's team; Chastain was often asked to repeat the gesture at sporting events where she was the guest of honor and politely declined (304). Jere Longman in his book *The Girls of Summer: The U.S. Women's Soccer Team and How It Changed the World* poses the question as to whether we can regard the success of the 1999 team as a watershed moment for women's sport if they are still largely recognized for their sexuality. Eminent sport historian Allen Guttmann would argue that we could. Guttmann, in his book *The Erotic in Sports*, suggests that to acknowledge the erotic aspect of the body is not to take away from the skill of the performance (35). Guttmann argues that "When an erotic element is too blatantly present to be overlooked, the customary reaction of the proponents of sports is promptly to condemn it" (4). Guttmann is arguing that athletes are often beautiful people who have attained a look and a skill that many of us strive for.

> The instinctive testimony of our senses all agree that men's and women's sports experiences can be and often have been suffused with a sense of erotic pleasure. The Greeks who gathered at Olympia for athletic festivals in honor of Zeus and Hera were candid about their pleasure. Perhaps, after two millennia of disavowal and denial, it is time for us to be as candid as they were [172].

U.S. society is certainly one that worships the body beautiful while lauding its sporting stars as heroes. By posing the question of whether this is problematic in terms of the 1999 World Cup team, but doing so in a non-academic tome, Longman is contributing to the world of sport studies by increasing the awareness of the issues the academy discusses and bringing these conundrums to a lay audience. To take away the agency of the 1999 team as world champions simply because Brandi Chastain was asked to take off her jersey by opportunistic promoters is going too far. However, we have to recognize the difference between the treatment of male and female sporting champions in U.S. popular culture and acknowledge that male and female sporting icons are not treated equally and thus the categorization of soccer as a feminine sport can be seen as detrimental to soccer's efforts to become more popular.

Soccer in the U.S. is predominantly a middle-class, suburban, white game. Of the winning U.S. team only goalkeeper Briana Scurry was not white, there were also no black administrators in the hierarchy of U.S. soccer, and only one black female women's coach at the Division 1 level of the NCAA (Longman 255). There was condemnation of the media in the U.S. after the game as most sport pages went with the picture of Chastain in a sport bra rather than a picture of Scurry making the winning save in the kicks from the mark. This was enhanced when ABC television pictures cut away from Scurry as she was about to receive her winner's medal and showed Mia Hamm who was next in line (284). Harry Edwards suggests that whether the snub to Scurry was deliberate or not it highlights the fact that Scurry and other black female soccer players do not fit the wholesome all–American image that is women's soccer in the U.S. (285).

Conclusion: The Future of Soccer on TV in the U.S. and Its Effect on the Sport

Those who are big supporters of soccer in the U.S., such as myself, have to look to TV to try and take soccer to the next level — that is to break into the big four of football, baseball, basketball, and hockey. We have seen from basketball and in particular football how television coverage galvanized the game, and I believe that it could do the same for soccer. For this to happen wholesale changes are needed to the way soccer has been historically shown on TV and how it is often depicted in popular culture. This is slowly happening. ESPN's 2010 World Cup coverage was intensely advertised and, as promised, was an integral part of their summer scheduling. More soccer from all over the world is being shown on U.S. TV than ever before, and it surely cannot be long before a serious soccer movie, in the ilk of the sport movies I mentioned earlier, is made and is successful. It has often been said that the youth of America are the key to soccer's future success — this is undoubtedly true but they need the assistance of the now middle-aged medium of television to really help the sport become a fundamental part of U.S. culture.

Notes

1. This is brilliantly lampooned by the TV show *The Simpsons* and is discussed later in the essay.

2. In the years leading up to the 1994 World Cup there were many stories in the European press about how Americans would change the game of soccer — one of the most popular, and as far as I can tell least reputable, was that the game would be changed from two halves to four quarters to allow for extra commercials. Needless to say this never happened.

3. See the discussion of Jim Rome later in this essay.

4. Although there is a history of women's professional soccer in the U.S. it has proved difficult to establish a sustained professional league. The Women's Professional Soccer League (WPS) ran from 2009 until it folded in early 2012. It has since been replaced with the National Women's Soccer League (NWSL) which began play in spring 2013.

5. For many years the series finale of *M*A*S*H* was famously the most watched TV program in U.S. history, this has changed with Super Bowl XLIV breaking the record in 2010

with 106.5 million viewers and Super Bowl XLV breaking the record again in 2011 with 111 million viewers.

6. There is also a debate here as to whether the years 1870–1930 were really when "modern mass societies" were established. Popular culture theorists such as Ray Browne would suggest that mass culture had existed for centuries and revisionist popular culture theorists such as Russell Nye would contend that modern mass culture began well before this date with the advent of the printing press.

7. This match has since been immortalized in the film *The Game of Their Lives* (2005) and the book of the same name (2005). Nineteen fifty was the first time England had entered the World Cup and many in England, and in the England team, still had the arrogant attitude that as they had invented the game they would easily go on to dominate any teams they played at the international level. The game was played in Belo Horizonte in Brazil and some British newspapers presumed there had been an error in the wire report sent back to the UK and reported the final score as England 10 U.S. 1—they could not entertain the idea that the mighty England had fallen to upstart USA.

8. Many soccer fans around the world are surprised to learn that the 1994 World Cup in the USA has the highest average attendance of any tournament—not bad for a country that apparently does not enjoy the game.

9. The name Dynamo is also quite controversial as it was the name given to many teams in Eastern Europe during the communist era. Dynamo Moscow, Dynamo Kiev, and Dynamo Bucharest were all famous teams with this moniker—all were associated with the secret police in their respective countries.

10. The career of Freddy Adu is of particular interest to this study. To many observers he was the "hero" that commentators, such as Dolores P. Martinez say the U.S. was holding out for. Sean Brown in his 2005 article "Can European Football Spur Interest in American Soccer? A Look at the Champions World™ Series and Major League Soccer," says of Adu and U.S. soccer: "American sports are driven by individual stars, even in team sports. Star athletes depend on media exposure…. Despite his being born in Ghana, it seems that Americans might be willing to embrace Adu as a great American soccer star…. If MLS can keep Adu in the U.S., playing in its league, then it is possible that his emergence could spur soccer in a way that it has not seen in almost a century" (Brown 59). Adu did not stay in the U.S. and is certainly not the world star that many in the U.S. hoped he would be (he recently returned from a spell playing in the second division of Turkish football to rejoin the MLS where he is a member of the expansion team the Philadelphia Union) but if such a star did come along it would be interesting to see if he (for the star would have to be male) could indeed increase TV figures for soccer in the U.S.

11. ESPN2 averaged a 0.2 U.S. rating and 254,000 viewers for its first two MLS Playoff telecasts in 2009. Houston Dynamo Vs. Seattle Sounders on October 29 drew a 0.2 and 274,000, while LA Galaxy vs. Chivas USA on November 1 drew a 0.1 and 233,000. ESPN Deportes averaged 63,000 viewers for the same two games, including 86,000 for Dynamo/Sounders and 39,000 for Galaxy/Chivas USA (Krishnaiyer).

12. Average attendance at the 1994 World Cup was around 69,000 with 3.6 million people in total going to the games across the nine host cities in the U.S.

13. Due to the recent nature of the World Baseball Classic and, it has to be said, its relative anonymity on the world stage, published figures for the event are difficult to find however the *bizofbaseball* and RBR/TVBR websites both suggest figures around those I quoted in the chapter. As a useful guide twice as many people watched the draw for the first round of the 2006 World Cup than watched the final of the 2009 World Baseball Classic.

14. The 2010-11 discussion of the value of the Connecticut women's basketball team beating the UCLA men's basketball teams consecutive games won record is a fine example of this.

Works Cited

BBC. "Champions League Final Tops Super Bowl for TV Market." *BBC Sport*. Web. 9 Feb. 2013.

_____. "Super Bowl XLIV breaks ratings record." *BBC News*. Web. 9 Feb. 2013.

Bourdieu, Pierre. *Distinction: A Social Critique of the Judgement of Taste*. London: Routledge, 1984. Print.

Brown, Maury. "World Series Averages 19.4 Million Viewers, Up 42% From 2008." *Bizof baseball*. Web. 9 Feb. 2013.

Brown, Sean Frederick. "Can European Football Spur Interest in American Soccer? A Look at the Champions World Series and Major League Soccer." *Soccer and Society* 6 no.1 (2005): 49–61. Print.

Douglas, Geoffrey. *The Game of Their Lives: The Untold Story of the World Cup's Biggest Upset*. New York: Perennial Currents, 2005. Print.

Edelman, Bob. "*The Goalkeeper*. Directed by S. Timoshenko, screenplay by Lev Kassil. U.S.S.R: Lenfilm, 1936." *Soccer and Society* 12 no. 1 (2011): 42–43. Print.

ESPN. "Major League Soccer Stats: Team Attendance — 2009." *ESPN Soccernet*. Web. 9 Feb. 2013.

FIFA. "No. 1 Sports event." *Fifa*. Web. 9 Feb. 2013.

Foer, Franklin. *How Soccer Explains the World: An Unlikely Theory of Globalization*. New York: Harper Perennial, 2005. Print.

Goldblatt, David. *The Ball is Round: A Global History of Soccer*. New York: Viking, 2006. Print.

Gramsci, Antonio. *Selections from Prison Notebooks*. Trans. Quintin Hoare and Geoffrey Nowell-Smith. London: Lawrence & Wishart, 1971. Print.

Green, Carlnita. "Snap, Crackle, Pop Culture and Communication Curricula." *Popular Culture Studies Across the Curriculum*. Ed. Ray B. Browne. Jefferson, NC: McFarland, 2005. 28–39. Print.

Guttmann, Allen. *The Erotic in Sports*. New York: Columbia University Press, 1996. Print.

Jensen, Rik, and Jason Sosa. "The Importance of Building Positive Relationships Between Hispanic Audiences and Major League Soccer Franchises: A Case Study of the Public Relations Challenges Facing Houston 1836." *Soccer and Society* 9 no.4 (2008): 477–490. Print.

Krishnaiyer, Kartik. "MLS Playoff Ratings on ESPN2 Continue to Beat Premier League." *Major League Soccer Talk*. Web. 9 Feb. 2013.

Lever, Janet, and Stanton Wheeler. "Mass Media and the Experience of Sport." *Communication Research* 20 (1993): 125–45. Print.

Longman, Jere. *The Girls of Summer: The U.S. Women's Soccer Team and How It Changed the World*. New York: Harper Collins, 2000. Print.

Markovits, Andrei S., and Steven L. Hellerman. *Offside: Soccer & American Exceptionalism*. Princeton: Princeton University Press, 2001. Print.

Martinez, Dolores P. "Soccer in the US: 'Holding Out for a Hero'?" *Soccer and Society* 9 no. 2 (2008): 231–243. Print.

Montague, James. "When U.S. postmen and miners humbled England." *CNN*. Web. 9 Feb. 2013.

Mottola, Greg, dir. *Superbad*. Columbia Pictures, 2007. Film.

Noverr, Douglass A. "Popular Culture in Sports, the Popular Culture of Sports: A Cross-Disciplinary Historical View.' *Popular Culture Studies Across the Curriculum*. Ed. Ray B. Browne. Jefferson, N.C.: McFarland, 2005. 167–180. Print.

Roth, David, and Jared Diamond. "Found at Last: A Tape of the First Super Bowl." *The Wall Street Journal*. Web. 9 Feb. 2013.

Rushin, Steve. "A Billion People *Can* Be Wrong." *Sports Illustrated*. Web. 9 Feb. 2013.

Sandvoss, Cornel. *A Game of Two Halves: Football, Television and Globalization.* London: Routledge, 2003. Print.
Szymanski, Stefan, and Andrew Zimbalist. *National Pastime: How Americans Play Baseball and the Rest of the World Plays Soccer.* Washington, D.C.: Brookings Institution Press, 2006. Print.
Tomasch, Kenn. "NASL TV: A Short History." *Kenn.com.* Web. 9 Feb. 2013.
Tomlinson, Alan, and John Sugden. "What's Left When the Circus Leaves Town? An Evaluation of the World Cup USA 1994." *Sociology of Sport Journal* 13 no. 3 (1996): 238–258. Print.
Trouille, David. "Association Football to Fútbol: Ethnic Succession and the History of Chicago-area Soccer, 1890–1920." *Soccer and Society* 9 no.4 (2008): 455–476. Print.
Wangerin, David. *Soccer in a Football World: The Story of America's Forgotten Game.* Philadelphia: Temple University Press, 2008. Print.
Woodward, Kath, and David Goldblatt. "Introduction." *Soccer and Society* 12 no. 1 (2011): 2–3. Print.

PART III: SOCCER IN AMERICAN SOCIETY

7

Perceptions of Hooliganism in American Soccer

CEDRICK G. HERAUX

"Some people believe football is a matter of life and death, I am very disappointed with that attitude. I can assure you it is much, much more important than that."—former Liverpool F.C. manager Bill Shankly, 1981

The image of association football ("soccer" to North Americans) is one that is tinged with violence due to certain high-profile incidents and a number of contentious rivalries present in Europe. Although sports in general are occasionally marred by violence, either on the field of play between participants or in the stands between supporters, soccer often appears to bear the brunt of criticism regarding this issue. Apocryphal tales abound of extensive, and continuous, acts of physical conflict among the supporters of certain teams ("clubs") and national sides, with a particular emphasis on England. While incidents involving national sides are typically explained as simple instances of nationalism taken to extremes, violence at the club level often involves teams playing within the same domestic competition, which is more difficult to account for.

Soccer has, in its current form, been in existence since the mid–1800s in England, with the first concerns over violent conduct following shortly thereafter. In contrast, this issue has not been prominent in the United States, despite the founding of the United States Soccer Federation in 1913 and the existence of the North American Soccer League from 1968 through 1984, until the relatively recent establishment of Major League Soccer in 1993. However, there remain persistent questions about the true extent of violence among supporters, with much of the difficulty stemming from definitional issues regarding "hooliganism" as opposed to spontaneous, isolated fan violence. The current work will examine the issue of hooliganism within the historical context of European soccer and the modern era of North American soccer in order to provide clarity, with particular emphasis on the perception of the extent and characterization of violence among supporters of Major League Soccer.

Hooliganism Abroad: History and Evidence

Early Soccer-Related Violence in Great Britain

Historically, soccer was played in medieval England with an inflated pig bladder as the ball, with the goal of the contest being to resolve disputes between neighboring villages. The earliest recognition of the potential for violence surrounding the sport saw Nicholas Farndon, the mayor of London, issue a proclamation banning soccer in 1314, followed by a further fifteen efforts through 1660 to ban the sport in various parts of England and Scotland (Carnibella et al. 19). As the game progressed through rule changes which brought it closer to the modern version, reported acts of violence persisted well into the early nineteenth century.

Codification of the rules of soccer in England occurred in 1863 as the Football Association, the governing body of English soccer, sought to further distinguish association football from rugby football (Mason 19). However, the modern era of the sport is generally considered to have begun in 1886 with the formation of the International Football Association Board (IFAB), which officially established the laws of the game (Giulianotti and Robertson 9). In that same year, Preston North End supporters fought with Queens Park Rangers supporters at a train station, marking the first known instance of football-related violence occurring outside of a match (Carnibella et al. 28). The trend of well-publicized incidents continued, with over six thousand spectators involved in a riot that injured fifty-four police officers at a 1909 match between Glasgow Rangers and Celtic Football Club, a pairing known as the "Old Firm" which has seen numerous displays of sectarian violence (Carnibella et al. 22). Following a lull during the First and Second World Wars, violence was renewed between 1946 and 1960, with a considerable increase from 1960 to 1980 (Carroll 89; White 155).

By the end of the 1950s, the British media had begun to focus significantly on stories of railway stations being destroyed, supporters moving onto the field of play (commonly referred to as "pitch invasions"), and fights between rival supporters occurring both within and outside of soccer stadia (Mignon, "Supporters Ultras et Hooligans" 46). This reached critical mass by 1961, considered the beginning of the modern era of hooliganism, with the relatively large increase in the number of instances of violence (Carnibella et al. 30). Media attention, in turn, resulted in the Harrington Report, which represented the first government-sponsored effort to investigate soccer-related violence, and the Lang Report, which marked the first attempt at proposed solutions to the issue (Frosdick and Marsh 87–88).

Defining Hooliganism

Despite the enormous amount of scrutiny from both government and media entities, as well as increasing social science research, there remained confusion regarding the distinguishing of hooliganism from more banal violence committed by supporters. As noted by Mignon, hooliganism has been loosely defined as including a vast array of activities, including: (1) confrontations sought out by supporters (either with rival supporters or with the police); (2) actions initiated by far-right political groups against perceived "outsiders"; (3) fights provoked by actions within the context of the match; (4) acts of vandalism; (5) pitch invasions; (6) use of flares; (7) use of insulting, particularly racist, language; and (8) drunkenness ("Supporters Ultras et Hooligans" 47). The same phenomenon is catalogued by Hourcade, who found that both media and law enforcement officials characterized as hooligans anyone who attempted to enter the stadium: (1) drunk; (2) with political emblems; or (3) in the possession of flares (16). This conflating of generalized (often individualized) disorder among spectators with more strictly-defined acts of hooliganism has resulted in what Stanley Cohen termed a "moral panic" over the issue of violence at soccer matches (Cohen 9; King, "The Postmodernity of Football Hooliganism" 584; Mignon, "Supporters et Ultras" 48; Roversi and Balestri 183; Ward 453).

There are also definitional difficulties resulting from the use, and confounding, of several different terms for individuals engaged in a variety of acts within the context of support. Indeed, Mignon notes that there was "a dramatic expansion of different forms of 'supporterism,' including hooliganism and the style of supporting associated with the ultras" ("Une autre Exception Francaise" 323). Thus, any violence or other disorder occurring before, during, or after a soccer match (given proximity and visual markers of supporterism, such as club shirts, scarves, etc.) is labeled as "hooliganism" despite ambiguity in cause. When taken together with the use of terms such as "firms" and "casuals," or attribution of hooliganism to the "lad culture," this definitional confusion expands the discussion beyond the bounds of utility.

Noting that much of the discussion of hooliganism is for the purposes of stigmatization, rather than objective analysis, Hourcade proposes that definitional clarity can only be obtained through an understanding of various aspects of the supporter culture. Thus, hooligans are defined as individuals who come to soccer matches specifically to seek out confrontation with opposing supporters or police, with little investment in overall stadium ambiance or the life of their club (Hourcade 23). That is, rather than attending a match for the purpose of spectatorship, supporting one's club through vocalization or the creation of "tifos,"[1] hooligans participate in soccer (either watching at the stadium itself, or at a pub near the stadium) primarily to demonstrate their superiority to the outgroup. As an example, King notes that "[f]ans' songs almost exclusively operate around the ... denigration of the opposition" ("The Postmodernity of Football Hooliganism" 585), while Ward argues that theoretical approaches to understanding hooliganism "signify the importance of 'we-group' versus 'they-group' antagonisms in the creation and maintenance of fan violence" (453).

In addition to differentiating themselves from rival supporters, hooligans are also adamant that they are superior to what has come to be known as "the prawn sandwich brigade."[2] With the sport increasingly corporatized and commodified, the stereotypically working-class youth comprising hooligan culture respond to being priced out of the best seats in the stadium by engaging in acts of physical violence and destruction, thus retaking soccer from the bourgeoisie (Taylor, "Football Mad" 355).

The final aspect of supporter culture to be discussed is that of politicized violence. Much of the research on violence at soccer matches in Italy and England focuses on the difference between apolitical ultras in the former and far-right extremist doctrine among hooligans in the latter. Mignon ("Supporters Ultras et Hooligans" 45) extends this thought, arguing that Italian-style ultras are predominant in France and Spain, with English-style hooliganism prevalent throughout the rest of Europe. However, this dichotomy is not absolute, as there are certainly far-right factions present in Spanish (e.g., Real Madrid C.F.[3]), French (e.g., Paris Saint-Germain F.C.[4]), and Italian (e.g., S.S. Lazio[5]) soccer, while not every instance of hooliganism in England is necessarily associated with political ideation. Yet there remains an undertone of racism and xenophobia accompanying much of the violence present at soccer matches in Europe.

Notable Incidents of Hooliganism in Europe

Hooliganism has touched matches at all levels of professional soccer within Europe, during both international (whether between national sides, or between clubs) and domestic competition. However, much of the violence has historically occurred within local rivalries known as derbies.[6] The latter matches occur in the majority of countries featuring large domestic competitions in their soccer leagues, and many are fraught with continual displays of disorder.

Of the derbies taking place in the United Kingdom, the most notorious is almost certainly the Old Firm Derby, contested in Glasgow, Scotland between Rangers Football Club and Celtic Football Club. The two most successful sides in Scottish soccer, they have faced off nearly four hundred times, with the number of victories for each club fairly even. Due to the sectarian nature of the contest, the Old Firm Derby has seen hooliganism lead to several fatalities and hundreds of assaults, with 1996–2003 notable as a particularly violent period (Foer 45).[7] There is one match within this rivalry, however, which stands out as an example of hooliganism. The 1980 Scottish Cup Final saw Celtic F.C. defeat Rangers F.C. by a score of 1–0, but is best remembered for the massive riot that took place at the conclusion of the match. Hundreds of supporters from both sides poured onto the pitch, engaging in a battle that featured wooden clubs, iron bars, bricks and bottles. As a result of the riot, nearly two hundred supporters were arrested, both clubs were fined £20,000,[8] and the sale of alcohol was banned at all Scottish soccer matches (Giulianotti, "Football and the Politics of Carnival" 193).

With respect to the rest of the United Kingdom, the fiercest rivalry is the Dockers Derby,[9] contested in London, England between Millwall Football Club and West Ham United Football Club. Having played nearly one hundred times, the clubs are separated by only a few victories and are almost equal with respect to the number of goals scored in those matches. The latest, and most notable, acts of violence occurred during a 2009 Football League Cup match between the clubs at Upton Park, the home of West Ham United's stadium, the Boleyn Ground.[10] The match, eventually won 3–1 by West Ham United, saw three separate pitch invasions from hundreds of supporters, as well as violence resulting in twenty injuries, including the stabbing of a Millwall supporter outside the stadium. Although both clubs were charged with failing to prevent their supporters from engaging in violent, threatening, obscene and provocative behavior, only West Ham United was found guilty by the Football Association (FA). In addition to the latter, West Ham United was also found guilty of failing to prevent their supporters from entering the field of play and were fined £115,000 by the FA ("West Ham Fined").[11]

In addition to their rivalry with West Ham United, the Millwall supporters have engaged in acts of hooliganism against a number of other clubs. The 1978 FA Cup match against Ipswich Town Football Club was marked by continuous violence, with Millwall supporters throwing bricks and stones at motor coaches carrying Ipswich supporters, as well as a large-scale pitch invasion ("1978 FA Cup Winners"). This was followed a few years later by the Kenilworth Road riot, in which the 1985 FA Cup quarterfinal match against Luton Town Football Club saw thousands of Millwall supporters follow their club to the away match. Eventually won by Luton Town 1–0, the violence erupted before the match even began, with Millwall supporters moving into the home stands to attack the Luton Town supporters with bottles and nails. Although the match started on time after the crowd was calmed, it had to be suspended after only fourteen minutes of play as the Millwall supporters began to rip out the seats of the main stand, throwing several onto the pitch at police officers; after a twenty-five minute delay, play was restarted. The end of the match was marked by more violence, with eighty-one people, including thirty-one police officers, sustaining injuries, and over thirty arrests made. Despite the extent of the violence, neither club was fined by the Football Association ("Luton v Millwall Cup Draw").[12]

Although these acts of violence began in earnest in 1960s England, it was not until the 1970s that "the British Disease" was exported to the European continent (Mignon, "Supporters Ultras et Hooligans" 46). One of the first such incidents occurred during the return leg of the 1974 UEFA Cup final, contested in Rotterdam, Netherlands between English club Tottenham Hotspur Football Club and Dutch club Feyenoord Rotterdam. During the match, the away supporters of Tottenham attacked the home supporters of Feyenoord, resulting in over two hundred injuries.[13] Although Feyenoord won the match 2–0, thus winning the 1974 UEFA Cup on an aggregate score of 4–2, the extensive violence marred the victory on what has since been referred to as "the day Dutch football lost its innocence" (Spaaij, *Understanding Football Hooliganism* 94).[14] This was followed the next year by violence in Paris, France after a controversial 2–0 win for German club Fußball-Club Bayern München e.V. over English club Leeds United Association Football Club in the 1975 European Cup Final contested at the Parc des Princes. Leeds United supporters, upset with having been denied two claims for a penalty kick and having had another goal disallowed, rioted in the streets of Paris, leading UEFA to ban the club from European competition for four years (Goldblatt 550).

The defining moment of hooliganism on the international stage arrived at the 1985 European Cup final, contested in Brussels, Belgium between Italian club Juventus Football Club S.p.A. and English club Liverpool Football Club at Heysel Stadium. An hour before the match was scheduled to kick off, the stands were already nearly full, with rival supporters separated only by wire-netting in a section of the stadium that was in a state of disrepair. As the Liverpool supporters pushed aside the security netting and rushed into a confrontation with the Juventus supporters, some of the latter attempted to escape the violence by exiting the other side of the stand. The resulting panic resulted in a mass of humanity concentrated in a vulnerable area, and several parts of the stands began to crumble. In total, thirty-nine people were killed, either by being crushed against the retaining wall as Juventus supporters pushed for a way out, or by being crushed under the retaining wall after it collapsed. Juventus supporters then attempted to rush towards the Liverpool supporters, but were stopped by police, resulting in a confrontation that saw the latter face a deluge of rocks and bottles. Despite the death toll, and an additional six hundred people estimated to have been injured during the incident, the match proceeded as planned, with Juventus winning 1–0.[15] The subsequent investigation into the violence resulted in an indefinite ban on English clubs from European competition,[16] with fourteen Liverpool supporters sentenced to three years imprisonment for involuntary manslaughter (Carter).[17]

Despite the events at Heysel, or perhaps due to the banning of club sides from European competition, English hooliganism continued unabated at the international level, with the focus shifted to the English national side. During the 1988 European Championship, held in West Germany, English supporters engaged in violence at all three matches featuring their national team. The first match saw England lose 1–0 to Ireland, with violence after the match, which strangely saw English and Irish hooligans band together to fight against German skinheads, resulting in eighty-nine English supporters arrested.[18] On the night before the second match, which England would lose 3–1 to the Netherlands, violence again erupted between the English and the Germans, resulting in massive damage to the Düsseldorf train station and hundreds of arrests. The aftermath of the third match, yet another England loss, this time 3–1 to the Soviet Union, saw over eighty arrests and the destruction of several pubs (Gammon).

The trend of violent confrontations during national team matches continued even after the ban on English club teams in European competition had been lifted. One illustrative incident occurred within the context of a 1993 World Cup qualifying match between England and the Netherlands. In the hours before the match, the streets of Rotterdam were filled with English and Dutch hooligans engaged in numerous acts of violence, including one instance of a homemade bomb filled with nails that injured an England supporter.

Dutch police made over six hundred arrests, claiming that most of those were of English hooligans (Connett and Cusick).

Although the violence abated over the ensuing decades, the media continued to emphasize isolated instances of violence during international competition, further propagating the notion that hooliganism was "the British disease." As an example, Garland and Rowe note that "the sensationalist way that the disorder during the World Cup [in 1998, held in France] was reported meant that many stories contradicted supporters' accounts of events" (41). This pattern was repeated at the 2002 World Cup, held jointly in Japan and South Korea, with Crabbe arguing that the media often focused on isolated acts in order to "feed the consumption of the spectacle of violence" (418), an assertion validated by Poulton ("New Fans, New Flag" 19). The tide began to shift slightly with the 2004 European Championship, held in Portugal, which was hailed for its distinct lack of violent incidents (Stott et al., "Variability in the Collective Behavior 75; Stott et al., "Tackling Football Hooliganism" 136).

Theories of Hooliganism

While relatively little research has been conducted regarding hooliganism within the United States (or North America more generally), the literature on theoretical explanations for that behavior has the potential to be applied across the soccer landscape. These theories have focused extensively on sociology, social psychology and anthropology in their efforts to describe and explain the organized violence characteristic of hooliganism.

Sociological Theories

The prominent sociological explanations of hooliganism highlight the presumed importance of sub-culture, often from a Marxist perspective. Based largely on the work of Taylor ("Football Mad"; "On the Sports Violence Question"; "Putting the Boot") and Clarke (*Football Hooliganism and the Skinheads*; "Football and Working Class Fans"), these theories argue that much of the violence performed by soccer supporters can be understood as the result of societal "fault lines," in which the typical working-class male is reacting to a perceived commodification of the sport to its, and his own, detriment. Just as Roy Keane railed against the "prawn sandwich brigade" at Old Trafford, decrying the influx of wealthier spectators who were in attendance to be seen rather than to see the athleticism on display, the traditional supporter sees that changing aspect of soccer as a personal affront to the working-class weekend (Weed 407). As Back et al. note, "the 'football hooligan' [has been] defined in romanticized terms as a defender of football's traditional working-class communitarianism against a growing embourgeoisement of the game" (424).

Clarke (*Football Hooliganism and the Skinheads* 6; "Football and Working Class Fans" 41) also argues that the inherent conflict in simply being a member of the working class results in a very specific type of hooliganism that is concerned with the maintenance of physical space as a valuable resource. Thus, territory in the soccer stands (the "terrace") is of utmost importance, and a primary means of demonstrating dominance is to invade the "away end" where opposing supporters are located. Indeed, the phenomenon of "taking the end" is described as essential in France (Hourcade 17; Mignon, "Supporters Ultras et Hooligans" 51), the Netherlands (Braun and Vliegenthart 800), Belgium and Germany (Ward 459), and Poland (Piotrowski 631). Giulianotti, in fact, argues that this type of activity is nearly universal, as hooligans use "grassroots territory-making tactics with respect to specific urban 'turf' [as in] most nations, young spectator sub-cultures have long held deep topophilic ties to their favoured stadium 'ends' which are defended in physical and symbolic terms from outside incursion" ("Sport Mega Events" 3298).

Social-Psychological Theories: The Figurational Approach

Although similar in approach to more general sociological theories, the figurational approach championed by what has become known as The Leicester School emphasizes the sub-cultural nature of violence, arguing that hooligans are simply reflecting the reality of working-class values and norms, rather than responding to conflict among social classes. Dunning (*Sport Matters*) and colleagues (Dunning, Murphy and Williams; Dunning et al.), therefore, propose that expectations of "civilized" behavior have failed to impact the "rough working class" which comprises the majority of persistent, hard-core hooligans. That particular group of (typically) males is viewed as valuing masculinity and aggression, often through a positive feedback cycle that involves "getting over," questionable sexual encounters and heavy drinking. Thus, violence serves a functional purpose for hooligans, allowing them to release aggression and meet their socially-constructed psychological need for emotional arousal and risk-taking (Gibbons 32; King, "The Postmodernity of Football Hooliganism" 585).

Importantly, some of the research building on the work of the Leicester School suggests that mere confrontation, rather than physical violence, is enough to meet most of these needs. In these moments, hooligans tend to express that aggression towards members of the out-group, who are most often opposing supporters or police officials (Abell et al. 97; King, "Football Hooliganism" 269; Roversi and Balestri 183; Spaaij, "The Prevention of Football Hooliganism" 2; Stott et al., "Tackling Football Hooliganism" 117). When responding to rival supporters, particularly if those rivals are seen as potentially violent, this has also resulted in the amplification of xenophobia and racism, as working-class males in this context are viewed as relatively intolerant. Stott, Hutchison and Drury, for example, note that "in-group members defined themselves through an explicit contrast with the 'hooligan' supporters of rival teams" (359), a phenomenon also described by Back et al. (427) and Ward (461).

With respect to the police, research indicates that confrontations and violence are interactional, with policing measures often put into place to deal with the "rough working-class" ironically resulting in an intensified potential for conflict. Thus, Stott and Reicher (353) argue that the police are participatory in creating hooliganism, as the former assume that all fans are potentially one of the latter. King ("Football Hooliganism" 270) confirms this, noting that "English fans increasingly saw their resort to violence as legitimate since the police had provoked them, but more importantly, the fans saw it as necessary." Indeed, Stott et al. propose that the main reason for the lack of violence at the 2004 European Championship was the non-paramilitary style of policing employed by the Portuguese during the event ("Tackling Football Hooliganism" 115).

Anthropological Theories

Much of the anthropological work related to hooliganism has focused on memoirs or ethnographies, with a particular emphasis on how those methods have helped to fuel the moral panic over the extent of violence. Built on the recent work of Poulton ("New Fans, New Flag"; "English Media Representation"; "'I Predict a Riot'") and Redhead ("Hooligan Writing"; "Little Hooliganz"; "Lock, Stock and Two Smoking Hooligans"; "Soccer Casuals"), this class of theories proposes that violence is not a central activity of the vast majority of supporters, and that much of the concern stems from exaggerated claims made by the media and the police. Importantly, some studies find that media attention often significantly worsens the problem of violence in the stands and the streets (Braun and Vliegenthart 796), while others suggest that the mythology of hooliganism is far more influential than the reality of said behavior (Melnick 3; Tsoukala 372).

Indeed, much of the more recent research on violence among supporters, regardless of theoretical orientation, has found that the "British disease" is not as prevalent as it was in past decades, nor is it as widespread currently as portrayed in the media. Observational studies conducted in England (Rookwood and Pearson 149), France (Hourcade 9–10), Italy (Roversi and Balestri 183), the Netherlands (Braun and Vliegenthart 796), and Portugal (Stott et al., "Tackling Football Hooliganism" 117) all note that the perception of hooliganism far outstrips current practice. This increasing realization has fortunately resulted in a slight shift in media coverage, as noted by Poulton:

> With the widespread prediction of trouble involving England fans failing to materialize, the 2002 [World Cup] appeared to witness a sea change in the media's agenda-setting. The most significant shift in the news values characterizing the reporting of this WC was the widespread and positive profile of ordinary English supporters, which contributed to a more accurate insight into English fan culture ["New Fans, New Flag" 19].

The USSF and MLS: Concerns Over Hooliganism in the United States

With the establishment of the United States Soccer Federation (USSF) in 1913,[19] North America truly entered the realm of international soccer, with a variety of domestic leagues formed over the next century. There is evidence that concerns over violence were present relatively early within this history, although much of that centered on incidents between players during the course of play (Hawley 3). While leagues such as the American Soccer League, the United Soccer Association, and the National Professional Soccer League waxed and waned in popularity, it was not until the formation of the North American Soccer League (NASL) in 1968 that significant interest was generated, increasing exponentially from 1975 to 1977 due to the presence of Brazilian superstar Pelé on the New York Cosmos.

Despite the dissolution of the NASL in 1984, soccer in the United States retained a modicum of popularity, with matches at the 1984 Olympics, held in Los Angeles, being well-attended. This was instrumental in securing the 1994 World Cup, awarded to the United States by the Fédération Internationale de Football Association (FIFA) on July 4, 1988. As a precursor to hosting the 1994 event, the USSF established Major League Soccer (MLS) in 1993 in order to provide a new structure for domestic competition, although the latter did not begin play until 1996. Thus, soccer in America had an eight-year period (1988–1996) during which to consider the type of atmosphere it wished to foster during international and domestic competition taking place on American soil.

Initial fears of hooliganism marring the 1994 World Cup (Barnum; Thomsen) proved unfounded as the event unfolded, with the relatively small number of arrests most often made for ticket-scalping rather than violence (Dwyre; Hersh) in spite of record attendance.[20] In fact, of the violence during, or related to, the event, the most notable incidents did not involve acts of hooliganism. The first incident saw Brazilian defender Leonardo elbow U.S. midfielder Tab Ramos in the head during a Round of 16 match, resulting in a skull fracture for the latter and a straight red card (and expulsion for the remainder of the 1994 World Cup) for the former. The second incident saw Colombian defender Andrés Escobar murdered upon his return to his country, ostensibly as retaliation for his own goal during the Opening Round loss against the United States, which contributed to Colombia's exit from the competition.

If the main fear during the 1994 World Cup had been importation of the "British disease" with the influx of foreign soccer supporters following their national teams to the United States, the concern surrounding the beginning of MLS play in 1996 was related to the level of competition on display. Doug Logan, the first commissioner of MLS, presided over a seemingly successful first season with respect to attendance, but he was summarily dismissed in 1999 after the league had lost an estimated $250 million during his tenure. In 2009, the former commissioner suggested that some of the league's financial struggles had been due to a reluctance to market increasingly world-class soccer to supporters more reflective of a world-class (read: European) atmosphere, arguing that "soccer audiences at their best have got to be a little dangerous. It's three guys with a beer cursing at the guy on the field. It's not a family activity" (Bachman).

Regardless of whether Logan's assertion was correct, prior research has clearly demonstrated that the notable lack of violence at North American soccer events is directly attributable to the fact that supporter demographics differ from those of European clubs and national teams. Early work (Guttman 127) noted that North American sports spectators have a variety of other sports from which to choose, and "due to differences in the historical development [of the game], soccer in Britain lends itself to crowd violence whereas soccer in North America does not" (Roadburg 265). This is borne out by recent research, which finds that most instances of violence involve individuals engaging in fairly typical drunken and disorderly behavior (Young 202), and that North American soccer does not experience the equivalent of European hooliganism (Lewis, *Sports Fan* 41; Roberts and Benjamin 163; Spaaij, "Football Hooliganism as a Transnational Phenomenon" 15).

In spite of the lack of instances of hooliganism, the continued rise of soccer as spectator sport in the United States resulted in renewed consternation over the identity of MLS with respect to European clubs and competition. Efforts to grow the league in terms of prestige began to focus on the two specific aspects that had been noted by former commissioner Doug Logan: (1) the quality of play on the pitch, reflected in the movement to attract (typically aging) European players, culminating in the implementation of the designated player rule in 2007[21]; and (2) the ability of MLS clubs to maintain a "European atmosphere" with respect to supporter noise and fervor without the (presumed) accompanying violence. Following a surprising performance from the U.S. Men's National Team in the 2002 World Cup,[22] and sparked by the building of soccer-specific stadia, interest in MLS resulted in increased profitability and attendance, with an average attendance of 18,807 for the 2012 MLS season placing the league in third place among domestic sports competitions in the United States.

With the renewed interest in soccer came some supporters who seemed to believe that being a "true supporter" meant emulating the style and actions of the hooligans on the terraces of 1980s England. Although these were thankfully few and far between, each instance of violence served to increase the rising moral panic within USSF and MLS ranks, much as the publication of hooligan memoirs had done in 1990s England.

The Changing Face of Major League Soccer: Supporters' Influence

From the opening matches of Major League Soccer in 1996, clubs have embraced official supporters' groups in an effort to generate enthusiasm in the stands, and from the beginning many of these groups adopted aggressive names and styles reflective of the notorious "firms" of English soccer. Of the nine remaining original MLS clubs,[23] six have official supporters' groups[24] using violent or aggressive names typically associated with hooliganism: (1) Columbus Crew — Hudson Street Hooligans; (2) D.C. United — Barra Brava,[25] District Ultras; (3) L.A. Galaxy — L.A. Riot Squad; (4) New York Red Bull[26]— Garden State Ultras; (5) San Jose Earthquakes[27]—1906 Ultras; and (6) Sporting Kansas City[28]— La Barra KC, Mass St. Mob. Another eleven clubs entered into MLS play after the inaugural season, of which ten are still in existence.[29] However, only four of the latter have official supporters' group with hooliganism-related names[30]: (1) Chicago Fire — Blitzer Mob, Fire Ultras 98, Ultras Red Side; (2) C.D. Chivas USA — Union Ultras; (3) Montreal Impact — Ultras Montreal; and (4) Real Salt Lake — La Barra Real. Thus, slightly more than 50 percent (ten of the current nineteen) of MLS clubs tacitly endorse supporter's clubs using names related violence and/or hooliganism, providing the media with a readily available negative connotation.

As noted, however, in spite of the attempts of MLS supporters to associate themselves with hooligan imagery, actual instances of violence in and around the stadia are relatively infrequent. Yet it is these few instances which provide fodder for moral panics. Benson, in describing New York Red Bull supporters' group the Empire Supporters Club (ESC), notes that "relations between the team and the supporters club have been strained, at times, by the determination of some of the fans to act out symptoms of what's known in Europe as 'The English Disease.'" Despite this description, there had been (at the time) no allegations of violence committed by the ESC independently confirmed.

As European clubs began to journey to America more often, both for matches against the MLS All-Stars as well as for friendlies against individual MLS clubs, concern over the importation of hooliganism persisted. Indeed, in 2007 the venerable institution National Public Radio (NPR) conducted an interview with former English hooligan Dougie Brimson in which the latter argued that violence could easily arrive in MLS stadia (Smith). The worst fears seemed realized in July 2008 when a friendly match between English club West Ham United and MLS club Columbus Crew erupted into violence at half-time, with over one hundred individuals involved in the fracas. The match, designed to provide a pre-season warm-up for West Ham[31] while exposing an American audience to European soccer, ended in a comprehensive 3–1 victory for the English side. It proved to be an interesting match-up, however, not merely due to the play on the pitch, but also because it ostensibly pitted the most notorious MLS supporter's group (the Hudson Street Hooligans) against some of the most notorious English hooligans (the Inter City Firm[32]). Various reports suggested that nearly thirty West Ham supporters moved into the Columbus Crew supporter's seating section after some spirited chants back and forth, with punches eventually being thrown (Leonard; Warner). However, only a single arrest was made during the incident, and officials from both clubs stated that the incident had been overblown by the media (Mitchell).

The mythologizing of MLS supporters continued to structure the narrative of the match-day experience, with Goode describing the drunken behaviors of a fan calling himself "A.J. Hooligan" and his fellow Barra Brava members at D.C. United home matches. Perhaps in light of this negative focus, MLS implemented a "Supporter's Code of Conduct" beginning in the 2009 season which stated that "the soccer experience [should be] free from fighting, ... thrown objects, attempts to enter the playing field, political or inciting messages, and disorderly behavior, including foul, sexist, racial, obscene or abusive language or gestures." While such rules of behavior for spectators are common in American sports, evidence continued to indicate that the number of individuals to whom the code applied was minimal. Yet, media reports again highlighted isolated incidents of supporter violence in 2010, noting that three Seattle Sounders fan physically attacked a Portland Timbers fan after the latter club registered a 1–0 preseason victory (McNerthney). This was followed shortly by New York Red Bull supporters throwing rocks at a motorcoach carrying Philadelphia Union supporters. However, in this instance the media response was slightly more restrained, as Straus noted that "while violence at MLS matches remains rare, there still is the occasional reminder that there are a few posturing poseurs in this country who think that acting tough and roughing somebody up are a key component of the 'authentic' soccer experience."

The officials responsible for marshaling Major League Soccer towards increasing success have been complicit in maintaining the moral panic over hooliganism in spite of a lack of evidence regarding the prevalence of such activities. While a profile of Philadelphia Union supporters group Sons of Ben noted that much of the presumed hooliganism was merely playacting, it also featured a quote from MLS commissioner Don Garber stating that he was "worried about a 'lunatic fringe' among MLS supporters, and about the 'dynamic' of travelling fans [singling] Philadelphia out twice" (Hankinson). Garber persisted with that line of thinking, noting recently that "[with] the supporters movement ... come challenges. There's a lot of thinking that we need to have in partnership with our clubs and our supporters leaders to ensure that our stadium environments are appropriate for everyone, not just for several thousand [hardcore] supporters. I continue to get frustrated and disappointed with the [profane] chants" (Wahl). In fact, the league went so far as to ban the Houston Dynamo supporters' groups from traveling to away matches during the 2012 season after an incident during the 0–1 loss to the L.A. Galaxy in the 2011 MLS Cup Final in which beer cans were thrown at Galaxy stars David Beckham and Landon Donovan (Dreier), furthering the perception such incidents represent a significant problem.

The Future of MLS: Battling Perceptions

Going forward, Major League Soccer continues to face the same two concerns that have plagued it over the past decade. The first is that the quality of play on the pitch is markedly inferior to that of European soccer. Questions regarding the overall sustainability, with respect to both profit and interest (i.e., attendance and television ratings), of the league loom within the media (Baxter) as well as at the highest levels of the sport, with FIFA President Sepp Blatter declaring that the United States does not have a strong professional league (Das). The second is the ever-present specter of hooliganism.

As has been discussed here, the pattern of "discovering" hooliganism and then overstating its prevalence that characterized 1980s and 1990s England has spread to the United States in the past decade. While most theorists (J. Lewis 41; Roadburg 265; Roberts and Benjamin 163; Spaaij, "Football Hooliganism as a Transnational Phenomenon" 15; Young 202) agree that incidents of violence at North American soccer events are quantitatively and qualitatively different than those in Europe, it is even more instructive to note that the true rarity of hooliganism in the former almost makes theorizing unnecessary. The simplest, yet most robust, explanation is that the fear of violence far outpaces actual incidents, with the media complicit in constructing a moral panic (Braun and Vliegenthart 796; Crabbe 415; Melnick 1; Poulton, "New Fan, New Flag" 19; Poulton, "English Media Representation" 330; Poulton, "I Predict a Riot" 28; Redhead, "Hooligan Writing" 16; Redhead, "Little Hooliganz"; Redhead, "Lock, Stock and Two Smoking Hooligans" 663; Redhead, "Soccer Casuals" 66; Ward 453; Weed 408). Indeed, the 2013 MLS season had not even begun when the question was raised yet again, with Black asking if "soccer hooliganism [could] invade America."

Notes

1. The Italian word "tifosi" was originally used to indicate individuals who were active supporters of their club, but has more recently been shortened to "tifo" as a description of any coordinated activity, such as the presentation of large banners depicting players, conducted by supporters' groups (Derbaix and Decrop 271).

2. The phrase comes from former Manchester United player Roy Keane who, in 2000, lashed out against the club's supporters, stating, "Sometimes you wonder, do they understand the game of football? Away from home our fans are fantastic, I'd call them the hardcore fans. But at home they have a few drinks and probably the prawn sandwiches, and they don't realize what's going on out on the pitch. I don't think some of the people who come to Old Trafford can spell football, never mind understand it."

3. Real Madrid Club de Fútbol, based in the Spanish capital city, are often derisively referred to as "the pet club" of the fascist General Francisco Franco.

4. Paris Saint-Germain Football Club, based in the French capital city, have had continual problems with a group of supporters known as the Boulogne Boys (now disbanded by government order), which is comprised mainly of members of the far-right French National Front political party.

5. Società Sportiva Lazio, based in the Italian capital city of Rome, was founded in 1900 by officers in the Italian army and was known to be the preferred club of fascist dictator Benito Mussolini. They have experienced persistent problems with a group of supporters

known as the Irriducibili (the "Unyielding") who engage in anti–Semitic and racist chants and displays.

6. The term "derby" has traditionally been used to denote athletic competition, regardless of sport, between two clubs located within the same town, but is most commonly used to refer to rivalries present in soccer. The origin of the term is unclear, but it is believed to derive from a horse race, known as "The Derby" established by Edward Smith-Stanley, the 12th Earl of Derby.

7. Rangers F.C. are historically supported by Protestant Unionists, while Celtic F.C. tend to draw their support from among the Catholic community.

8. This is the current equivalent of £73,205 or $117, 669, given inflation and currency conversion rates as of September 2012.

9. The name is a reference to the fact that West Ham United was founded by members of the Thames Ironworks, while many early Millwall players came from the Millwall/London/Surrey Dockyards. Enmity between the sides resulted from the latter breaking a dock workers' strike.

10. Under the terms of sponsorship, at the time the Football League Cup was known as the Carling Cup. Due to a change in sponsors, the competition is currently known as the Capital One Cup.

11. This is the current equivalent of £131,000 or $210,609, given inflation and currency conversion rates as of September 2012.

12. Although Luton Town F.C. and Millwall F.C. were both initially fined, all penalties were withdrawn on appeal.

13. European soccer competitions between different club sides often use a home-away system of matches. The first leg of the 1974 Union Européenne de Football Association (UEFA) Cup final was contested at White Hart Lane (the home stadium of Tottenham Hotspur F.C.) on May 21, while the second leg was contested at Stadion Feijenoord, also known as De Kuip (the home stadium of Feyenoord) on May 29.

14. In home-away matches for European competition, the overall winner is determined by aggregating the score from both matches.

15. Although the Hillsborough disaster, in which ninety-seven Liverpool F.C. supporters died in a crush, is often mentioned during discussions of the Heysel Stadium disaster due to their similar results and circumstances of fatalities, it is generally acknowledged that the latter was precipitated by hooliganism, while the former occurred under circumstances of neglect.

16. The ban was lifted for all English clubs, with the exception of Liverpool F.C., for 1990–1991 competition. The ban was lifted for Liverpool F.C. the following year, allowing them to participate in 1991–1992 European competition.

17. Twenty-seven Liverpool supporters were extradited to Italy to answer charges of manslaughter, which was the only extraditable offense that could be applied to the events at Heysel.

18. The violence that occurred after the match, which took place in Stuttgart, is notorious for having resulted in the expulsion from Germany of Paul Scarrott, nominal leader of the English hooligans, with the latter arrested upon his return to England for having jumped bail.

19. The organization began in 1913 as the U.S. of America Foot Ball Association. See Dettmar in this collection for a discussion of the history of soccer in the United States.

20. The 1994 World Cup, with a total of 52 matches held in 9 host cities, averaged 68,991 spectators per match, totaling 3.59 million spectators over the entire event. The average and total attendance still stand as FIFA World Cup records, despite the tournament expanding from 24 to 32 teams beginning with the 1998 World Cup.

21. MLS' designated player rule is commonly referred to as the "Beckham Rule" as the first player signed under the salary cap exemption was England star David Beckham, who

received a contract with the Los Angeles Galaxy worth $6.5 million a year in guaranteed salary.

22. The USMNT quarterfinal loss 0–1 to Germany marked a watershed moment in supporter fervor, as a perceived handball from Germany midfielder Torsten Frings on the goal-line resulted in angry reactions from U.S. fans.

23. There were ten original clubs that began MLS play in 1996. The Tampa Bay Mutiny were disbanded at the end of the 2001 season.

24. Supporters' groups were deemed to be official if they were listed on a club's official website linked through www.mlssoccer.com/.

25. The term "barra brava" is taken from Latin American supporter culture, having originated in 1950s Argentina, and has become synonymous with hooliganism in a number of countries.

26. The club entered MLS competition in 1996 as the NY/NJ Metrostars.

27. The club entered MLS competition in 1996 as the San Jose Clash.

28. The club entered MLS competition in 1996 as the Kansas City Wizards.

29. The Miami Fusion entered into MLS competition in 1998 and were disbanded at the end of the 2001 season.

30. Two other clubs have unofficial supporters' groups with such names: (1) Philadelphia Union — Broad Street Hooligans; and (2) Vancouver Whitecaps F.C. — North Gate Ultras.

31. Most European domestic leagues, including England's Premier League, hold their season from August through May, providing them with a break from play over the hotter summer months. Major League Soccer, in contrast, holds its season from March through December.

32. Indeed, after the violence had subsided, a group of English supporters unfurled a large banner that read "ICF: 30 years undefeated."

Works Cited

Abell, Jackie, Susan Condor, Robert D. Lowe, Stephen Gibson, and Clifford Stevenson. "Who Ate all the Pride? Patriotic Sentiment and English National Football Support." *Nations and Nationalism* 13.1 (2007): 97–116. Print.

Bachman, Rachel. "Pitched Battle to Marketing MLS in Portland and Beyond: Rough and Rowdy versus Family-Friendly." *The Oregonian* 4 July 2009. Web. 4 Jan. 2013.

Back, Kes, Tim Crabbe, and John Solomos. "Beyond the Racist/Hooligan Couplet: Race, Social Theory and Football Culture." *The British Journal of Sociology* 50.3 (1999): 419–442. Print.

Bairner, Alan. "The Leicester School and the Study of Football Hooliganism." *Sport in Society: Cultures, Commerce, Media, Politics* 9.4 (2006): 583–598. Print.

Barnum, Art. "Police Bracing for World Cup: Suburban Cops Want to Be Ready for Crush of Fans." *Chicago Tribune* 1 Feb. 1994. Web. 4 Jan. 2013.

Baxter, Kevin. "MLS Still has Growing Pains." *The LA Times* 23 Dec. 2012. Web. 12 Jan. 2013.

Benson, Josh. "Red Bulls Fan Club Gets Loud, English-Style." *The New York Observer* 13 Aug. 2007. Web. 12 Jan. 2013.

Best, Shaun. "The Leicester School of Football Hooliganism: An Evaluation." *Soccer and Society* 11.5 (2010): 573–587. Print.

Black, Alan. "Could Soccer Hooliganism Invade America?" *San Francisco Gate* 10 Jan. 2013. Web. 27 Jan. 2013.

Braun, Robert, and Rens Vliegenthart. "The Contentious Fans: The Impact of Repression, Media Coverage, Grievances and Aggressive Play on Supporters' Violence." *International Sociology* 23.6 (2008): 796–818. Print.

Carnibella, Giovanni, Anne Fox, Kate Fox, Joe McCann, James Marsh, and Peter Marsh. *Football Violence in Europe: A Report to the Amsterdam Group.* Oxford: The Social Issues Research Centre, 1996. Print.
Carroll, R. "Football Hooliganism in England." *International Review for the Sociology of Sport* 15 (1980): 77–92. Print.
Carter, Jon. "Rewind: The Heysel Aftermatch." *ESPN Soccernet* 2 June 2011. Web. 4 Jan. 2013.
Clarke, John. "Football and Working Class Fans: Tradition and Change." *Football Hooliganism: The Wider Context.* Ed. R. Ingham. London: Interaction, 1978. 37–60. Print.
_____. *Football Hooliganism and the Skinheads.* Birmingham: Centre for Contemporary Cultural Studies, 1973. Print.
Cohen, Stanley. *Folk Devils and Moral Panics.* London: MacGibbon and Kee, 1972. Print.
Connett, David, and James Cusick. "England Supporters Fall Foul of Dutch Police." *The Independent* 14 Oct. 1993. Web. 12 Jan. 2013.
Crabbe, Tim. "'The Public Gets What the Public Wants': England Football Fans, 'Truth' Claims and Mediated Realities." *International Review for the Sociology of Sport* 38.4 (2003): 413–425. Print.
Crisp, Richard J., Sarah Heuston, Matthew J. Farr, and Rhiannon N. Turner. "Seeing Red or Feeling Blue: Differentiated Intergroup Emotions and Ingroup Identification in Soccer Fans." *Group Processes and Intergroup Relations* 10.9 (2007): 9–26. Print.
Dart, Jon. "Confessional Tales from Former Football Hooligans: A Nostalgic, Narcissistic Wallow in Football Violence." *Soccer and Society* 9.1 (2008): 42–55. Print.
Das, Andrew. "Blatter Critical of M.L.S. in Interview." *The New York Times* 31 Dec. 2012. Web. 4 Jan. 2013.
Derbaix, Christian, and Alain Decrop. "Colours and Scarves: An Ethnographic Account of Football Fans and their Paraphernalia." *Leisure Studies* 30.3 (2011): 271–291. Print.
Dreier, Frederick. "Houston Dynamo Fans Rebound from Bad Behavior." *USA Today* 15 Nov. 2012. Web. 12 Jan. 2013.
Dunning, Eric. *Sport Matters: Sociological Studies of Sport, Violence and Civilization.* London: Routledge, 1999. Print.
Dunning, Eric, Joseph Maguire, Patrick Murphy, and John Williams. "The Social Roots of Football Hooligan Violence." *Leisure Studies* 1.2 (1982): 139–156. Print.
Dunning, Eric, Patrick Murphy, and John Williams. "Spectator Violence at Football Matches: Towards a Sociological Explanation." *The British Journal of Sociology* 37.2 (1986): 221–244. Print.
Dwyre, Bill. "World Cup USA '94/The First Round: Hooligans, Schmooligans: Peace Reigns in Orlando." *The Los Angeles Times* 26 June 1994. Web. 15 Dec. 2012
Foer, Franklin. *How Soccer Explains the World.* New York: HarperCollins, 2004. Print.
Frosdick, Steve, and Peter Marsh. *Football Hooliganism.* New York: Taylor and Francis, 2013. Print.
Frosdick, Steve, and Robert Newton. "The Nature and Extent of Football Hooliganism in England and Wales." *Soccer and Society* 7.4 (2006): 403–422. Print.
Gammon, Clive. "Those Thugs Again: To Some Fans, the European Soccer Championships Were Just an Excuse for Violence." *Sports Illustrated* 27 June 1988. Web. 15 Dec. 2012.
Garland, Jon, and Michael Rowe. "The 'English Disease'—Cured or in Remission? An Analysis of Police Responses to Football Hooliganism in the 1990s." *Crime Prevention and Community Safety: An International Journal* 1.4 (1999): 35–47. Print.
Gibbons, Tom, Kevin Dixon, and Stuart Braye. "'The Way It Was': An Account of Soccer Violence in the 1980s." *Soccer and Society* 9.1 (2008): 28–41. Print.
Giulianotti, Richard. "Football and the Politics of Carnival: An Ethnographic Study of Scottish Fans in Sweden." *International Review for the Sociology of Sport* 30.2 (1995): 191–220. Print.

———. "Sport Mega Events, Urban Football Carnivals and Securitised Commodification: The Case of the English Premier League." *Urban Studies* 48.15 (2011): 3293–3310. Print.
Giulianotti, Richard, and Francisco Klauser. "Introduction: Security and Surveillance at Sport Mega Events." *Urban Studies* 48.15 (2011): 3157–3168. Print.
Giulianotti, Richard, and Roland Robertson. *Globalization and Football.* London: Sage, 2009. Print.
Goldblatt, David. *The Ball is Round: A Global History of Soccer.* New York: Penguin, 2008. Print.
Goode, Harlan. "In the Trenches with Soccer's Craziest Fans." *The Washington Times* 25 June 2008. Web. 4 Jan. 2013.
Guttmann, Allen. *Sports Spectators.* New York: Columbia University Press, 1986. Print.
Hankinson, Andrew. "America's Football Factory." *GQ Magazine* 4 Feb. 2011. Web. 15 Dec. 2012.
Hawley, Lindsay. "Ethnics, Violence, and Truth: Soccer's American Past." *Constructing the Past Online-Only Journal* 5.1 (2004): n.p. Web. 4 Jan. 2013.
Hersh, Phil. "It is a World Cup Teetering on the Brink Between Ineffable Sadness and Transient Joy." *Chicago Tribune* 10 July 1994. Web. 4 Jan. 2013.
Hourcade, Nicolas. "Hooliganisme, Ultras et Ambiguïtés en France." *Esport e Sociedade* 3.7 (2008): 1–40. Print.
King, Anthony. "Football Hooliganism and the Practical Paradigm." *Sociology of Sport Journal* 16 (1999): 269–273. Print.
———. "Outline of a Practical Theory of Football Violence." *Sociology* 29.4 (1995): 635–651. Print.
———. "The Postmodernity of Football Hooliganism." *The British Journal of Sociology* 48.4 (1997): 576–593. Print.
Leonard, Tom. "West Ham Fans Brawl with Columbus Crew as Football Hooliganism Hits the US." *The Telegraph* 21 July 2008. Web. 14 Dec. 2012.
Lewis, Jerry Middleton. *Sports Fan Violence in North America.* New York: Rowman & Littlefield, 2007. Print.
Lewis, R.W. "Football Hooliganism in England before 1914: A Critique of the Dunning Thesis." *The International Journal of the History of Sport* 13.3 (1996): 310–339. Print.
"Luton v Millwall Cup Draw Brings Back Chilling Memories from Football's Dark Days." *The Daily Mail* 28 Jan. 2013. Web. 1 Feb. 2013.
Maguire, Joseph. "The Emergence of Football Spectating as a Social Problem." *Sport in Society: Cultures, Commerce, Media, Politics* 14.7–8 (2011): 883–897. Print.
Mason, Tony. *Association Football and English Society, 1863–1915.* Brighton: Harvester Press, 1980. Print.
McNerthney, Casey. "Police: Sounders Fans Beat Portland Fan after Preseason Game: Attackers Covered Faces with Sounders Scarves." *Seattle Post-Intelligencer* 16 Mar. 2010. Web. 4 Jan. 2013.
Melnick, Merrill J. "The Mythology of Football Hooliganism: A Closer Look at the British Experience." *International Review for the Sociology of Sport* 21.1 (1986): 1–21. Print.
Mignon, Patrick. "Supporters Ultras et Hooligans dans Les Stades de Football." *Communications* 67 (1998): 45–58. Print.
———. "Une autre Exception Française: Un Football sans Hooligans?" *Revue Internationale de Criminologie et de Police Technique et Scientifique* 56.3 (2002) : 323–347. Print.
Mitchell, Shawn. "Official Condemns Violence after West Ham, Crew Fans Trade Blows in Stands." *The Columbus Dispatch* 21 July 2008. Web. 12 Jan. 2013.
"1978 FA Cup winners." *British Broadcasting Corporation* 19 May 2008. Web. 4 Jan. 2013.
Piotrowski, Przemyslaw. "Coping with Football-Related Hooliganism: Healing Symptoms versus Causes Prevention." *Journal of Applied Social Psychology* 36.3 (2006): 629–643. Print.

Poulton, Emma. "English Media Representation of Football-Related Disorder: 'Brutal, Short-Hand and Simplifying'?" *Sport in Society: Cultures, Commerce, Media, Politics* 8.1 (2005): 27–47. Print.

_____. "'I Predict a Riot': Forecasts, Facts and Fiction in 'Football Hooligan' Documentaries." *Sport in Society: Cultures, Commerce, Media, Politics* 11.2–3 (2008): 330–348. Print.

_____. "New Fans, New Flag, New England? Changing News Values in the English Press Coverage of World Cup 2002." *Football Studies* 6.1 (2003): 19–36. Print.

Poutvaara, Panu, and Mikael Priks. "Hooliganism and Police Tactics." *Journal of Public Economic Theory* 10.2 (2011): 72–86. Print.

Pratt, John, and Mick Saller. "A Fresh Look at Football Hooliganism." *Leisure Studies* 3.2 (1984): 201–230. Print.

Redhead, Steve. "Hooligan Writing and the Study of Football Fan Culture: Problems and Possibilities." *Nebula* 6.3 (2009): 16–41. Print.

_____. "Little Hooliganz: The Inside Story of Glamorous Lads, Football Hooligans and Post-Subculturalism." *Entertainment and Sports Law Online-Only Journal* 8.2 (2010): n.p. Web. 12 Jan. 2013.

_____. "Lock, Stock and Two Smoking Hooligans: Low Sport Journalism and Hit-and-Tell Literature." *Soccer and Society* 11.5 (2010): 627–642. Print.

_____. "Soccer Casuals: A Slight Return of Youth Culture." *International Journal of Child, Youth and Family Studies* 1 (2012): 65–82. Print.

Roadburg, Alan. "Factors Precipitating Fan Violence: A Comparison of Professional Soccer in Britain and North America." *The British Journal of Sociology* 31.2 (1980): 265–276. Print.

Roberts, Julian V. and Cynthia J. Benjamin. "Spectator Violence in Sports: A North American Perspective." *European Journal on Criminal Policy and Research* 8 (2000): 163–181. Print.

Rookwood, Joel, and Geoff Pearson. "The Hoolifan: Positive Fan Attitudes to Football 'Hooliganism.'" *International Review for the Sociology of Sport* 47.2 (2010): 149–164. Print.

Roversi, Antonio, and Carlo Balestri. "Italian Ultras Today: Change or Decline?" *European Journal on Criminal Policy and Research* 8 (2000): 183–199. Print.

Smith, Robert. Interview with Dougie Brimson. *National Public Radio* 10 Nov. 2007. Web. 14 Dec. 2012.

Spaaij, Ramón. "Football Hooliganism as a Transnational Phenomenon: Past and Present Analysis: A Critique — More Specificity and Less Generality." *The International Journal of the History of Sport* 24.4 (2007): 411–431. Print.

_____. "The Prevention of Football Hooliganism: A Transnational Perspective." *Actas del X Congreso Internacional de Historia del Deporte*. Ed. J. Aquesolo. Seville: CESH, 2005. 1–10. Print.

_____. *Understanding Football Hooliganism: A Comparison of Six Western European Football Clubs*. Amsterdam: Amsterdam University Press, 2006. Print.

Spaaij, Ramón, and Alastair Anderson. "Soccer Fan Violence: A Holistic Approach: A Reply to Braun and Vliegenthart." *International Sociology* 25.4 (2010): 561–579. Print.

Stott, Clifford, Otto Adang, Andrew Livingstone, and Martina Schreiber. "Variability in the Collective Behavior of England Fans at Euro 2004: 'Hooliganism,' Public Order Policing and Social Change." *European Journal of Social Psychology* 37.1 (2007): 75–100. Print.

_____. "Tackling Football Hooliganism: A Quantitative Study of Public Order, Policing and Crowd Psychology." *Psychology, Public Policy, and Law* 14.2 (2008): 115–141. Print.

Stott, Clifford, Paul Hutchison, and Jon Drury. "'Hooligans' Abroad? Inter-group Dynamics, Social Identity and Participation in Collective 'Disorder' at the 1998 World Cup Finals." *British Journal of Social Psychology* 40 (2001): 359–384. Print.

Stott, Clifford, and Steve Reicher. "How Conflict Escalates: The Inter-Group Dynamics of Collective Football Crowd 'Violence.'" *Sociology* 32.2 (1998): 353–377. Print.

Straus, Brian. "New York–Philly Debut Marred by Hooligan Wannabes." *AOL News* 26 Apr. 2010. Web. 4 Jan. 2013.

Taylor, Ian. "Football Mad: A Speculative Sociology of Football Hooliganism." *The Sociology of Sport: A Selection of Readings.* Ed. E. Dunning. London: Frank Cass, 1971. 352–377. Print.

_____. "On the Sports Violence Question: Soccer Hooliganism Revisited." *Sport, Culture and Ideology.* Ed. J. Hargreaves. London: Routledge, 1982. 152–197. Print.

_____. "Putting the Boot into Working Class Sport: British Soccer after Bradford and Brussels." *Sociology of Sport Journal* 4 (1987): 171–191. Print.

Taylor, N.A.J. "Football Hooliganism as Collective Violence: Explaining Variance in Britain through Interpersonal Boundaries, 1863–1989." *The International Journal of the History of Sport* 28.3 (2011): 1750–1771. Print.

Thomsen, Ian. "The Hooligan Threat Hangs Heavily over World Cup '94." *The New York Times* 6 Oct. 1992. Web. 15 Dec. 2012.

Tsoukala, Anastassia. "Constructing the Threat in a Sports Context. British Press Discourses on Football Hooliganism." *Violence and Sport.* Ed. J. Aquesolo. Seville: University Pablo de Olavide, 2006. 372–379. Print.

Wahl, Grant. Interview with Don Garber. *Sports Illustrated Magazine* 29 Nov. 2012. Web. 14 Dec. 2012.

Ward, Russell E. "Fan Violence: Social Problem or Moral Panic?" *Aggression and Violent Behavior* 7 (2002): 453–475. Print.

Warner, David J. "Fans of West Ham, Columbus Crew Behave Just Like You Think They Would." *AOL News* 21 July 2008. Web. 4 Jan. 2013.

Weed, Mike. "Ing-Ger-Land at Euro 2000: How 'Handbags at 20 Paces' Was Portrayed as a Full-Scale Riot." *International Review for the Sociology of Sport* 36.4 (2001): 407–424. Print.

"West Ham Fined £115,000 for Carling Cup Crowd Disturbance." *The Guardian* 15 Jan, 2010. Web. 4 Jan. 2013.

White, Anita. "Soccer Hooliganism in Britain." *Quest* 34.2 (1982): 154–164. Print.

Young, Kevin. "A Walk on the Wild Side: Exposing North American Sports Crowd Disorder." *Fighting Fans: Football Hooliganism as a World Phenomenon.* Eds. E. Dunning, P. Murphy, I. Waddington, and A.E. Astrinakis. Dublin: University College Dublin Press, 2002. 201–217. Print.

8

Becoming Apple Pie
Soccer as the Fifth Major Team Sport in the United States?

GLEN M.E. DUERR

Soccer's Rapid Growth in the U.S.

Although soccer is still seen as a "foreign sport" by many people in the United States, the recent growth of Major League Soccer (MLS) provides some evidence that soccer is penetrating the American market and is establishing a permanent place in the sporting culture of the country. Moreover, when one considers the popularity of soccer amongst the youth of America and amongst immigrant groups, there is the potential that soccer could continue to grow into the twenty-first century to become a fully entrenched part of the American culture. It is, however, important to evaluate where soccer is in the current cultural landscape of the United States. Soccer has long been considered something alien to the United States and this may not reflect the current reality.

Three fairly recent books have mapped the changes towards the perception of soccer in the United States. Over the course of the 2000s decade, soccer went from being part of an American "exceptionalism" to a more natural part of the national sporting scene, albeit one in which Americans simply watch European soccer games on television rather than attending domestic MLS games. In this essay, the current state of soccer in the United States is further examined to build on the sentiments of these three major books evaluating the success of the sport.

Scholars Andrei Markovits and Steven Hellerman, writing in 2001, argue that soccer is an extension of American exceptionalism — that the United

States is qualitatively special compared all other countries. There is an exceptionalism in that people of the United States — on the whole — do not play, watch, or follow soccer at a rate that people in most other countries do. The same is also historically true of the Indian subcontinent, Canada, Australia, and New Zealand, but soccer is largely popular elsewhere in the world.

Markovits and Hellerman posit an interesting thesis, which, in many respects, was true of the late 1990s when they were writing. Their analysis, for example, examines the *Boston Globe* newspaper and argues that most newspapers in major cities cover in excess football, baseball, and basketball (and in some cities, hockey), and only these sports (Markovits and Hellerman 10). The authors argued that soccer still has no place in the U.S. sporting market despite upwards of 19 million registered youth soccer players in the country (Markovits and Hellerman 10). At that point in American history, their analysis was right.

Author David Wangerin, writing in 2008, maps the rise of soccer in the United States and notes the historical difficulties with growing the sport. He notes some of the changes going on within American soccer in the first decade of the twenty-first century. For example, Wangerin notes that the 2002 World Cup performance put the U.S. on the global soccer map, and that even despite a poor performance in the 2006 World Cup, more Americans attended games in 2006 than all of the other World Cup tournaments in history combined (except the 1994 World Cup, which was hosted in the United States) (Wangerin 6). Growth has been slow, but positive.

Writer Simon Kuper and economics professor Stefan Szymanski, writing in 2009, argue that soccer is popular in the United States, but has done so without the requirement of a strong domestic men's professional league (164). Essentially, they argue that soccer has become quite popular in the United States, but soccer followers spend much more time on the couch watching Fox Soccer Channel. The authors argue that MLS is just a tiny piece of the mosaic that is American soccer because there are plenty of other types of soccer such as kids soccer, college soccer, indoor soccer, and leagues from Mexico to England to Spain that capture the imagination and attention of Americans. All of this is true, but it understates the recent rise and impact of MLS on the American sporting scene.

This essay builds on some of the arguments presented here and directly contrasts with others. The arguments presented in this essay note that a confluence of three different factors — the growth of MLS, popularity amongst large immigrant populations, and high levels of youth participation have contributed to the conclusion that soccer has quietly, in the twenty-first century, become the fifth major team sport in the United States, and perhaps challenges ice hockey for the fourth spot. This is not to claim that soccer will remain popular — a downturn could occur — but that at least for now, soccer has created for itself a significant place in the sporting culture of the United States.

The Quiet Rise of Major League Soccer

When MLS kicked off its inaugural season in 1996, there was much excitement surrounding the new league. The World Cup, which was hosted by the United States in 1994, provided a major impetus for this new league. In fact, hosting the World Cup was contingent upon the creation of a new professional league because many senior members of the FIFA — the world's governing body of soccer — wanted the legacy of the World Cup to be the long term growth of the sport in the United States, not just a one-time event. MLS started with ten teams split into two five-team geographic east-west conferences. Very quickly, MLS expanded to Chicago and Miami in 1998 and the league looked like it was starting well. Although MLS attendance had decreased significantly from the inaugural season, the league seemed to be somewhat constant when inaugural commissioner Doug Logan stepped down in 1999 and new commissioner Don Garber was appointed.

However, after financial difficulties continued to mount and revenues remained stagnant, MLS contracted two teams — Tampa Bay and Miami — and the league decreased back to ten teams following the 2001 season. Television contracts were sparse, market exposure was minimal, and there were only three ownership groups in the whole ten-team league including the Anschutz, Hunt, and Kraft families. It should also be noted that the Anschutz family, at one point, owned more than half of the franchises in the league. MLS was in a very precarious financial position in the early 2000s and was essentially propped up solely by the Anschutz and Hunt families in particular.

Since 2005, however, MLS has rapidly expanded from 10 teams to 19 in 2012. Moreover, as the number of teams increased, so did league attendance, recognition, and revenue. Real Salt Lake and Chivas USA (Los Angeles) were added in 2005; Toronto F.C. became the first Canadian team in 2007; San Jose rejoined the league in 2008 after the original franchise was moved to Houston following the 2005 season; Seattle became the league's first team in the Pacific Northwest in 2009; Philadelphia Union was added as the league's sixteenth team in 2010; Vancouver Whitecaps and Portland Timbers were both added in 2011 rekindling the Cascadia Cup between the three largest cities in the Pacific Northwest; and the Montreal Impact became MLS's nineteenth team in 2012, the league's third Canadian team, and the first team in a majority Francophone community. Expansion has been rapid and frequent since 2005. With the New York City Football Club, the league will continue to grow — albeit at a slower rate — into the future.

In fact, as with all "State of the League" addresses by MLS commissioner Don Garber, the subject of expansion remains a frequent one. MLS has plans to further expand the league in the next few years possibly increasing to twenty-two teams. For several years, MLS officials have publicly announced the desire to place a second New York team within the physical limits of the city (most likely in Queens). Furthermore, MLS executives have also expressed a desire to put a team in the Southeast of the United States, probably in Atlanta, Tampa, Orlando, and/or Miami (Borg). This, in many respects, is seen as a way for the league to expand its geographic appeal since the contraction of the league after the 2001 season in which both Florida-based teams were contracted.

One reason for purporting the success of soccer in the United States is because the footprint of MLS is spread broadly across the entire country, with the exception of the southeast. Soccer has become a major part of the sporting scene in the Pacific Northwest with development of an intense trilateral rivalry between Portland, Seattle, and Vancouver that was historically present in the era of the North American Soccer League (NASL) in the 1960s and 1970s as well as in the lower divisions before all three teams were granted entrance into MLS. As the NBA has largely left the Pacific Northwest with the movement of the Vancouver Grizzlies to Memphis, Tennessee, and the Seattle Supersonics to Oklahoma City, Oklahoma, soccer now has the most franchises of any of the major five sports in the region. MLS also has a major presence in California with three teams, as well as four teams in the Northeast, and two teams in Texas. MLS also has the second highest number of teams in Canada behind the NHL and the league has taken advantage of the desire for major league sports in Canada's largest and richest three cities in a way that MLB, NBA, and the NFL have failed to do. MLS has a footprint in the heartland of America with teams in Denver, Salt Lake City, Kansas City, and Columbus (Ohio). For all of these reasons, MLS has helped soccer become like apple pie in the United States. Not only does the league have a footprint in major cities like New York, Los Angeles, and Chicago, but MLS is having an impact in places that the other major leagues have either ignored or abandoned.

Soccer-Specific Stadiums

Perhaps the main reason for the growth of MLS since 2005 — except for the increase in the number of franchises — has been the development of soccer-specific stadiums (SSS). Since 1999, when the Columbus Crew became the first team in MLS to open a SSS, there has been a proliferation of new, smaller, but more intimate SSS across North America. This remedied a major problem in MLS that its teams played in cavernous NFL stadiums and were not able to create a good atmosphere. Even 20,000 ravenous fans seemed dull in 80,000 seat American football stadiums.

Table 1: The State of MLS in 1996 and League Attendance

Year	Attendance	#Teams	%Teams with SSS	Notes on SSS
1996	17,406	10	0%	N/A

Source: mlssoccer.com.

Table 1 shows that MLS had a very successful inaugural season with an average of over 17,000 attending games. This "honeymoon" period was sparked by the 1994 World Cup and, on the surface it looked like soccer would succeed in the United States where it had failed numerous times before. The "honeymoon" period did not last, however, as attendance began to decline in the latter part of the 1990s and reached a nadir in the 2000 season when average attendance dipped below 14,000 as shown in Table 2. Even though MLS expanded by two teams in the 1998 season, low attendance and financial losses caused the league to contract by two teams at the end of the 2001 season. The outlook for MLS looked fairly dire at this point. What can also be drawn from Table 2, though, is the development of SSS in Columbus, and then in Los Angeles during this period, which preceded some pretty dramatic growth in MLS. This period, from 1997 to 2004, was difficult, but ultimately set the league in the right direction moving into the latter part of the 2000s decade.

Table Two: The State of MLS from 1997 to 2004 and League Attendance

Year	Attendance	#Teams	%Teams with SSS	Notes on SSS
1997	14,619	10	0%	N/A
1998	14,312	12	0%	N/A
1999	14,282	12	8.3% (1)	Columbus Crew Stadium in Columbus
2000	13,756	12	8.3% (1)	N/A
2001	14,961	12	8.3% (1)	N/A
2002	15,822	10	10% (1)	N/A
2003	14,898	10	20% (2)	The Home Depot Center (HDC) in Los Angeles (Carson)
2004	15,559	10	20% (2)	N/A

Source: mlssoccer.com.

Table 3 shows the dramatic rise of MLS since 2005 to the present (2012). Since the addition of Chivas USA and Real Salt Lake in 2005, MLS has undergone a dramatic transformation and is barely recognizable from the league pre–2005. Other new teams like Toronto F.C. and the Seattle Sounders have added much to the perception of MLS by consistently attracting large crowds. MLS also added teams in San Jose, Philadelphia, Vancouver, Portland, and Montreal, and many of these cases have been considered successful.

Table 3 also shows the proliferation of SSS in MLS. Dallas opened their new stadium in 2005. This was followed in short succession with new SSS in Chicago, Toronto, Denver, Salt Lake City, New York, Philadelphia, Kansas City, and Montreal. Only some of these SSS are actually in the downtown core of these cities, but many of these SSS are well positioned and provide easy access to both urban and suburban residents of these cities.

Table Three: The State of MLS from 2005 to 2012 and League Attendance

Year	Attendance	#Teams	%Teams with SSS	Notes on SSS
2005	15,108	12	33.3% (4 — Chivas USA also in HDC)	Pizza Hut Park in Dallas (Frisco, TX)
2006	15,504	12	41.6% (5)	Toyota Park in Chicago (Bridgeview, IL)
2007	16,770	13	53.8% (7)	BMO Field in Toronto, and Dick's Sporting Goods in Colorado (Commerce City)
2008	16,460	14	57.1% (8)	Rio Tinto Stadium in Salt Lake City (Sandy, UT)
2009	16,037	15	53.3% (8)	N/A
2010	16,675	16	62.5% (10)	Red Bull Arena in New York (Harrison, NJ), and PPL Park in Philadelphia (Chester, PA)
2011	17,872	18	61.1% (11)	Livestrong Sporting Park in Kansas City
2012	18,807	19	68.4% (13)	BBVA Compass Stadium in Houston, and Stade Saputo in Montreal

Source: mlssoccer.com.

After compiling data on MLS and SSS, two, quite basic statistical tests were conducted in order to see the statistical correlation between league attendance and the proliferation of SSS. First, the correlation between average league attendance and the percentage of teams with SSS for all years (1996 to 2012) is .697 and is statistically significant at a p<.01 level using a one-tailed test. This provides some, reasonably strong evidence that there is a positive correlation between building SSS and increased attendance for MLS. If more stadiums are built, the correlation results imply that MLS attendances will continue to increase. The r^2 (coefficient of determination) is still only .485, however, so other factors also have a bearing on attendance, not just stadiums.

A note of caution is important, though. A correlation merely shows that there is a relationship between the two variables: in this case, a relationship between the number of SSS and average attendance in a given year. However, a correlation does not mean that one variable causes the other. A correlation only shows that an association exists between the two variables, not that one variable caused the change in the other variable. There are other factors that have contributed to increased attendance in MLS, all the correlation shows is that a strong, positive relationship exists between the two variables.

A second statistical test — a basic bivariate regression — builds on the correlation and shows that as the independent variable — the percentage of teams with SSS — increases, the dependent variable — average attendance — also increases. This is shown most concisely in Chart One such that for every 1 percent increase in SSS, an average of 38 extra people attends MLS games. Consider that with almost 20 teams, one SSS accounts for 5 percent of the total and an average of an extra 190 fans per game.

The regression line of best fit increases with the addition of new soccer specific stadiums. There is evidence then that each MLS team should, if possible, build its own soccer specific stadium as there is a strong correlation between increased attendance and SSS. Although the sample is only seventeen years, the results provide an interesting rationale for more soccer specific stadiums to be built.

Although it would be foolhardy to predict future success for MLS, the recent signs have been very positive given the growth of SSS. Furthermore, with new SSS across North America, MLS has a much better chance to do well because teams control tickets, concessions, parking, and all other forms of revenue associated with a owning a stadium. In fact, SSS are so important to the growth of MLS that commissioner, Don Garber, has noted that future expansion — especially in the southeast cities of Atlanta or Orlando — must include the building of a SSS (Borg).

When compared to the other major leagues in North America — Major League Baseball, the National Football League, the National Basketball Association, and the National Hockey League — MLS does not typically rival any of the leagues in terms of revenues, salaries, or television viewership. However, in terms of attendance, MLS attracts more fans than the NBA and the NHL. For example, in 2011, MLS attracted 17,872 fans, compared to 17,323 for the NBA, and 17,132 for the NHL (Coombs 231). And, in a select number of cities, the MLS team is either the most popular team or competes for second. This is the case in cities like Seattle, Montreal, Columbus, Houston, Portland, Salt Lake City, and Vancouver. So, even though many commentators and analysts continue to overlook soccer and the growth of soccer in North America, a more nuanced investigation shows that, especially in MLS cities, soccer has quietly become much more popular and a much more entrenched part of American society than is normally considered.

Despite the positive signs from the data, it should be noted that the r^2 only accounts for 48.5 percent of the explanation for the rise in MLS attendance. Other factors are noteworthy and serve as important limitations to the correlation coefficient and bivariate regression. For example, perhaps the Seattle Sounders serve as an outlier to the model here given that their average attendance is well above the league average. The numbers, however, only tell part of the story. One reason for the growth of attendance in MLS is the Seattle Sounders have averaged 30,943 fans in 2009, 36,174 fans in 2010, 38,496 fans in 2011, and 43,144 fans in 2012, and do not have a SSS. The Sounders traditionally cap capacity in the much larger Seahawks stadium, but do, on occasion, play matches with full capacity, thus leading to a rise in average attendance. This is the first major limitation to the study. A second potential pitfall of the study is that the increase of MLS attendance has also coincided with the iconic David Beckham joining the league. Since Beckham announced his retirement from the league following MLS Cup XVII on December 1, 2012, MLS will lose one of its top marketing tools. How the league responds in 2013 and beyond will be important for the continued rise of MLS. A third and final shortcoming of the study is that the league has only been in existence for seventeen years and the sample of observations is not large enough to draw absolute conclusions.

What is known is that MLS has nineteen teams and while this is still well below the NFL at thirty-two and MLB, NBA, and the NHL at thirty, soccer is growing and beginning to take a place in the sporting landscape of the United States. Soccer's world governing body, FIFA, has imposed a limit of eighteen teams in any domestic league, but this has been violated in a number of countries. Moreover, since MLS spans both Canada and the United States, MLS could claim an exception, but this too violates another FIFA principle of separate domestic leagues for each country. Despite FIFA's objections, there is a path through which soccer could continue to develop and grow in the United States.

MLS, like other major sports leagues in the United States, is now part of the cultural landscape. Baseball has long been America's pastime, football has a major part of Sunday and major holidays like Thanksgiving, and basketball is very popular in urban and suburban areas. Soccer does not rival any of these sports, but soccer has become popular on July 4 in some cities, is wildly popular in suburban areas, but is also breaking into urban areas, and some soccer events like the World Cup have become so popular that they must be considered an American pastime in the twenty-first century.

Soccer and Immigrant Groups in the United States

In addition to the growing popularity of MLS, soccer remains highly important to immigrant communities throughout the United States. In some places these two points are highly interlinked. For example, even with a cursory examination of amateur men's league teams across the country, numerous international and/or ethnic team names predominate. What is interesting about the teams, typically, is that they are not solely defined by ethnicity; membership is for the most part open to family, friends, or connections. To provide two anecdotes, a Moroccan friend of the present author invited him to join a German team, and a British friend invited him to join a Croatian team. Although these examples are merely anecdotal, the existence of ethnic-based teams provides some rationale that soccer remains popular amongst immigrant groups in the United States. A full test here is beyond the scope of this essay, but a survey of men's leagues in the United States reveals an ethnic background to a range of teams even if those teams do not display ethnic homogeneity in their teams.

Immigration has long been part of the United States and it is often noted that the country is built on immigration. According to Department of Homeland Security (DHS) statistics, the United States started granting legal permanent resident status (in modern vernacular, green cards) en masse in the 1820s. Immigration grew steadily from the 1820s through 1910 increasing from a mere 128,000 to over 8 million, but immigration was essentially European in origin (DHS 6). For example, from 1890 to 1900, the United States granted legal resident status to just over 3.69 million people, 3.57 million of which were from Europe (DHS 6). Immigration began to decline in the 1910s and 1920s to 6.3 and 4.2 million respectively, but then dropped dramatically in the 1930s to under 700,000 (DHS 8). In the 1920s, immigration became less Euro-centric with a smaller majority of 2.5 million of the total 4.2 million coming from Europe. By contrast, almost 500,000 people came from Mexico specifically in the 1920s (DHS 8). Immigration began to expand slowly again in the 1940s and has increased in every decade since then. The number of people obtaining legal resident status only surpassed the zenith of the 1900–1909 decade of 8.2 million in the 1990s when 9.7 million people received green cards (of which only 1.3 million were of European origin) (DHS 8). In the 2000s, the trend continued with over 10.3 million people obtaining green cards.

Immigration, as measured through green cards, has been a staple of the

United States for long periods of its history. At times immigration was much more tightly limited and also very Euro-centric in nature, but in recent decades, immigration has increased and become very global in nature. For example, in the 1990s, of the 9.7 million people receiving green cards; 2.8 million were from Asia, including over 500,000 people from the Philippines, and over 350,000 from both China and India; in Central America and the Caribbean, 2.7 million people came from Mexico, 1.1 million people came from the Caribbean, and over 600,000 people came from Central America, including almost 275,000 people from El Salvador; over 550,000 people arrived in the United States from South America, including over 100,000 people from both Colombia and Peru; almost 350,000 people came from Africa, from both northern Africa and sub–Saharan Africa; and 1.3 million people arrived from Europe, including over 400,000 people from Russia, almost 175,000 people from Poland, and over 150,000 people from the United Kingdom (DHS 8–9).

The roots of soccer's appeal to immigrant communities is longstanding. For example, an examination of past U.S. Open Cup winners underscores a number of prominent ethnic community teams such as the New York Hakoah, Greek American AA, Philadelphia Ukrainian Nationals, Brooklyn Hispano, Ponta Delgada, New York German-Hungarians and Maccabi Los Angeles among others ("U.S. Open Cup"). Major cities like St. Louis, Missouri, also became popular soccer cities in the early 20th Century, in many respects due to the large immigrant (in this case, Irish) populations (Wangerin 28). Kearny, New Jersey, is a similar early soccer success story given the larger number of Scottish immigrants who impacted the area such that the most successful soccer team — the Kearny Scots — was named after the immigrant group and won several of the early competitions in the first era of professional soccer in the United States (Wangerin 28). Similarly, another case like Falls River, New Jersey, provides another example of a city where soccer was popular even over a century ago. Falls River, New Jersey, became a popular soccer area with a mixture of French-Canadian, British, and Irish immigrants collectively working together to create a successful soccer town (Wangerin 28). Even in the late nineteenth century, thousands of British immigrants would turn out to watch teams in cities across the northeast of the United States (Abrams).

Later waves of immigrants had a similar impact on local areas within the United States. However, following major reductions in immigration following the 1930s and 1940s, soccer had a much more difficult time finding a lasting place on the American sporting scene. An earlier professional soccer league, the American Soccer League (ASL) failed to gain traction in the United States given a confluence of four factors including: the Depression, restrictions on immigration, an overreliance of an ethnic fan base, and significant competition with other major sports leagues (for a fuller overview, see Duerr 2013).

The nature of immigration has changed in the post–World War II era such that immigration is much less Euro-centric. As a result of this change, in many major American cities, leagues have increased that specifically cater to the Latin American heritage community. For example, the Chicago Latin American Soccer Association was founded in 1969 given the perception of bias towards ethnic European teams on the part of the Chicago National Soccer League (Iber et al., 210–211). The soccer league started with ten teams but quickly grew to become a major attraction in Chicago's amateur sporting scene.

Immigration and soccer remain tightly woven together. Even in the modern MLS, one team — Chivas USA — was created to appeal more readily to the Hispanic population of the United States and, more narrowly, the Mexican American population of Southern California. Chivas USA has underperformed in the league and does not rank amongst the top teams in terms of attendance. However, Chivas USA has maintained a multicultural playing and coaching staff, which does not rest solely on appealing to the Hispanic or Mexican American communities. This may change under Jose Luis Sanchez Sola — otherwise known as "El Chelis" — but it is still too early to know whether Chivas USA will change dramatically and become a much more ethnic oriented team.

Although soccer has long been tied to immigrant groups in the United States, immigrant participation in soccer provides a strong base of support. Journalist Simon Kuper dedicated a chapter of his popular book, *Football against the Enemy*, to the notion of "short, dark, Americans" in reference to the popularity of soccer amongst Latino immigrant communities, which provides a basis for community for immigrant populations (189). Scholar, Douglas Massey argues that the soccer club is the most important voluntary association in the United States for the bi-national migrant (105). Although the main purpose of soccer clubs is recreation, Massey argues that they also serve the needs of migrants and also to expand social contacts.

Soccer has been a big beneficiary of the growing Mexican American population in the United States because many people in this community are soccer fans (Kuper and Szymanski). Many Hispanics (specifically Mexican Americans) support teams in Mexico such as Chivas Guadalajara and Club America, but many are also following and supporting MLS teams as well.

The trouble for soccer is that it has been difficult to maintain support for the sport after successive generations. If an immigrant enters the United States, it has historically proven to be more difficult for said immigrant to pass along his/her love of the sport to his/her children. There are two major reasons for this. First, with immigration to the United States, there has been a sense of assimilation that comes with living in the country and that includes sports. Particularly in the periods around World War I, the interwar years, and World War II, an obvious sense of a carefully defined national identity was created and protected in the United States, and this included participation in "American" sports like baseball, basketball, and football, rather than soccer. There was a level of cultural autonomy for immigrants, but this was largely maintained through religious practice, cuisine, and cultural events (Diner 101). Second, the history of professional soccer in the United States has been inconsistent at best. The failure of both the American Soccer League in 1933 and the NASL in 1984 made it difficult for people to watch professional soccer, because, in many respects, watching sports together is a way that love for a sport can be passed from one generation to the next. Both of these major points account for the main reason that, over time, soccer has diminished in popularity despite the fact that millions of soccer fans have immigrated into the United States over the last century.

Immigration is part of the United States and the sport of soccer is a part of the lives of many immigrants. In some senses, then, soccer has been as American as apple pie all along; the population just did not know it until now. The enjoyment of soccer by immigrants has spilled over into the youth population of the United States and growing support for the domestic league, MLS. It is likely that the United States will continue to accept immigrants in the decades to come and, since much of the world likes and plays soccer, it is also likely that many immigrants coming into the United States will continue to support and grow the sport of soccer in the country.

Youth Participation in Soccer

In alignment with the growth of MLS and the continued popularity of soccer amongst many immigrant groups is a third factor contributing to the argument that soccer has become the fifth major team sport in the United States: youth participation in soccer also remains high. While it is true that many young adults stop playing soccer after high school, the same is true of many other sports as well. So, taken together, soccer should be noted for its emergence as a more entrenched part of American culture.

Soccer is extremely popular amongst America's youth. The United States Youth Soccer Association (USYSA), for example, claims that it has 3.2 million members between the ages of 5 and 19 ("History: Largest"). Additionally, the American Youth Soccer Organization (AYSO) also claims to have over 600,000 members ("History of AYSO"). To provide some perspective, the USYSA started with just 100,000 members in 1974 and has grown enormously since then. So the growth of soccer in the United States has been dramatic.

Soccer's growth has been so substantial that by 2002, 1.3 million more kids played soccer in the United States than Little League baseball (Foer 244). In terms of youth participation, this could have a dramatic effect on sports culture in the United States in the years and decades to come. Much depends on what these kids do, play, and watch later in life, but this change at the youth level could mark a dramatic shift in the United States. Baseball will likely remain very popular, especially MLB, for decades to come, but the shift in participation could change the sporting trajectory of the country.

More than 20,000 high schools in the United States also have at least one soccer team accounting for approximately 700,000 players (Wangerin 316). Many of these players probably also play within the USYSA and AYSO systems, but this number still adds to the total youth participation in the United States. Furthermore, there are 2,000 college teams accounting for another 40,000 players (Wangerin 316). Unofficially, many colleges and universities also have reserve teams that do not factor into official numerical counts, nor do highly popular intramural leagues. Soccer, then, is very popular amongst people that range from four to eighteen years of age, but also up to the age of twenty-two.

Figures range as to the actual number of soccer players in the United States. A sporting goods manufacturer, for example, estimated almost 18 million players in 2002 (Wangerin 315). Another figure estimated 19 million soccer players (Markovits and Hellerman 10). Yet another figure estimated the number of players as 24 million according to a survey conducted by a company for FIFA (Kuper and Szymanski 182). According to this list solicited by FIFA, the United States is ranked second in the world behind China for the largest number of soccer players, which is a significant finding that could have global ramifications. Regardless of the actual number, it is obvious that millions of young people in America play soccer. In youth culture, soccer is firmly implanted as part of the society.

There are, however, some additional factors that should be noted. Included within these numbers is the large number of girls that also play soccer. In many countries, soccer is a male-dominated sport and is overtly masculine in its viewership and participation. This has changed over time in many countries, but there is a still a large asymmetry between support for men and women in soccer. In the United States, there is much more parity. Moreover, with Title IX enabling women to participate equally in collegiate sports, female soccer players actually have an advantage over male soccer players. If there are an equal number of men's and women's athletic scholarships, then women have an advantage because men's soccer has to compete with (American style) football, which does not have a female alternative. For example, there are numerous large universities that have football programs and no men's soccer program such as the University of Alabama, Auburn University, the University of Minnesota, the University of Nebraska, the University of Iowa, the University of Illinois, Purdue University, and Kent State University (Solomon; McVicker).

Franklin Foer, writing in 2004, argues that the growth of soccer has largely been in more liberal, urban/suburban, and educated circles such that where soccer is popular amongst the working classes across the world, soccer is most popular amongst children of white collar parents in the United States. Foer notes that, in contrast to much of the world, participation in soccer is most popular amongst the upper-middle class rather than the working class, which is more frequently cited across the rest of the world. Over half of the total number of soccer players in the United States come from families that make over $50,000 per year (Foer 239). As with the patchwork argument presented in the introduction — where soccer has grown in patches rather than holistically — soccer has become an entrenched part of the culture amongst the youth of America, especially those from middle to upper-middle class backgrounds.

Soccer is not just popular until people reach the age of twenty-two. In fact, over the course of the last two decades, the number of semi-professional soccer teams has increased rapidly. Although soccer's minor league system does not rival that of baseball's in any profound way, the Premier Development League (PDL)—which is roughly the equivalent to Single-A baseball—featured a total of 73 teams in the 2012 season across Canada and the United States ("PDL 2012"). While many high school and collegiate players also play in the PDL, this league remains an option for post-collegiate players because of long term explicit provisions allowing for paid players and players over twenty-three to participate. Moreover, other significant amateur leagues like the National Premier Soccer League (NPSL), which was composed of 48 teams in the 2012 season, also provide a venue for post-collegiate players to continue playing soccer at a high level ("NPSL 2012"). Summing up the number of teams from both the PDL and the NPSL, there were more than 120 post-collegiate, semi-professional teams in North America in 2012.

Soccer, therefore, has become much more of an option for young adults wishing to play in collegiate, post-collegiate, and semi-professional leagues. In many respects, this qualitatively places North American soccer on par with some of the top soccer playing countries across Europe and South America.

The success of the United States at the major international competitions does not yet rival Europe or South America, but there are projections that as the United States continues to participate in the sport and gains experience, this will begin to change (Kuper and Szymanski).

Despite the rise in popularity, however, youth soccer is still only popular in mainly suburban and more densely populated areas. In some rural schools with small enrollments, soccer is often not an option as the desire remains to field a stronger football team and/or limited resources must be streamlined into a few chosen sports (which might not include soccer).

The other major issue with youth participation in soccer is that once children become adults, the question is whether they will continue to participate in soccer? Given the rise in average attendance at MLS games and viewership of the World Cup or the Euro, there is some evidence that more and more young people are continuing to watch soccer even after they no longer participate in youth soccer. Many of these young people watch other sports too, but the big difference is that soccer remains part of their lives and pocketbooks.

The youth of the United States has, in some respects, changed the world. This is the generation of Facebook, Twitter, and other modes for social media. President Obama specifically targeted young people as part of his coalition and many young people voted, campaigned, and overall worked hard for his reelection (young people also worked hard for Governor Romney as well and have shown an active involvement in politics). This is also the generation that has played and supported soccer in greater numbers than in any prior generation. The vibrancy and energy of young Americans has in many ways changed the world. Now, this soccer playing generation is also changing the country.

Conclusion

A confluence of three factors—the growth of MLS, high levels of participation and support amongst immigrant groups, and youth participation—has quietly made soccer into the fifth major sport in the United States. This is not to say that the popularity of soccer will remain indefinitely—and soccer's popularity could rapidly decline for several reasons—but that soccer has quickly and quietly become much more entrenched on the national sporting scene than most commentators and analysts would recognize. Moreover, soccer's surge has also coincided with the recent economic downturn, from 2008 to the present (early 2013). Soccer, especially MLS, has seemingly thrived during this time. This can be viewed in two different ways. First, it shows that soccer has done well economically even during a very difficult financial period for many period, which bodes very well for the future of the sport in the United States. A second view, in contrast, implies that many people are using soccer as a substitute for watching other, more expensive, sports, and will no longer watch soccer once the economy recovers. The second view is unlikely, but the major business leaders of soccer and MLS owners should continue to work very hard to provide entertaining — and affordable — soccer for people even as the economy improves.

Nonetheless, regardless of potential pitfalls, there is evidence that soccer has become a more entrenched part of American culture. This essay updates and, in some senses, refutes the Markovits/Hellerman, Wangerin, and Kuper/Syzmanski books. Given the confluence of three factors, soccer has become more like apple pie in American culture, and has done so quite rapidly. MLS has grown rapidly since 2005 and has set a solid business course with the proliferation of new SSS. Soccer remains highly popular amongst immigrants groups, especially the large Mexican American immigrant group. And, finally, youth participation in soccer remains very high, which helps build the overall conclusion that soccer has become a mainstay in American culture.

Works Cited

Abrams, Nathan. "'Inhibited but Not Crowded Out': The Strange Fate of Soccer in the United States." *The International Journal of the History of Sport*, 12.3 (1995): 1–17. Print.

Borg, Simon. "Garber: MLS Expansion to South Requires New Stadiums." *Major League Soccer*. Major League Soccer. 26 November 2012. Web. 3 December 2012.

Coombs, Danielle. "Don't Tread on Me: Soccer in the United States" in Danielle Coombs and Bob Batchelor, eds. *American History Through American Sports: From Colonial Lacrosse to Extreme Sports*, Santa Barbara: Praeger, 2013. 225–241. Print.

Department of Homeland Security. *2011 Yearbook of Immigration Statistics*. September 2012. Web. 25 November 2012.

Diner, Steven. *A Very Different Age: Americans of the Progressive Era*. New York: Hill and Wang, 1998. Print.

Duerr, Glen. "Soccer's Own Goal: Immigration, Economics, and the Decline of American Soccer in the Early 1930s" in Danielle Coombs and Bob Batchelor, eds. *American History Through American Sports: From Colonial Lacrosse to Extreme Sports*. Santa Barbara: Praeger, 2013. 217–227. Print.

Foer, Franklin. *How Soccer Explains the World: An Unlikely Theory of Globalization*. New York: HarperCollins, 2004. Print.

"History: Largest Youth Sports Organization Celebrated 35th Anniversary." *United States Youth Soccer Association*. U.S. Youth Soccer. Web. 3 December 2012.

"History of AYSO." *American Youth Soccer Organization*. American Youth Soccer Organization. Web. 3 December 2012.

Iber, Jorge, Samuel Regalado, Jose Alamillo, and Arnoldo De Leon. *Latinos in U.S. Sport: A History of Isolation, Cultural Identity, and Acceptance*, Champaign, IL: Human Kinetics, 2011. Print.

Kuper, Simon. *Football Against the Enemy*, London: Orion Books, 1994. Print.

Kuper, Simon, and Stefan Szymanski. *Soccernomics: Why England Loses, Why Germany and*

Brazil Win, and Why the U.S., Japan, Australia, Turkey — and Even Iraq — Are Destined to Become the Kings of the World's Most Popular Sport. New York: Nation Books, 2009. Print.

Markovits, Andrei, and Steven Hellerman. *Offside: Soccer and American Exceptionalism,* Princeton: Princeton University Press, 2001. Print.

Massey, Douglas. "The Social Organization of Mexican Migration to the United States." *Annals of the American Academy of Political and Social Science,* 487 (1986): 102–113. Print.

McVicker, Micah. "5 Big Ten Universities Fail to Provide Varsity Men's Soccer Programs," *Indiana Daily Student.* Indiana Daily Student. Web. 11 January 2013.

"NPSL 2012." *National Premier Soccer League.* National Premier Soccer League. Web. 3 December 2012.

"PDL 2012." *United Soccer Leagues.* United Soccer Leagues. Web. 12 October 2012

Solomon, John. "Why Don't Alabama, Auburn Have Division I Men's Soccer Programs?" *Alabama.com.* Alabama. Web. 11 January 2013.

"U.S. Open Cup," *US Open Cup.* U.S. Open Cup. Web. 14 January 2013.

Wangerin, David. *Soccer in a Football World: The Story of America's Forgotten Game.* Philadelphia: Temple University Press, 2008. Print.

9

Pitch Perfect

How the U.S. Women's National Soccer Team Brought the Game Home

DANIELLE SARVER COOMBS

Olympic fever reached extraordinary heights on Thursday, August 9, 2012. The gold medal match to determine the best team in the world's most popular sport drew the attention of audiences from around the globe. Twitter exploded with second-by-second reports, with fans screaming in collective joy when goals were scored and metaphorically shaking their heads via text-speak when opportunities were missed. As the hotly contested ninety minutes drew to a close, a nation celebrated. The United States had brought home the gold. As the Nike shirts the players immediately donned in the wake of their victory declared, greatness was found on the pitch that day.

While tales of American athletic achievements dominate headlines throughout the Olympic season, this was different. Unlike traditionally popular "American" Olympic sports like swimming, gymnastics, or track and field, soccer during the Games often has been an afterthought. NBC, the official broadcaster for the London 2012 games, did not even show the match in real time on a commonly accessible channel, instead relegating it to an upper-tier channel. Despite this lack of prominence in official channels, the American people were paying attention. This was a team that managed to capture the viewing public's attentiveness—and hearts—by playing hard and, perhaps more importantly in terms of public attention and affection, winning. Far from relegated to afterthoughts (as members of the U.S. men's national soccer team so often are), the United States women's national team (USWNT) stars have become household names. Abby Wambach, Hope Solo, Alex Morgan, Megan Rapinoe, and the rest of the women on the squad have managed to do what their male counterparts have not: consistently win major tournaments and get the American public excited about the beautiful game. This is uniquely American; as Markovits and Hellerman noted, "Nowhere else is women's soccer the cultural equivalent of— or even superior to — the men's game, as it is in the United States" (14).

While commentators often emphasize the perceived resistance to soccer in the United States, the women's game is proving to be a growing force. This phenomenon is important to understand for two reasons in particular: first, because it subverts the typical sporting structure that elevates men's teams as the gold standard and women's teams as inferior, substandard also-rans, as often is the case in basketball, baseball/softball, and hockey; and second, it provides an unusual context to examine the importance of success in gaining national attention for team sports.

This essay will examine the USWNT both in the context of their historical success and their popular appeal. Specifically, I will trace their emergence as a globally dominant team and the corresponding media attention they have drawn, focusing particularly on two rosters who seemed to capture lightening in a bottle: the 1999 World Cup champions and the 2011/2012 iteration that lost to Japan in the World Cup finals but then rebounded to beat them in the Olympics final the next year. This essay will be both a celebration of the USWNT and an examination of how their success has subverted a media culture that privileges male sports and athletes over females, making soccer success a marker of national pride rather than a "backseat" sport.

Building a Foundation

As detailed elsewhere in this volume, soccer in the United States has followed a very different trajectory than in most other countries. While most of the world embraces the "beautiful game," the U.S. remains focused on its own indigenous sports: baseball, basketball, and American football. Various explanations have been posed for this example of "American exceptionalism" (Waddington and Roderick 28), the end result is the same: until the explosion of youth soccer teams in the 1980s and '90s, "few American citizens had any idea what soccer was beyond a vague image of a black-and-white ball" (Shugart 5–6). Despite the "obliviousness of the average American to soccer as a major sport" (Stossel), however, the game began to take root in the U.S. with the passage of Title IX.

A key component of the Education Amendments Act of 1972, Title IX forced schools to offer equal sporting opportunities for women and men in order to receive federal funds. In the ensuing decades, women's participation in athletic competitions would skyrocket, particularly in terms of team sports like soccer. In the wake of Title IX, "Soccer emerged as a primary beneficiary; physical yet not violent, athletically demanding but not requiring exceptional size, bulk, or upper-body strength, it was constructed as a sport suitable for women and an acceptable outdoor female team sport to balance male football programs" (Henry and Comeaux 278). Because of these advantages, soccer programs for girls and women created "a farm system for female athletes.... This, in turn, has spawned skilled athletes equipped for professional sports and an enormous base of little girls to worship them" (Hammel and Mulrine).

The impact of Title IX on the development and success of women's soccer in the United States cannot be overestimated. Girls were playing on the pitch alongside boys, testing their mettle, forming their game, and learning skills that would benefit our national team for years. When soccer's international governing body, the Fédération Internationale de Football Association (FIFA), organized the first Women's World Cup in 1991, the United States was ready to play, having "dominated the sport on a world level as its most consistent and successful performer" (Markovits and Hellerman 20). They won the tournament, hoisting the inaugural cup in China. Upon their return to the States, however, they faced the cold reality that being crowned champions of the world did not translate into mass appeal: "As the players and then-coach Anson Dorrance walked out of the baggage area, they were applauded by maybe a dozen people.... The historic witnesses included three reporters, one photographer, several U.S. Soccer Federation officials, a referee from New York and Swiss Air officials, who gave each player a rose" (Lewis).

The emergence of a competitive international environment for women's soccer coincided with increased attention to women's sports in general. NBC, the official broadcaster of those Olympics, publicly declared their intention to increase coverage of women's sports — and team sports in particular — in their coverage of the 1996 Summer Olympics in Atlanta, Georgia. This was an important step in allowing for the emergence of a women's sports team into popular consciousness, since "any Olympics is a constructed event and becomes thoroughly mediated by its producing organizations, especially the American network broadcasters" (Eastman and Billings 142). In other words, the broadcasters have the power to reshape the Games through their production decisions; by declaring that women's sports would play a central role in coverage, NBC created an Olympic environment designed to highlight and normalize their athletic achievements. In the wake of this new media environment, the United States was primed to fall in love with the 1999 national women's soccer team.

Breakout Success: The 1999 World Cup

While the USWNT historically was one of the most dominant teams in the world, it took one event — the 1999 Women's World Cup, hosted in the U.S.— to capture America's attention and imagination. In anticipation of the event, media partners ABC announced that all matches would be broadcast on ESPN and ESPN2, with the final match airing live on ABC itself. As the tournament approached, media coverage began to approach a fever pitch: "Particularly significant in the case of the U.S. women's soccer team is that media coverage of it and its members slightly before, during, and following the 1999 Women's World Cup was excessive, lavish by any standards, even as compared to coverage of men's sports" (Shugart 4). The press could not get enough of the players, clamoring for interviews and photo opportunities. Even late night talk show host David Letterman got into the spirit. He "referenced the women on his show nearly every night.... Dubbing the team 'babe city' and its members 'soccer mamas'" (Shugart 20).

Throughout the tournament the American women embraced the spotlight and lived up to the hype, attracting bigger crowds and more attention as they continued to win. They inspired throngs of young girls, and during matches "Legions of pre-teen 'mini–Mias' were out in force, wearing the jersey of the sport's biggest star, No. 9 Mia Hamm, and going hoarse as they chanted 'U-S-A!'" (Hammel and Mulrine). They managed to expand their appeal beyond the preteen set, however, appealing across a broad spectrum while attracting new fans to the game. The combination of good looks, American wholesomeness, positive attitudes, and a winning record proved irresistible, generating a "media frenzy was phenomenal, possibly more intense than any coverage of a men's championship in any sport and certainly more intense than any coverage, ever, of a women's championship" (Shugart 7).

World Cup Finals

As the American women continued to win against opponents, the fervor grew. Finally, on July 10, 1999, the championship match began, pitting the U.S. women against their Chinese rivals. The teams played in front of the largest crowd ever gathered to watch a women's sporting event as 90,185 fans packed the Rose Bowl. A closely matched and intensely fought battle, the final came down to kicks from the mark. With the U.S. up by one and only one chance left, the championship came down to Brandi Chastain. When her attempt went past the Chinese goalkeeper and into the back of the net, "Chastain fell to her knees like Bjorn Borg after winning Wimbledon and ripped off her jersey, waving it above her head to the thundering crowd" (Wahl, "Out of This World"). Photographs of Chastain's celebration instantly became iconic, symbolizing "the spectacular success of the 1999 World Cup" (Stossel).

The reaction to this team and their victory was diametrically opposed to the dearth of attention they received in the wake of the 1991 World Cup win. No longer was their celebration limited to a group small enough to be listed in a magazine column; instead, the entire country was watching and joining in (Lewis). *Sports Illustrated*'s soccer reporter, Grant Wahl, quoted Michelle Akers' explanation for the difference:

> It was like all the stars configured perfectly, and we won in such a dramatic way," says Akers. "I still don't understand why that captured so many people's imaginations, but something about it was very special. It changed people inside.... It was just pure. And I think that's what it was about us, that team and that time. It was just pure. That resonated with people, the purity of competing ["Green Acres"].

Beyond the purity of competition, this team also was one of the first American soccer teams with whom the general public developed an emotional connection. Primed by the previous year's men's World Cup tournament also held in the States, the public saw firsthand the type of passion and excitement felt by the rest of the world toward their football teams. When the women's team — among the favorites going into the tournament — won so dramatically, it was a victory on a much larger scale: "The main reason, of course, was that American fans were following their own team, suffering with it, waiting for that one tiny advantage that finally came in the shootout" (Wahl, "Out of This World"). As Wahl wrote in his 2011 profile on Michelle Akers, published as the new iteration of America's soccer sweethearts prepared to take to the pitch, the import and magnitude of this win continued to increase with time: "With each year that passes, the cultural breakthrough of the '99 U.S. Women's World Cup team appears more like a transcendent achievement in the women's movement, not just in sports" (Wahl, "Green Acres").

After the Final Kick

Attention to and interest in the USWNT continued post-tournament, with claims that the "women's World Cup marked the first step in creating a passion for soccer and an understanding of why it's the world's most popular sport" (Thomsen). A week after their Rose Bowl victory the team "recorded the unprecedented feat of making the cover of America's four largest news weeklies: *Time, Newsweek, People* and *Sports Illustrated*! The team broke more hearts than saturated fat and achieved fame and adoration levels matched only by the 1980 U.S. Olympic Hockey Team" (Taylor)

The team was named *Sports Illustrated*'s Sportswomen of the Year, an honor bestowed to such luminaries as Roger Bannister (1954), Sandy Koufax (1965), and Wayne Gretzky (1982), as well as the Associated Press's Sports Story of the Year. Coach Tony DiCicco "has become the role model for all soccer coaches in this country. He will go down as the first American to win an international tournament while coping with high expectations and intense scrutiny at home" (Thomsen). The team itself became celebrities, with the public and mainstream media clamoring for more. The women made guest appearances on a number of television shows during their "magical victory tour" (Lewis). To echo Wahl's sentiment above, it is important to remember that "These women didn't turn into star athletes overnight, nor did they do it without a sea change in the way culture viewed the role of sports in their lives" (Hammel and Mulrine). The increased media attention to women's sports that began in the mid-'90s and the competitive opportunities offered by Title IX had culminated with this phenomenon: the public's utter absorption in a team of women who played a sport that was not traditionally part of the American viewing experience. Women athletes were no longer an anomaly; these women came into viewers homes and hearts, inspiring a generation of young girls to play hard in hopes of being "just like Mia."

The elevation of a group of women athletes to iconic status was almost unprecedented in American sporting history, which tended to focus on individual events associated with traditional "feminine" characteristics like grace and elegance instead of physical, aggressive "masculine" team sports. Celebrating these women on the front pages of magazines and fêting them on television shifted the way media addressed women athletes, which had "the potential for drastically altering the perception of women in all forms of society" (Eastman and Billings 145–146). This coverage was not entirely unproblematic, however, since "general references to the team, too, featured the same dynamic of acknowledging athletic prowess while framing it as sexual shtick" (Shugart 13).

As scholars at that time noted, these women were popular because they were presented as heterosexually attractive: "If their representation had been congruent with the prevailing stereotype of athletic lesbians, the enthusiasm for this team might have been considerably less" (Knoppers and Anthonissen 362). Emphasis on traditional feminine beauty, roles as wives and mothers, and sometimes upfront sexuality created controversy over the coverage, and this emphasis preceded their success: "Much of the (mediated coverage) occurred prior to coverage of the team in their athletic capacity, including Hamm's selection as one of *People Weekly*'s 50 Most Beautiful People; Foudy's appearance in a swimsuit in the pages of *Sports Illustrated*; and Chastain's nude posing for *Gear* magazine" (Shugart 8). Debates over the meaning and import of this continued long after the tournament concluded, particularly for three women considered central to the success of the team: Mia Hamm, Brandi Chastain, and Michelle Akers.

Generally considered "the most famous women's soccer player of all time" (Wahl, "Green Acres"), Mia Hamm also is considered one of the best: she joined Michelle Akers as the only two women — and only Americans — on a list of the "100 greatest living players chosen by Pelé and approved by FIFA" ("Hamm, Akers Named"). While her prowess on the pitch was unmistakable, it was Hamm's looks that were considered central to her appeal as the player "whose conventional beauty attracted the advertising dollars of, among others, Nike and Gatorade. She was also named the official spokeswoman for the new soccer Barbie, that icon of feminine beauty" (Shugart 8). Hamm was a sought-after endorser, signing on with Nike, Powerbar, Dreyer's Ice Cream, Earthgrains, Fleet Bank, and Gatorade, "earning in excess of $1 million a year" (Spencer and McClurg 333).

Perhaps Hamm's best-remembered advertisement was a 30-second spot for Gatorade that pitted her athletic skills against a man then widely considered to be the best in the world: basketball player Michael Jordan. Set to an aggressive, pop-punk rendition of "Anything You Can Do, I Can Do Better," the two went head-to-head in a variety of sports, including basketball, soccer, fencing, and tennis. "Certainly, linking Mia Hamm with arguably the greatest endorser of the 20th century (i.e., Michael Jordan) has enhanced the marketability of female athletes" (Spencer and McClurg 341).

Best known for her iconic post-goal celebration, Brandi Chastain was among the most vocal proponents for acknowledging the usefulness of looks and sex appeal to help gain media attention. Pointing out that she "had worked hard to obtain her well-muscled physique" (Spencer and McClurg 322), Chastain opted to pose nude in *Gear* magazine before the tournament began. When she removed her jersey to reveal a full-coverage sports bra that offered considerably more modesty than what would be found on a beach any given day, the ensuing attention offered a lens to examine the ways sexuality defined coverage: "The most blatant way in which sexualized performance characterized coverage of the women's soccer team was the 'controversy' over Chastain's removal of her shirt upon scoring the winning, championship goal of the Cup tournament.... Indeed, that image and the ensuing notoriety defined the team, then and now" (Shugart 12).

Considered the "sport's first superstar" (Wahl, "Green Acres"), Michelle Akers' impact on the team was unparalleled. Despite suffering from a number of physical ailments that often limited her playing time, including chronic fatigue syndrome, Akers role as the team's powerful leader gave them the defensive strength needed to prevail. Although not as glamorous as her teammates, her sheer skill and power meant true soccer aficionados paid attention when she was on the pitch. The accolades paid to Akers' prowess were echoed by her fellow USWNT athletes: "So go ahead, lionize Akers. Her teammates do. They call her Mufasa, after the gallant feline in The Lion King, ostensibly for her long mane of curly hair but just as much for her unsurpassed strength" (Wahl, "Out of This World). During the tournament she even gained the attention of then-president Bill Clinton: "Then Akers, who DiCicco calls the best woman player ever, couldn't resist repeating what President Clinton had told her when he visited the U.S. locker room after the game: 'From someone who knows how to take a hit, I really admire you'" (Wahl "Out of This World").

Despite the recognition that Akers' role in the team was essential to her success, the media coverage of her tended to emphasize her age and physical frailty. Bigger and more physically imposing than her teammates, Akers did not fit the mold of the sexually attractive girl next door that Hamm and Chastain embodied. According to Shugart,

> This consistent mediated representation of Akers as old and physically ravaged cast her not merely as distinct from her teammates but diametrically opposed to their youth and "sexy" physical wholesomeness. Indeed, this dynamic was crystallized, as in Scurry's case, in media coverage that cited Akers' disapproval of the other team members' actions in using sexuality to market the team [25].

Moving On and Losing Momentum

Even as the initial excitement abated, a continued expectation held that this tournament, this victory, and this team constituted a tipping point in American sporting history. Scholars claimed, "There can be little doubt that soccer — particularly women's soccer — will feature prominently on the playing fields and TV screens of the USA in coming years" (Black and Hebdige 531), noting that "viewers of both sexes are likely to be attracted to compelling coverage of dramatic competition on the world's most important sports stage regardless of whether the competitors are men or women" (Tuggle and Owen 179). It was in this context that the Women's United Soccer Association

(WUSA)—the world's first professional women's soccer league—launched with sponsors including such major American brands as Allstate, Bud Light, Gatorade, McDonald's, and Nike, boasting "a combined value of $6 million" (Spencer and McClung 331).

Despite the promise of building on the team's momentum, the excitement around women's soccer in the United States proved to have a limited shelf life. Much of the blame was directed at the U.S. Soccer Federation, which was accused of committing "a world-class marketing blunder" (Taylor) when they refused to settle Coach DiCicco's contract for months and, more problematically, balked at giving the world champions a pay raise that would eliminate the pay disparity between their team and the men's national side (a team that notably had not enjoyed nearly the same level of success). In the midst of negotiations, players were "asked to go on a boondoggle tour of Australia without a contract. When they unanimously rejected this offer, U.S. Soccer replaced them with a scab team. Net: we sold America's soccer team down the river for a few measly dollars" (Taylor).

The USWNT had a difficult time bouncing back from the negative publicity and stalled momentum of this period. Women's professional soccer leagues also failed to catch fire, with WUSA collapsing in 2003 after only three seasons. While professional women's soccer struggled, the national team also failed to recapture the public's interest in the first decade of the twenty-first century despite continuing to play well. This changed, however, when the 2011 World Cup "relaunched the USWNT and its players into the American collective consciousness" (Coombs 229), sweeping the team and its players back into the media spotlight.

World Beaters: The 2011 World Cup and 2012 Summer Olympics

Unlike the 1999 tournament where the American women were among the clear favorites to win, they were not a sure bet in 2011: "The global landscape of women's soccer has undergone upheaval from 15 years ago, when the U.S., China, and Norway dominated" (Wahl, "The Power to Rule"). Other teams had caught up in terms of size and power, the traditional strengths of the American side, but this iteration of the team boasted considerable skill as well as a new approach to play: "If the early years of U.S. women's soccer were defined by East Coast athleticism, today's team is symbolized by a more freewheeling West Coast vibe" (Wahl, "Unquiet American"). Perhaps most tellingly, the 2011 team also boasted individual players who again were capturing America's imagination, with "a new golden generation ... stepping to the fore" (Deitsch). As online sports website *Bleacher Report*'s Ott wrote, "The on-field product is tremendous. They're competitive, play games down to the wire and stir up quite the dramatic moments. The off-field personalities are captivating...."

As was the case in 1999, the cultural zeitgeist began to build around the team before the World Cup tournament began. The tournament itself was recognized as the true world championship, and it was recognized that the last American victory in the Cup was now long past. In both 2003 and 2007 the USWNT lost in the semifinals, not even making it to the final match. A reminder of past victories was impossible to forget since they were reminded each time they put on their shirts:

> Two stars. When the U.S. players pull on their uniforms at the Women's World Cup in Germany, that's what will be above the shield on their jerseys, twin symbols of soccer glory: the U.S.'s titles in 1991 and '99.... And while the pride that accompanies them is palpable, so too is the awareness that 12 long years have passed since Brandi Chastain's penalty kick against China clinched the Americans' last World Cup crown in a sold-out Rose Bowl [Wahl, "The Power to Rule"].

Would 2011 finally be the year to reclaim glory?

World Cup 2011

The mission to win rested on the shoulders of a team that had long been preparing for this stage. Captain Christie Rampone was a veteran of the '99 World Cup squad, and other team members — including goalkeeper Hope Solo — had been on board for a number of major tournaments as well. Heading into the event, however, the USWNT's best chance of winning was clear: "To reclaim the title against a deep field in Germany, the U.S. must harness its most potent weapon: the strike force of veteran Abby Wambach and phenom Alex Morgan" (Wahl, "The Power to Rule").

The road through the tournament was bumpy, with outstanding play and lucky breaks regularly required to get the American women out of trouble and into the final match. Once there, they faced off against a small, fast, and skilled Japanese team in "one of the most gripping World Cup finals anyone had ever witnessed" (Wahl "Guts and Glory"). As was the case in '99, the final match came down to the kicks from the mark. Despite having beat Brazil on the kicks just a few short days earlier, the United States lost its mojo, lost the match, and lost the Cup. During a post-match press conference the two teams demonstrated the respect they had for each other, with the USWNT members praising their opponents. The women recognized the magnitude of the victory for Japan in the wake of the massive tsunami that had wreaked destruction across the island. After all, "only the heartless would begrudge them their World Cup title, and if we know one thing about the U.S. players, they aren't lacking heart" (Wahl, "Guts and Glory").

While the USWNT did not manage to eke out a third World Cup title, they did succeed in bringing attention back to the sport. Social media platforms that had not even been conceived during the '99 tournament were ablaze during the match, and the German stadia were filled with crowds cheering on the squads:

> Yet the timing was perfect for women's soccer, which reached new heights of competitiveness and captivated a global audience. At the end of U.S.-Japan, Twitter was logging 7,196 posts per second, an alltime [sic] high and a figure that dwarfed the Super Bowl. The host Germans filled the stadiums as they do for the biggest men's events, and ESPN's ratings for the final nearly doubled its previous best for a World Cup match, the men's U.S.-Algeria game from last summer [Wahl, "Guts and Glory"].

The television audience averaged 13.458 million viewers, making it "the most-watched and highest-rated soccer telecast on an ESPN network" (Vanderberg) and "the second most-watched daytime telecast ... in cable history, behind the Rose Bowl on ESPN " (Seldman).

While the World Cup loss was heartbreaking for the members of the USWNT, they had to quickly recover and begin preparing for the next major tournament: the 2012 Summer Olympics. Unlike men's soccer which has a two-year gap between the Games and the World Cup, the timing of the women's World Cup — held the year before the Summer games — means there is a chance to build on momentum established. In 2012, this worked to the USWNT's advantage. Even though they had not won the tournament, their success still translated into public attention and affection. It was up to them to capitalize on this.

The 2012 Summer Olympics

The USWNT had a history of success at the Olympics, winning the gold medal in all but one Games since women's soccer was introduced in 1996 (Norway took the top honors in 2000; the USWNT came in second). Held in London, the 2012 Summer Olympics offered the American women a shot at redemption where they were "favored to win their third consecutive Olympic gold medal.... Says Wambach, 'Americans like a good old-fashioned comeback story, and the Olympics gives us a platform in order to achieve that" (Deitsch). The women on the team clearly understood what was at stake in London, particularly those who had toiled in the shadows of the early-2000s squads — teams that had enjoyed success but had failed to become part of the cultural zeitgeist. Recognizing the import of building on the World Cup momentum, goalkeeper Solo noted, "'It's simple.... If we show America that we're a winning team, we're going to have lifelong fans.' And if you don't? 'People are going to forget all about us'" (Romano).

The status of women's professional soccer in the United States was particularly precarious as the Games approached. A second attempt to build a women's professional soccer league — Women's Professional Soccer (WPS) — was launched in 2009, but that tenure was even shorter than that of WUSA. In the wake of owner disagreements and organizational struggles, the plug was pulled in 2012. Within this context, "the squad will be under a lot of pressure to defend its 2008 gold medal and avenge last summer's narrow World Cup loss, relying on its strength, grit, and experience to counter Japan's technical skill and the graceful, creative play of Brazil and France" (Romano). Clearly, expectations for the quality of play — and level of excitement — in women's soccer had been raised, and the USWNT embraced the challenge.

After a series of tough matches that tested the team, the American women made it to the finals at Wembley, where they would once again meet Japan. Media referred to this as "one of the most anticipated events of the entire Summer Games" (Ott). The match lived up to the hype. Full of DVR-rewind moments and Tweet-worthy incidents, the final game was played in front of 80,203 fans — making it "the best attended women's Olympic soccer match ever" (Greenberg). While television audiences were smaller in large part due to timing (the match was played on a weekday and in the middle of typical work hours) and being on a relatively obscure channel, an average audience of 4.35 million gave it the largest viewership in NBC Sports Network's history. Perhaps even more impressively, the match also "generated nearly 1.5 million live streams on NBCOlympics.com, more than any previous Olympic event. That exceeds other streams from London: Usain Bolt winning the 100-meter race (1.289 million) and the United States women's gymnastics all-around gold medal victory (1.463 million)" (Sandomir). Clearly, this team was something special: "At the risk of sounding too grandiose, these women seem to embody some sort of Olympic ideal, one that's been gradually eroding since the introduction of the Dream Team in the 1992 Games. Though their matches are serious and highly-pressured affairs, they seem — at least to this eye — always more like play" (Burke).

Individual Stars

As was the case with the '99 team, a large part of the appeal for the 2011-12 USWNT iteration was derived from individual players. Sports journalists noted, "A handful of the players are transcendent" (Burke); sports marketing expert Bob Dorfman was quoted as saying, "The final was an epic match, it likely drew a huge audience, and it made household names of Wambach, Solo and [Alex] Morgan" (Thomaselli). Those three players, along with Megan Rapinoe, generated substantial media attention throughout the two tournaments.

As co-captain and one of the more senior players on the squad, Wambach is a "proven threat" and an "aerial warrior whose strike rate (118 goals in 157 international games) surpasses that of Mia Hamm" (Wahl, "The Power to Rule"). She dominated in the Olympics, scoring five goals and leading her team through smart, savvy play, referred to as "one of the best women's players in history" (Burke). As of the end of 2012, Wambach trailed only Hamm in total goals scored for the USWNT, and her performance led to her selection as the FIFA Woman's World Player of the Year. Notably, this is only the third time an American woman has been selected for the honor, with Hamm winning in 2001 and 2002.

Well-muscled, makeup free, and her short hair pulled back with a stretchy headband, Wambach's look does not fit with a team "whose longstanding mass appeal has been based in part on its ponytailed girl-next-door aura" (Wahl, "Unquiet American"). Her more masculine appearance has not put off sponsors, however, and Solo and she had the most bargaining power coming out of the World Cup. Unlike her goalkeeping colleague, however, Wambach has shied away from the more public, performance-based endorsements because "It just doesn't fit her personality" (James). The striker was introduced to the world of endorsements and marketing by Hamm, and Wambach benefited from the superstar's expertise in this area while simultaneously developing into an international striker under Hamm's mentorship. In the 2011–12 seasons, Wambach returned the favor by helping up-and-coming striker Alex Morgan get her sea legs on the global stage as well.

As the youngest player on the World Cup team at 22 years old, Morgan's prowess as a striker combined with her sunny, all–American good looks have engendered numerous comparisons to the legendary Hamm. Nicknamed "Baby Horse" by her teammates due to her colt-like running style, Morgan's commercial appeal is undeniable. After she scored in the final match of the 2011 World Cup loss, Wahl wrote: "By the time Morgan slid into a celebration with her teammates, you could almost hear Madison Avenue buzzing from

4,000 miles away" ("Guts and Glory"). In fact, her media appeal was such that she was cited as "one of the country's most recognizable female athletes" (Ott).

Perhaps the most controversial member of the squad was goalkeeper Hope Solo. Once an outcast from the team after criticizing a former coach's decision to replace her with a more seasoned keeper between the sticks in a pivotal 2007 World Cup match against Brazil (that the USWNT went on to lose 4–0), Solo had worked her way back into a starting role. After a stint on television's *Dancing with the Stars*, the release of her autobiography, and the first failed drug test in U.S. Soccer history (later explained as a result of a premenstrual medication prescribed by her doctor), Solo went into the Summer Games ready to battle and in many ways representing the soul of the American public:

> Not to get mystical or anything, but at a time when America itself feels increasingly rattled, it makes a certain kind of sense to have a survivor like Solo as our avatar at the Olympics.... We're competing in a globalized game that we can't really dominate. We're not earning as much as we'd like. We're striving, even now, to level the playing field for women. We're struggling to strike the right balance between what's best for us and what's best for the team. And so is Solo. The question is whether she — whether we — can still win on the world stage, regardless [Romano].

Midfielder Megan Rapinoe's creativity and drive were central to the team's success in the 2011–12 seasons, serving crosses that allowed her teammates to score fantastic goals while also occasionally hitting the back of the net herself. Representing the new breed of American women's soccer, Pinoe, as known to her teammates, brought a new style to the team:

> Truth be told, Pinoe is the most un–American player in U.S. women's soccer, and that's a compliment. For decades the U.S. has thrived on strength and speed more than skill. Rapinoe is different. With a build that more closely resembles Twiggy than tigress — she models her look on actress Tilda Swinton — Rapinoe relies instead on clever dribbling, fluid movement and visionary passing. It's a little bit of Barcelona in red, white and blue [Wahl, "Unquiet American"].

Perhaps Rapinoe's greatest and most lasting legacy to American soccer will have happened off the pitch. In the weeks leading up to the Summer Games, Pinoe became the first American international footballer to come out in the media as gay. This brave step demonstrates the shift in perceptions of sexuality and femininity from that experienced by the 1999 squad. In the past, women who considered coming out were all too aware of the risks associated: "While there is not a problem with wanting to convey a 'feminine' image, the problem arises when lesbians in sport are perceived as the 'problem' and therefore asked to become invisible as a result" (Spencer and McClurg 341). Rapinoe's experience, however, offers hope that women athletes can now more comfortably acknowledge and publicly discuss their sexuality.

Marketing the Team

While decisions to pose either nude or in minimal clothing generated controversy for the members of the 1999 women's squad, this seemed much more commonplace for the '11/'12 iterations. Solo and Wambach were photographed nude for *ESPN the Magazine*'s "Body Issue" series in 2011 and 2012 respectively, and Morgan wore only a painted-on (literally) bikini for the 2012 *Sports Illustrated* Swimsuit Edition. While historically "successful female athletes carried the added burden of conveying traditional notions of femininity" (Spencer and McClurg 341) as seen in Morgan's shots, both Solo's and Wambach's photos demonstrate power, muscles, and athleticism. Of the three athletes, Solo best bridges the traditional divide between masculine and feminine, connoting muscle-based power while maintaining long hair and boasting a "leonine bone structure" (Romano). These women are savvy about what it takes to be successful in this era of marketing madness:

> For Solo, who will turn 31 later this month, it's all part of being a female athlete circa 2012. "An NFL player never has to do any endorsements, and he's fine," says Solo. "But it just doesn't work that way for us. My soccer salary would only make me an average living. So we can't just market to little girls constantly. We need to start selling tickets to the masses. To middle-aged men. To all walks of life. At the end of the day, these stupid photo shoots are about bringing more recognition to the game, getting bigger contracts, and putting our selves [sic] on the same level as the men" [Romano].

Unlike the internal debates within the '99 squad over what was appropriate for players in terms of marketing sexuality, today's team seems to recognize that sex appeal can have its advantages. In an *ESPN* article, James quotes Wambach as saying she believes her teammates will "be successful in that genre of marketing. I think Hope and Alex [Morgan] both bring that level of sex appeal, if you will, to the sport.... I think Mia brought a level of that as well. She'd probably be the first one to say that's not true, but I think you have to take advantage of the things you have."

Much more than in the past, women on today's USWNT—particularly the super stars and rising stars—are aware of and willing to do what needs to be done to attract marketing deals in order to help promote the sport as a whole. In the wake of the 2011 World Cup loss, Wambach was quoted as saying, "If you're a female athlete today, you should hope the generation after you will make more money than you can," she says. Of the U.S.'s prospects in 2012, she says: "We have unfinished business. What better marketing can you get? I think that will be attractive to sponsors" (Berfield). This focus on improving the financial situation for future athletes was echoed by Solo, who commented: "I think a lot of female athletes want to please everybody by saying, 'Oh yeah, we'll take pay cuts.' 'We'll play professionally without health insurance.' And I always say it's not all about pleasing people. It's about looking after yourself as an athlete. To grow the sport, for future generations. That's something that's hard for women sometimes'" (Romano).

This sense of stewardship of the team, thereby improving the lots of future women footballers, weaves through discussions on marketing and sponsorships. Unlike in other sports, it seems, the women of the USWNT recognize that their time in the spotlight is fleeting, and it is up to them to maximize their impact to benefit both themselves and others: According to Wambach, "There's a really short period of time the light shines so bright on women's soccer, and one is the World Cup and the other is the Olympics.... And if it is my goal to leave this game better than I found it, I really need to keep dedicating [myself]" (James). In other words, for at least some of the stars of the USWNT, the endorsements and marketing opportunities that come with success can lead to broader improvements and better conditions for the next generation of women to play.

While this type of consciousness about marketing and attracting target audiences may undermine the purity associated with the game—the purity that Akers felt was essential to the 1999 World Cup team capturing the hearts and minds of Americans—a savvy business approach could be just what women's professional soccer needs. The first iteration of a professional soccer league, WUSA, was created in the wake of the most successful and beloved team in the history of women's sports in America, yet it failed to take hold. A second attempt, launched in the middle of a recession yet managing to anticipate the growing interest in the USWNT, fell apart within months of the team's second-place World Cup final.

In late 2012, a third attempt was introduced: the National Women's Soccer League (NWSL). Consisting of eight teams across the United States, the league is partially supported by investment from the U.S. Soccer Association, Canadian Soccer Association, and the Federation of Mexican Football. In order to help make the league pay competitive for professional athletes, each of these organizations will subsidize the salaries of players: up to twenty-four of the United States national team players and up to sixteen for the other two nations. The success of the NWSL is by no means guaranteed; in fact, "the optimistic perspective suggests waiting to see how the talent is distributed before judging anything. The pessimist perspective has history on its side" (Becker). Despite the associated pessimism, hope prevails that the league will be able to tap into cultural excitement around women's soccer and the USWNT, particularly in terms of the appeal held by its stars.

Conclusion

As this essay has demonstrated, women's soccer in the United States has emerged as the premier women's sport and, for now at least, the dominant national side. Will NWSL and the players be able to capitalize on Olympic success to build a lasting relationship with fans that will transcend international tournaments? That remains to be seen. What we do know, however, is that the option to play soccer will continue to appeal to young American women, including among the growing immigrant groups. Increased immigration from countries where football is king will continue to bring attention to the sport domestically. Likewise, women emigrating from countries where soccer is almost exclusively the domain of men are coming to a place where the gender neutrality of the sport gives them the opportunity to join in the action on the pitch: "Hundreds of Latinas are playing soccer expanding the limits of traditional female roles and perhaps transforming the norms of femininity in their own families and in their communities" (Cuadros 228). These potential "futboleras" have the potential to deeply impact future USWNT iterations, and it is likely that future squads will reflect this increased diversity.

While the USWNT still only has two stars, a chance for a third is only a few years away with the 2015 women's World Cup to be played in Canada. With an almost home team advantage and time-zone friendly scheduling, the tournament is the best chance the U.S. women have to bring home the gold in front of record-setting audiences. Whether or not they do, they surely will give the American public something exciting to watch.

Works Cited

Becker, Josie. "A New League and Another New Dawn for US Women's Soccer." *Guardian*. Guardian, 18 Dec. 2012. Web. 11 Jan. 2013.
Berfield, Susan. "Selling Abby Wambach." *Business Week*. Business Week, 20 Oct. 2011. Web. 11 Jan. 2013.
Black, Michael, and Dick Hebdige. "Women's Soccer and the Irish Diaspora." *Peace Review* 11.4 (1999): 531–537. Web. 12 Dec. 2012.
Burke, Monte. "U.S. Women's Soccer: The Most Compelling Team in American Sports." *Forbes.com*. Forbes, 9 Aug. 2012. Web. 11 Jan. 2013.
Coombs, Danielle Sarver. "Don't Tread on Me: Soccer in the United States." *American History*

Through American Sports. Eds. Danielle Sarver Coombs and Bob Batchelor. Westport, CT: Praeger, 2012. 225–241. Print.
Cuadros, Paul. "We Play Too: Latina Integration Through Soccer in the 'New South.'" *Southeastern Geographer* 51:2 (2011): 227–241. Web. 12 Dec. 2012.
Deitsch, Richard. "Chasing the Dream." *Sports Illustrated* (2012): 42–45. *EBSCOhost*. Web. 26 Dec. 2012.
Eastman, Susan T., and Andrew C. Billings. "Gender Parity in the Olympics: Hyping Women Athletes, Favoring Men Athletes." *Journal of Sport & Social Issues* 21.2 (1999): 140–170. Web. 26 Dec. 2012.
Greenberg, Chris. "U.S. Women's Soccer Wins Gold, Defeating Japan in London Olympics Final." *Huffington Post,* 10 Aug., 2012. Web. 26 Dec. 2012.
"Hamm, Akers Named to 'FIFA 100' List." *USSoccer.com*. United States Soccer, 4 Mar. 2004. Web. 11 Jan. 2013.
Hammel, Sara, and Anna Mulrine. "They Got More Than Just Game." *U.S. News & World Report* 127.2 (1999): 54. *EBSCOhost*. Web. 26 Dec. 2012.
Henry, Jacques M., and Howard P. Comeaux. "Gender Egalitarianism, in Coed Sport: A Case Study of American Soccer." *International Review for the Sociology of Sport* 34.3 (1999): 227–290. Web. 12 Dec. 2012.
James, Brant. "Hope Solo, Abby Wambach Take Different Paths." *ESPNW.* ESPN, 24 Oct. 2011. Web. 11 Jan. 2011.
Knoppers, Annelies, and Anton Anthonissen. "Women's Soccer in the United States and Netherlands: Differences and Similarities in Regimes of Inequalities." *Sociology of Sports Journal* 20.4 (2003): 351–370. Web. 26 Dec. 2012.
Lewis, Michael. "Firsthand: Combating a Myth from Women's World Cup '91." *Sportsillustrated.cnn.com*. Sports Illustrated, 14 July 1999. Web. 11 Jan. 2013.
Markovits, Andrei S., and Steven L. Hellerman. "Women's Soccer in the United States: Yet Another American 'Exceptionalism.'" *Soccer, Women, Sexual Liberation, Kicking Off a New Era.* Eds. Fran Hong and J.A. Mangan. London: Frank Cass, 2004. 14–29. Web. 14 Dec. 2012.
Ott, Alex. "Olympic Soccer TV Schedule: Japan vs. US Rematch Will Top 2011 World Cup Final." *Bleacher Report*. Bleacher Report, 7 Aug. 2012. Web. 26 Dec. 2012.
Romano, Andrew. "It Takes a Lot to Rattle Me (Cover Story)." *Newsweek* 160.4/5 (2012): 20–25. *Academic Search Complete*. Web. 26 Dec. 2012.
Sandomir, Richard. "With Women's Soccer Final, NBC Sports Sets a Record." *London2012. blogs.nytimes.com*. New York Times, 10 Aug. 2012. Web. 11 Jan. 2013.
Shugart, Helene A. "She Shoots, She Scores: Mediated Constructions of Contemporary Female Athletes in Coverage of the 1999 US Women's Soccer Team." *Western Journal of Communication* 67.1 (2003): 1–31. Web. 26 Dec. 2012.
Spencer, Nancy E., and Lisa R. McClung. "Women and Sport in the 1990's: Reflections on 'Embracing Stars and Ignoring Players.'" *Journal of Sport Management* 15.4 (2001): 319–349. Web. 12 Dec. 2012.
Stossel, Scott. "As American as Women's Soccer?" *The Atlantic* June 2001. Web. 26 Dec. 2012.
Taylor, Rod. "How Soccer Is Shooting Itself in the Foot." *Brandweek* 41.6 (2000): 22. *Academic Search Complete*. Web. 26 Dec. 2012.
Thomaselli, Rich. "World Cup Loss Costs U.S. Team $10 Million in Endorsements." *AdAge*. Advertising Age, 18 July 2011. Web. 11 Jan. 2013.
Thomsen, Ian. "Back in the Back." *Sports Illustrated* 91.4 (1999): 70. *EBSCOhost*. Web. 26 Dec. 2012.
Tuggle, C.A., and Anne Owen. "A Descriptive Analysis of NBC's Coverage of the Centennial Olympics: The Games of the Woman?" *Journal of Sport & Social Issues* 23.2 (1999): 171–182.

Vanderberg, Marcus. "Women's World Cup Final Highest-Rated Soccer Match in ESPN History." *Mediabistro.com.* 18 July 2011. Web. 26 Dec. 2012.

Waddington, Ivan and Martin Roderick. "American Exceptionalism: Soccer and American Football." *The Sports Historian* 16.1 (1999): 28–49. Web. 26 Dec. 2012.

Wahl, Grant. "Green Acres." *Sports Illustrated* 115.1 (2011): 98–102. *Academic Search Complete.* Web. 26 Dec. 2012.

_____. "Guts and Glory." *Sports Illustrated* 115.3 (2011): 34–41. *Academic Search Complete.* Web. 26 Dec. 2012.

_____. "Out of This World." *Sports Illustrated* 91.3 (1999): 38. *EBSCOhost.* Web. 26. Dec. 2011.

_____. "The Power to Rule." *Sports Illustrated* 114.26 (2011): 50–53. *Academic Search Complete.* Web. 26 Dec. 2012.

_____. "Unquiet American." *Sports Illustrated* 117.5 (2012): 58–60. *Academic Search Complete.* Web. 26 Dec. 2012.

Part IV: Interviews

10

Scholarship and Soccer: Alex Galarza

Yuya Kiuchi, Interviewer

Popular culture studies began with a series of battles within the academy. Ray Browne, Russel Nye, and other pioneers of the discipline faced severe criticism from the academic establishment that claimed that popular culture did not deserve scholarly attention. Thanks to their efforts, academics today produce diverse scholarship in the field with prosperous organizations such as the Popular Culture Association, the American Culture Association and others, and academic journals including *The Journal of Popular Culture* and *The Journal of American Culture*. Outside of the field, however, there still remains a lack of awareness that popular culture can be a subject of study. Students seem surprised when they learn that their favorite TV show or singers can be studied in a classroom. The public seems to believe studying works by Shakespeare is, for some reason, more academically appropriate than studying the cultural meaning of a Shakespeare bobble head.

The same is true with soccer. Studying soccer, of course, is fun. But it is also a serious topic. Soccer can be a significant part of any course in history, anthropology, English, philosophy, and others, let alone in science, kinesiology, and engineering. This is exactly why Alex Galarza is a significant figure in the field of soccer studies. He is a founding member of the Football Scholars Forum, based in the Department of History at Michigan State University. Galarza launched this online community with his co-founder, Peter Alegi, in 2010, to bring journalists and academics of various backgrounds together to discuss their work. Currently, the forum's website contains an archive of discussion recordings, a list of scholars and journalists in the field, a repository of sample course syllabi, and many other sources.

Galarza, as he continues his doctoral dissertation research, is well aware of what soccer means in society. Soccer is where a community happens. Soccer drives communities. As an expert on Argentinian soccer and society, he also sees some parallel between South American communities and immigrant communities in the U.S. As soccer gains a larger foothold in the U.S., not only among middle class suburbanites but also among urban immigrant communities, Galarza's findings will be increasingly pertinent in the U.S.

The value of his contribution, however, is not limited to his scholarship. As he has made the Forum open to the public, he is engaged in the accessibility and openness of his works. In this interview, he elaborates on the importance of his colleagues producing scholarship with non-academics in mind. Regardless of the topic of study, scholars have a lot to learn from Galarza. Furthermore, for those who study popular culture, this approach is probably more significant. Soccer scholarship should not be confined in the ivory tower. Just as this book aims to be intellectually sound, legitimate, and meaningful while being relevant and accessible to any soccer fan, soccer scholarship bears the responsibility to exist with soccer communities.

Kiuchi: First, can you tell us about your background and your work?

Galarza: I look at soccer clubs in the Argentine capital of Buenos Aires, and I look at them throughout the twentieth century but mostly right in the 1950s, 1960s, and 1970s. The reason I look at soccer clubs is it's a way to examine urban history through a civic association and a site of everyday life. While my research, of course, looks at the professional teams and the league itself, how it was structured, results, who were the important teams, I really take more of a sharper interest in how the larger clubs are able to bring tens of thousands of people together as members, and then more tens of hundreds or thousands of people as fans behind the social life of the club. So, the most concrete example of how I use soccer clubs to look at urban history is this failed stadium complex which was a mix between a stadium and a theme park. One of the most popular clubs, Boca Juniors, tried to become more socially relevant because while they were either the first or second most popular team in the country depending on who you asked, they didn't have as much social infrastructure. So they didn't have as many facilities and activities to offer their fans or their members whereas at River Plate, there's even a school in the stadium. So, you could do anything if you were a member of River Plate, so much so that if you lived around River, you would be a member of the club just to use their facilities and things even if you weren't a fan. There was a president at Boca Juniors for twenty years whose name was Alberto Armando, and the current stadium is named after him. It's called the Alberto

Armando Stadium. So anyway, this guy was the tenth richest man in Argentina. He wanted to expand the club's social infrastructure. So he saw building this stadium, sports complex, theme park, and general leisure space as a way of attracting new members to Boca and making Boca like a prominent place for activity in the city. The government donated not land, but actually water in the river, and then they filled in with seven artificial man-made islands and built most of what this complex was supposed to do. But they never built the stadium. So, the stadium was started in the early 1970s, but it became clear it was not going to get built by 1976, by the time of the military coup. So that was actually supposed to be where the 1978 World Cup was played, but since it was never built, it never happened. I look at this project. I look at cases like Boca and a couple other urban projects in these clubs to look at how both the government, the directors of the clubs, and the members of the clubs themselves viewed soccer clubs as a way to expand the urban infrastructure. It was going to be a very middle class leisure space, kind of imagination of what these activities would look like so that project had a drive-in movie theater, eighteen tennis courts, and a theme park for kids. These were activities that were kind of part and parcel of what Argentina in the 1950s and 60s was looking at as kind of desirable leisure, middle class consumptive spaces.

Kiuchi: That's interesting because when a lot of people want to know more about soccer or any sport, they tend to look at just soccer or they tend to look at just baseball, and then they are obsessed with stats. They are so obsessed with the history of the team, but not necessarily the history of that urban area. So what got you into that topic?

Galarza: Well, I first needed to look at a topic in Argentine soccer that allowed me to look at more than just soccer. What landed me in Buenos Aires in the first place was that I looked at how clubs exist in a city and it's just that there are too many people who exist here in the city who aren't necessarily that interested in the professional team for this to be explained merely by professional soccer. There are too many women and children and men who aren't going to the stadium every day to say this club exists because of this professional team. My first time at Boca Juniors, I went into the library and was talking with older ladies in a knitting club. Anything you want to do, you can do through your club. The way I explain it to a lot of Americans is imagine your YMCA, your church group, your intramural teams, and your professional sports teams all wrapped up into one, and your civic association all wrapped up into one, and that's what the clubs are. I needed to look for a way to make Argentinian soccer relevant beyond just the sport itself. When I started looking at how vibrant the life of the clubs was, I said this is something I can look at as a way to understanding how people constitute their communities, and that came from realizing, less so today but still even very strong today, that a lot of the clubs have such strong neighborhood identities. Boca is a national team. The neighborhood itself has a very important mythical status in the club's identity, but has since moved far outside of the neighborhood, but still that neighborhood is rooted in the identity of its team, even though River Plate came out of the same neighborhood and there were other teams that came out of that neighborhood. A lot of neighborhoods, especially on the west side of Buenos Aires, somewhere like Velez Sarsfield, if you live in that area there is a high probability that you have either looked at becoming a member of that club or are a member of Velez Sarsfield just because there are so many things you wouldn't be able to do unless you were induced to get into the gym and use it or have your kid play on the soccer team. That's how I looked for a way to go beyond just the history of the team and instead look at more of an institutional history of the club. When you look at the club itself, you start to find how involved it is in local politics, municipal politics, national politics, and the fabric of the city itself being woven largely by soccer clubs in many instances.

Kiuchi: I may be asking you to condense a book-length project into fifty words, but when you think about soccer or clubs, do you see them as a vehicle of community building or community engagement? Or is it where a community happens? How do you characterize it?

Galarza: The tension I like to talk about is between the clubs as nonprofit civic associations, which they have legal status as, and the reality of business logics. I look at how that tension was always in play though, from the times when the Argentinians were first forming youth teams to then become the larger teams. There was a question of amateurism, bringing in amateurs but you pay them. There was always a tension of "Are we just a club providing a field for its youth" or "Are we a club that's trying to win and grow and become the best it can be." In the earliest twentieth century you have to look at them as institutions for vehicles of community building. But I think the question that is a little more interesting for me, moving out of that original period of professional leagues and the more prominent clubs that stuck around is how this explains everyday life in the city. Once those communities are even established, how do they change over time, how are the people in those clubs using the clubs as way to lobby politicians for expanded fields or more opportunities for the club? There's always an aspect of community building going on there, but after a period we have to talk about not just the building of the community but the democratic life of the community itself, how that fits into the neighborhood, how that fits into the national or urban conception of what it is to live in a certain area and belong to a certain club and perform your everyday business in that club.

Kiuchi: When you compare what you study to what you see how soccer is played in the United States, do you experience any similarities between the two or do you see more differences, especially when you think of high school or college soccer?

Galarza: I see some similarities in that even from my own personal experience, especially in youth soccer, I saw youth leagues really act as points where I saw my parents meet a lot of their friends because I played with their kids. Now their involvement with the municipality was far more limited than we would see in the kind of research that I do. And I think it would be a stretch to take that comparison beyond that this is a place of sociability. But in a far more limited way, in the United States, at least in my personal experience. With immigrant communities, historically speaking, we can see lots of parallels to the most vibrant communities of soccer in Buenos Aires. If you look at early twentieth century United States immigrant communities that would launch a lot of the famous teams that would arise either around a place of work or around an immigrant community would participate in the first kind of professional leagues here. There are similar parallels to how even in the 1920s, '30s, and '40s the clubs in Argentina were developing. I think one of the key differences in the United States is the trajectory of historical professional sports that kind of foreclosed the space around what soccer was going to become. It is not an urban male leisure activity whereas it is in Argentina. The other key difference that I look at in Buenos Aires is that a third of the population in Argentina is in one city, and its most storied clubs are in that city. The professional league now has a little bit more of a national character to it, but for a long period of time the majority of professional teams were from Buenos Aires. I see parallels around looking at soccer as a place of sociability, but I don't see either in the late twentieth or present day any examples of U.S. soccer clubs having such a strong role in the everyday life of a community at large where a chunk of the city is saying a lot of life in that chunk of the city goes through the club itself.

Kiuchi: For those of us who study soccer and society, it's quite obvious that there is a huge connection between soccer and society, and there are many of us studying it. Years ago you started Football Scholars Forum. Can you tell us a little bit more about that?

Galarza: You can correct me if I'm wrong, but I believe that four or five of us went to the Peanut Barrel [a local bar] after a seminar that Peter Alegi was teaching on global sports. The short story is I met Peter Alegi and I said this is a guy who is very well connected to other people who study soccer and it would be great just to mooch off of his contacts. I talked to him and asked if there was maybe a way we could get the people you know over Skype and talk about them about their work. And he said, "Yeah, I think that's a great idea" and so it started in a very limited focus around identifying a couple books that would be relevant to people here at Michigan State either moving through the seminar or who were interested in soccer. I asked if we could get a few people he was close with on Skype just to talk about their research. Since then, that's still the kernel of the group but since then it's evolved more into a platform for soccer scholarship in an academic community. Beyond the academics, we have journalists and enthusiasts who participate in the forums as well and professionals in the industry like Ray Hudson who is a commentator and former player in the NASL. What Peter and I and the members who have been most active in the group have been trying to do with the group is just to have it perform two functions: to be a venue for the presentation of research and a sounding board for those who are presenting their research to get feedback. Very simply, it's just who are the people who care about my work and can I get them to talk more about my work. It's been successful in that regard so far and we've been able to a few neat things like get a syllabus repository together and I think that's been a very popular item because I've known a lot of professors who might not have the depth or the grasp of the literature of soccer but are content experts in their fields and know about soccer in their particular context but don't necessarily know the wider literature about soccer. Looking at someone else's syllabus you can see they used it in a specific way around the unit around immigration, let's say. I can see myself doing that. I don't have to become a soccer expert I can just give a small lecture on that or assign a small reading on that. I think that's a nice tool to provide people with syllabus repository because people can go in and see how others are teaching with this link between soccer and society either a whole course kind of way or just a few weeks or a unit kind of thing.

Kiuchi: How popular is soccer as a course topic?

Galarza: I'm very biased but I think it's enormously popular. I think it's a very popular subject because you see this generation being one that maybe not necessarily has pushed for but has been the recipient of greater media coverage around soccer and a more polished consumer package around professional soccer in this country. When I was growing up, you could not find soccer on television, aside from very prominent international matches or the World Cup or Champions Leagues, but you would be looking in the newspaper for results, at least anyone who couldn't afford an incredible satellite connection. You see now where ESPN 2 and the main ESPN channel are covering the most prominent games from the Premier League and you have dedicated soccer channels that are part of the normal sports package on most cable providers. I think the access to professional leagues especially in Europe but also elsewhere is now at a point where the kinds of people that are attending four year institutions have a familiarity with soccer both as participants and with fans which I think was the crucial link. I grew up with many people that played soccer but then never took an interest in it as a professional league. That I think has alerted more people of my generation that even if they care nothing about the sport, or actually don't like the sport, that they get that it's a big deal in the rest of the world. That's a conversation that I have frequently when I say I study soccer. I think putting soccer into courses or designing courses around soccer gets at an effort in universities to have a global studies focus. I think soccer is a perfect link for that because it allows you to get at culture, politics, and economics in a global sense with the carrot dangling in front of students like hey we're studying soccer, this is kind of fun. But, it's the perfect segue into what they might perceive as more serious topics such as economics, politics and the link between societies. I think my one experience with Peter Alegi as with an undergraduate course around soccer, a lot of them were enthusiasts, but not all of them, and the ones that were enthusiasts by the end realized that soccer is always more than just the game itself, it has all these built-in characteristics that make it part of the social, economic, political fabric of the community itself. I think it's a very popular course topic. I think the key for educators and people who are designing syllabi is to make that kind of a sell and say it's not just about soccer. It allows us to talk about other things as I have done in the past, and to also make them realize that it's kind of a false dichotomy that we're setting up in the first place that we have to separate the political side of soccer from the sport itself. I think that's an easy sell once you have good examples out there of how to do it.

Kiuchi: When it comes to scholarship, I see a lot of journalists writing about soccer and society and right now I also see some scholars writing about that as well. What do you think about the proper stylistic balance?

Galarza: One of the most exciting things about, personally as a scholar, that I'm so happy to be involved in studying soccer, is I believe very strongly that academics need to be writing in a more journalistic mode. I think it would be unfair to say they've done a poor job but they haven't covered themselves in glory as a community of scholars with making their research relevant to a widely accessible public audience. There are always scholars who have been the exception. We rightfully idolize many of these people like Howard Zinn who wrote books and took their scholarship and said I want to make it accessible to as many people as possible. I think soccer is a no brainer because most of us are in this because we like having those kinds of conversations with people; it's rare to find the soccer scholar, at least in my opinion, who just wants to be left alone in the archive. They want to talk to people about soccer. I think we're a group who is blessed with that opportunity. At least speaking from my own discipline, from history, the outgoing president of the AHA [American Historical Association] who had a great outgoing presidential talk at the last annual meeting, said that cutting edge research is one of the most important aspects of growth as a discipline, but nobody else will know about that unless we revert to the more familiar forms of telling stories. One of these more familiar forms is the rich tradition of journalistic soccer coverage that is for the thinker as well, not just the stats, not just the bar fights that the players get into, but the story behind the club itself. France is playing Germany in Paris today. Then you need to know about the historical, political, economic history between those two countries to realize there is also soccer rivalries there just because they're great teams, but you need to know about France and Germany as nations themselves, to understand why people get worked up about that match and why it's something that even if it's friendly I'm going to watch it or I want to watch it. I think what that outgoing president of the AHA said is very relevant and it's an opportunity for soccer scholars to look and say that we're blessed with a topic that it's very easy to make that jump from maybe the more erudite journal or monographed design research that we're doing to put that into a podcast, to put that into a story, say in *the Blizzard*. There's resurgence now of football fanzines I think with *the Blizzard* and *the Howler* and *Quarterly XI*, and just content that's out there that people write on their own. People say "oh, this is a really neat story." I think that journalistic production of soccer pundits and journalists who are taking or who have always taken an interest in the historical and political aspects of soccer is something to be looked at as an incredible opportunity. I think that's what we try to do as football scholars as well is we try to identify not only monographs that have been published by University Presses but we watch films, we've read books written by journalists, and I think those two types of media as well are what people are actually consuming when they say "hey are you into soccer?" And you say "yeah" and then they start to list their favorite books and favorite films on soccer. And they'll say "Have you read the Miracle of Castel di Sangro?" "Yeah, yeah I've read this it's such an interesting story." Or "Have you watch *Pelada*?" "Oh yeah, they go and they play pick up around the world." Those are just neat stories, and those are perfect venues to us to say, it's very neat because it's a compelling story but look at everything about the human condition that we can also learn about by making that link between soccer and society.

Kiuchi: The publication of *Quarterly XI* is exciting. This book is going to have David Keyes contributing an essay, by the way. You were talking about the competition of journalistic scholarship and traditional scholarship. Do you think that's going to be the direction to go in the future?

Galarza: Yeah, I think so. I think it has to be. I think there's a number of factors that are pushing humanistic social scientists to make their scholarship more relevant to a wider audience, one on the funding side of public universities and budget cuts that have to be confronted with evidentiary based claims saying this is important stuff that cannot be eliminated from your universities. So I think that designing courses and producing scholarship that you can point to and say I didn't just write a monograph that was sold to a couple hundred libraries. There is an audience out there and it's important to the student body, it's important to a wider audience in our community beyond the student body. It's important globally because I have people visiting my website from all these different places. I think that's a good way to make that argument. I think also there's an ethical imperative to make efforts even if not just journalistic modes of writing that's designed for wider audience but stuff that's more accessible in terms of not being behind a pay wall, not being in an academic journal that is owned by a large publishing company that you have to pay an enormous subscription to get to. I think if scholars start to push in that direction, we already see that people are very intrigued by it even on the largest most popular football podcasts, they have scholars that are looking at soccer on their podcasts. Or there are journalists who are academically trained, people like David Goldblatt who bring that background to their journalistic coverage of the sport as well. I think when academics are funded at public universities like this one, Michigan State, I think at least I have an ethical obligation to make my research available towards the local community that I'm studying in. So I want Argentines to care about what I'm writing. I also want the public taxpayer in Michigan who is paying for my Ph.D. funding to be able to access my work. They might not care as much about it as much as say an Argentinian soccer fan. But that it's out there, that it's accessible, and it's written with them in mind, I think, is an ethical imperative to take seriously as well. This is where I think a conversation about not just the journalistic mode of writing, not just the question of audience, and taking seriously the question of audience, but the question of looking at the forms of scholarly communication we have: publication, and the economics and politics we have with that situation, you scratch at one and then you start to realize it's implicated in the other. You say "Oh well, I don't write in the more journalistic way because I do need that monograph to get tenure." Or say, "I do that journalistic stuff whenever possible." If we had a system of promotion and tenure that was more receptive to the idea that the monograph wasn't the only coin of the realm, or at least that it could be supplemented and taken seriously with other sources, then there would be a department and a community of peers that would say it's great that you do that podcast, and we see that as scholarship we don't see that as so and so is just having fun with their topic. No, it is fun, but it's also something that we take very seriously as a part of our role as scholars.

Kiuchi: I think when we study history we realize that at any moment in history, they thought that they were living the most special moment. I may be doing exactly that right now but when I think about, for example, Black Studies, the 1960s was the moment when it started. So in thirty or forty years from now, do you think we will look back and say, "Probably the 2010s, that was the moment soccer studies started"?

Galarza: I think there was a moment where the classics that were written in the 1970s and 1980s, and sports sociologists and people that were playing with real social theory and trying to look at the issues of sport and thinking about people like Bourdieu, people who looked at class in Britain and related it to working class activity like soccer. Those works will always be classics and they're important foundational works for people who then, people like Peter Alegi's generation who then said I want to do my dissertation about soccer and here's the social theory, here's the real proof that this is significant. I can relate this to social theory; this isn't something that I have to do alone. I can stand maybe on some key shoulders here. I think those two generations will always be assigned in comprehensive readings; they'll be a part of the literature and fantastic scholarship. But I think maybe you're right in that we're reaching a point of critical mass of the people that are looking at the subject itself, and I think the compression of time and space and technology with things like Skype and things like collaboration online are maybe allowing this community to reach a critical mass where it starts to think of itself as a subfield. People might have already considered it a subfield for a long time now, maybe for decades. What they consider a subfield and what their peers consider a subfield is a key question. I think we're getting to a point now where there is going to be enough people in departments that have written an article or a book or incorporated it into a syllabus where people say "Oh, that's kind of its own thing, that's kind of its own subfield that's not even just sports." Those are the people looking at soccer as a unique position as a global sport. That does speak to so many different audiences. Maybe we are a little bit special but I don't think we're the most special, yet. I think there is going to be a point maybe in the next ten years or so that we will look at the Football Scholars Forum as part of an ecosystem of scholars, soccer scholarship. It can be another organization or a group. I think at this point Football Scholarship

Forum has tried its hardest at least in English and Spanish speaking worlds and a bit in Europe as well to kind of just at least catalog everyone that's out there studying soccer scholarship. But if we can all be more on each other's radars I think that will be where were getting closer to a point where we say this is kind of a generational block now, we can talk about kind of a cohort that's looking at more edited volumes together, more specific conferences together, at web platforms like the football scholars forum where we can make this kind of accessible to our peers and our colleagues who don't study soccer.

Kiuchi: I'm going to ask you one last question. You talked about technology allowing us to have this forum, and you also work with technology quite a bit, in the Digital Humanities. For most people that are not aware of the Digital Humanities, Arts and Letter, Humanities, and other disciplines don't really mix well with technology. I think many traditional fans of soccer say, including probably FIFA, that soccer would not mix really well with technology. What's your take on that?

Galarza: I think technology is coming to the game. I think a system is from a fan's perspective. I think a system in which there is a tennis-like assessment of whether the ball has crossed the line for example is something that would not alter the dynamics of the game radically. I think you could do it in ways like if it has passed the line, the ref has a little buzzer go off on his belt or something. He still has the ultimate decision of saying I know that physically the ball crossed the line but I can still see if there was a foul, all these other factors that go into that decision. I think technology is coming and I think there will be experimentation. There have been successful models saying we'll introduce it in a lower tier league and then promote it up. Technology in the academic sense, I think the Digital Humanities is a very interesting topic because that term itself is just a strategic term. I'm in the College of Social Science here. I'm a social scientist. I'm not a humanist at MSU. Here, in Matrix, we don't call it our Digital Humanities Center, but it is part of that ecosystem of Digital Humanities Centers. One of the assistant directors is an archeologist, again, Social Science. There are lots and lots of people that are working in the Digital Humanities that are not humanists. I recognize that the term has strategic value to it because it encapsulates some characteristics and values that are part of the DH community like open access, trying to bring others into the use of technology for their teaching, project oriented scholarship that doesn't necessarily put the monograph or the journal article as the only unit of scholarly production. These are characteristics of the DH community. It's really just a strategic term, I prefer the term digital scholarship because I think we'll get to a point where we're just using technology just like you're using a word processor to achieve your aims as a scholar. It's just a way to make the writing faster. There are parts of technology that change the nature of the scholarship we produce. The closer we can get to saying these are things that move us closer to producing. That there are people who are going to be providing enough examples that say, "Yes, this person is using all kinds of neat technology but really it's an argument about history and anthropology." It could be in a monograph as well and it could be taken just as seriously. I think with soccer and technology in the academic sense, soccer in the Digital Humanities has an opportunity to overlap with that goal of open access, overlap with that question of taking wide audiences as the point of reference for our writing from our inception, rather than as an afterthought for after we get our real scholarly production off. How can we build an exhibit on a webpage that is designed to invite the readers not just to read the text but engage with the sources itself, maybe download the sources and produce their own scholarship. In Argentina, I know lots of people who are using blogs and just taking pictures of their sources as amateur historians and writing stories about those sources and saying there are no academics producing those histories. The amateur historians use the web as a way to collect more data, as a way to collect stories from others, to connect with others who might know more about collecting the memorabilia of the club for example. I think soccer scholarship and digital scholarship has some opportunities to work together on these kinds of things. Part of what I'm trying to do is in the community of Digital Humanities say look there are subjects like soccer that are inherently interesting to a wide audience, and that audience is on the web. How can we publish on the web for a way that's accessible to them? How can we bring that scholarly rigor and that long-form argument to a place where it's consumable at more of like a fanzine format?

Kiuchi: People say that those who can't do teach. When it comes to soccer scholars, are they good soccer players?

Galarza: I would rate myself as a very average player. But I would rate some of my colleagues as very talented soccer players. We were just talking about Andrew Guest before this interview. He was the original captain of one of the professional teams here in the U.S., the Michigan Bucks. I played with him a few times and he's quite impressive. Peter Alegi played college ball here, and is still in his forties, an excellent player. My advisor as well played at Georgetown. The Argentinians I play with are pretty good too. Now an economist, one guy who is in his late fifties, I'd say who I play pickup with on a weekly basis, he is a phenomenal. You can tell in his younger days, he could've gone down a different path and had things work differently for him. There are plenty of good players out there. There are also some average players I've played with, but I think that's part of the diversity of soccer itself. How many of the most rabid fans in the world can we give a ball to and they won't be able to do much with it? That's kind of part of soccer anyway. There are a lot of people who are enamored with the sport and would die for their team, but aren't particularly gifted. I think Eduardo Galeano, big writer in soccer, talked about how he was the last picked on all of his teams. This was part of the allure for soccer for him that he could never be good at it, so he felt that his love would be best captured in kind of writing about the game instead of being a good player.

11

Japanese Referee in the MLS: Toru Kamikawa

Yuya Kiuchi, interviewer

Soccer undoubtedly is an international sport. One's excellence in the sport is often affirmed with a success in the international arena. Unlike American baseball players' relative reluctance for playing on their national team for the World Baseball Classic (Bartkowiak and Kiuchi 141–142), the dream of many young and current elite soccer players is to play in the World Cup. Nothing is different for coaches or referees. Many of them find satisfaction and pleasure in working with youth or helping local soccer communities. But for many other aspiring members of the soccer family, representing their country at the World Cup is often their ultimate goal.

In this essay, we will hear from Toru Kamikawa, a former referee on the FIFA International Panel. Born in Kagoshima, Japan, in 1963, he played semi-professionally until 1992. As he retired as a player, he enrolled in a referee development program that was established to train former soccer players for top-level officials for J-League, Japan's top professional league. Kamikawa then debuted as a referee for J-League in 1996. Two years after, he was appointed as one of the seven male FIFA referees. Until he retired from officiating at the international level due to a knee injury at the end of 2006, Kamikawa refereed a total of 730 matches. This includes over 80 international matches, and over 230 J-League games. His most notable achievements are his appearances at the World Cups in Japan and Korea in 2002 and in Germany in 2006. He officiated the bronze medal game between Germany and Portugal on July 8, 2006. Currently, he serves as the Chair of the Japan Football Association's (JFA) Referee Committee and a member of FIFA's Referees Committee (Kamikawa 238–239).

11. Japanese Referee in the MLS: Toru Kamikawa (KIUCHI)

Kamikawa has a unique perspective, not simply because of his World Cup achievements. He is one of two Japanese Football Association referees to have officiated in Major League Soccer (MLS). He wrote in his autobiography, "The more J-League games I officiated, the less fun the experience had become. Of course I was still a young referee with little experience. But I did not feel any sense of achievement at the end of a game. During and after games, players did not seem to respect referees." He recalled that in Italy the relationship between players and referees is based on trust and respect. The future referee thought that obtaining experiences abroad might allow him to be a better official (Kamikawa 112–115).

A while after Kamikawa expressed his interest in refereeing abroad to the Referee Committee, he learned that the JFA was pursuing the possibility of referee exchange with MLS to improve the quality of referees in both countries. MLS was still in its first year in 1996. The JFA decided to send Kamikawa to the U.S. for a month starting mid–June 1997 (Kamikawa 116). He was exposed to not only a different style of soccer in the U.S., but also to a large cultural gap between Japan and the U.S.

Kiuchi: Thank you very much for your time and for agreeing to share your experiences with us today. Before we delve into your experiences, could you tell us what your responsibilities are in the JFA?

Kamikawa: I am the Chair of the JFA Referee Committee. Until recently, I primarily worked to develop and train top-level referees. But now that I have assumed this new position, I oversee everything that is related to refereeing, including futsal referees and female referees. Of course, I cannot be involved in every detail. I oversee the entire referee-related activities. We have men's soccer, women's soccer, futsal, and beach soccer as categories. I also have to work with local prefectural associations.

Kiuchi: Does your work include grassroots?

Kamikawa: I do not personally work in that area. But I need to know what prefectural football associations are doing, what their concerns are, and how they want the JFA to help them as it relates to grassroots. I must keep my ears open and listen to their ideas. So I am somewhat distanced from the actual soccer field.

Kiuchi: But you still inspect and assess referees on site, right?

Kamikawa: Yes, I do. But the number of games I attend as an inspector or an assessor has gone down.

Kiuchi: I remember that you assessed a game in Chicago two years ago.

Kamikawa: That is true. Aside from my responsibilities with the JFA, I continue to be on the Referees Committee for FIFA and AFC (Asian Football

Confederation) and work as an assessor for them. So that part has not changed. I still go abroad for that purpose.

Kiuchi: I see. Speaking of your international experiences, could you tell us how you began to be involved in soccer in the U.S.?

Kamikawa: I wanted to referee abroad to refine my officiating skills. I wanted to learn. Of course, I was going to pay my own expenses. So I asked the J-League via the Referee Committee if that was possible. It just happened that the J-League was examining the possibility of a referee exchange for the purpose of referee development.

Kiuchi: You were already a Class 1 referee at the time.[1]

Kamikawa: Yes, I was. I was already on the referee list for the J-League. The J-League kindly recommended me to participate in the exchange program for a month.

Kiuchi: Where did you go in the U.S.?

Kamikawa: I first went to Los Angeles. I did not have a game there, though. Then I went to Kansas just to watch a game. I moved around quite a bit, but the first match was an A-League match in Milwaukee.[2]

Kiuchi: What game did you watch in Kansas?

Kamikawa: It was an MLS game. I first watched a few games before I stepped onto the field with a whistle. From there, I went to New York.

Kiuchi: It was a big trip from the west coast to the east coast.

Kamikawa: Actually, I went back and forth twice. In a matter of about twenty days, I had seven games.

Kiuchi: That is a tough schedule.

Kamikawa: Yes, it was. But I was young. Speaking of the game in Milwaukee, remember that I was not a FIFA referee yet. It was my first game in the U.S., but it was my first outside of Japan, as well. I was so nervous.

Kiuchi: The rest of your crew, I imagine, was all American.

Kamikawa: Exactly. My assistant referees and fourth official were all American. In Japan, team staff brings their own team roster. But in the U.S. team captains brought them to us in the referee locker room. I was not expecting that. That made me even more nervous. I exchanged a few words with them. It was completely different.

Kiuchi: Were there many procedural differences?

Kamikawa: There were quite a few. Just as I said, it was already different before the game started. In a case of a tie, there was going to be a shoot-out. But I was told that if it happened, I was not charge of that. My fourth official was an experienced referee. So he was going to take care of the shoot-out for me. I think it was within five seconds, you had to take a shot. In addition, the clock in the stadium was different. It counted down from forty-five. Once it hit zero, there was a horn and I was supposed to blow my whistle. That was another difference. If I wanted the clock to stop, I was supposed to gesture to the person in charge by crossing my arms above my head. The first game was not easy.

Kiuchi: How was communication with your assistant referees and fourth official?

Kamikawa: There were no issues. But I made a mistake. I was so nervous. After giving a second caution to the same player in the game, I failed to send him off. I wrote down the player number in the wrong column on my notebook. There were not many fouls, though. Granted I had given a red card earlier in the game, so I did not have to call many fouls. The game was going smoothly in general. In the second half, I gave a yellow card. I looked at the assistant referee nearby just to make sure that everything was good. Nothing seemed to bother him at the time. But at the next stoppage of play, my fourth official called me over. He asked me who the yellow card was for. I told him who. He says, "That's a second one." I was at a loss. I had never made that mistake before. It was the only time in my career. I was just so nervous. But surprisingly enough, players did not appear upset, despite my mistake.

Kiuchi: Once you corrected your error, did everything go well?

Kamikawa: I know at least one thing was definitely wrong. Let's say, if you made the same mistake on a professional game, what would happen?

Kiuchi: That would be a major discussion topic, at least.

Kamikawa: Right? It would be a huge deal if you did that in Japan. My mistake did not affect the outcome of the game. On my way home, I was very disappointed. Alfred Kleinatis was my assessor of the game and he drove me back to the hotel. He said, "Your next game is an MLS game." I was relieved that I did not have to be sent home for my mistake. But I also thought that to appoint a referee that would make such a mistake, he must have gone through a lot of trouble. But I was happy that I was given another chance. My second game was in New York, on an artificial turf field. It was a baseball park. The turf was so soft because it was for baseball, and it was not easy to run on. There were so many field markings. I had only refereed in Japan until then. Japanese way of officiating is nothing different from international way of officiating. But procedural differences and confusing field markings were definitely different.

Kiuchi: What about communication with players? Did you feel any differences between Japanese players and American players?

Kamikawa: Of course, the language barrier was an issue. But for many American players, seeing a Japanese face on the field did not seem to matter to them. Probably I was more self-conscious that I needed to be. But before I went to the U.S., I had a lot of stress. Japanese players would work so hard to trick referees. There was no sense of respect toward referees. So I wondered if that was what soccer was supposed to be. That was primarily why I wanted to referee abroad. I admit I had one rough match. But including the game in Milwaukee, overall players listened to me. They accepted me. They even came to shake my hand after the game.

Kiuchi: What about dissent from players?

Kamikawa: There was almost none. Japanese players have a tendency not to complain to non–Japanese referees. I wondered if that was the case in the U.S. and that they were just being extra nice to me.

Kiuchi: So you had no issues with managers and coaches?

Kamikawa: To my knowledge, I had no issues. Maybe I was not paying enough attention and everyone else thought there were issues. But I really felt that was a cultural difference. They respected the sport. They respected the referee. It was engrained in my heart over the course of seven games.

Kiuchi: Was the stadium atmosphere different?

Kamikawa: It was definitely different. Japanese fans don't give you a standing ovation when you enter the field with the players. That was new to me. Of course, they are cheering for their players. But there was a very positive message in that act. I felt the warmth of fans. I felt welcomed. Around the stadium, there were many shops and events. Teams entertained their fans. It was not just a stadium. It was a park where fans could have a good time.

Kiuchi: In 1997, J-League teams did not have many fan events, did they?

Kamikawa: No, not in 1997. There were a few teams that had events, but American stadiums definitely had a different atmosphere. That was stimulating.

Kiuchi: What did you think about the national anthem? J-League games don't play the national anthem, whereas MLS games always do.

Kamikawa: For many of us, when we think about American sports, we think about Major League Baseball. So I felt like I was witnessing one of those games.

Kiuchi: After your experience in the U.S., you were nominated as a FIFA referee.

Kamikawa: Yes. 1998 was my first year as a FIFA official. Actually, while I was in the U.S., I was told that the JFA was recommending me to FIFA to be on its panel.

Kiuchi: In 1998, you received your FIFA badge for the first time and started officiating internationally. From that experience, have you ever noticed any difference among Japan, the U.S., and the rest of the world? It may be different styles of play. It may be different styles of officiating. Maybe just by looking at a referee, you can tell he is from South America.

Kamikawa: When I think about refereeing styles, I noticed in the U.S. that quite a bit was formulated and standardized there.

Kiuchi: I see.

Kamikawa: From signaling mechanics to other aspects of refereeing, I felt that everyone looked exactly the same.

Kiuchi: So did you feel Japan had more flexibility?

Kamikawa: Yes. In Japan, we have some basic guidelines. For mechanics, we instruct how to point, for example. But relatively speaking, there is quite a bit of individual differences. When I went to the U.S. for the referee exchange, it was the first time to travel abroad to referee. So I might have been overly observant. But the posture was another thing that seemed to be consistent across referees. They would push your chest out to assert their control and dominance. In Asia, I did not see too many differences. But once I started refereeing outside of Asia as a FIFA referee, I began to realize that without expressing your strength and dominance, you cannot manage players. Fans also judge you. So you need to show you are in control through your posture, mechanics, and presence. I did not think about this when I was in the U.S., but as I refereed more and more international games and meet referees from the world, it came to my mind how important this was. Without that sense of strength, you cannot survive in international soccer. In Japan, it is not as tough. The same with the rest of Asia.

Kiuchi: Do you think that difference has anything to do with the stereotypical view of the Japanese being so courteous and polite whereas Americans being assertive, and possibly arrogant, at least in some people's view?

Kamikawa: I didn't really think that stereotype about Americans was true.

Kiuchi: Maybe Japanese fans may complain but not as much as American fans? Or to put it differently, you can survive in Japanese soccer as a referee without having strength and confidence.

Kamikawa: That may be the case. As we often hear, there is not much sense of urgency in Japan, in general. You just say to yourself, "they're booing again," but you can leave it there.

Kiuchi: In the U.S., there have been several incidents where parents of youth players get too excited. They prevent a youth referee from leaving the field, for example. Or they push young referees and create a referee abuse case. Does that happen in Japan?

Kamikawa: No. That does not happen here. I just had a meeting with the technical development team and reaffirmed that youth referees must be nurtured and well taken care of by other referees, as well as players and coaches. JFA's Technical Committee has been extremely helpful on this matter. We grow them together. So the Technical Committee constantly communicates to coaches of youth teams how important their role is. We don't experience any of those issues.

Kiuchi: Do most youth referees, after they get their Class 4 badge, continue to referee without quitting?[3] In the U.S., there are many youth referees that take an introductory clinic but that quit within a year or two.

Kamikawa: We share the same concern. Or many quit when they graduate from high school and move on to college. So we are trying to create an environment in which they are encouraged to continue refereeing. That is one of the reasons why we should train and nurture them as a soccer community, not just inside the Referee Committee. It does not mean we just praise them. But we treat them as adults. We recognize their efforts.

Kiuchi: Is it at age thirteen when you can first enroll in a referee class?

Kamikawa: Actually you can be as young as an elementary school student. That has not happened yet. It would be too difficult. But we are witnessing an increasing number of youth referees in Japan.

Kiuchi: Do you know how many youth referees there are?

Kamikawa: I think there are 60,000 to 70,000 registered youth referees.

Kiuchi: That is out of over 200,000 registered referees.

Kamikawa: Yes. We have about 220,000 registered referees with the JFA. The number may be getting close to 250,000. When we say, "youth referees," that includes all the referees up to age twenty.

Kiuchi: That is up to the second year in college, for many.

Kamikawa: Exactly.

Kiuchi: What about female referees? As for the Nadeshiko League, I understand that the JFA tries to have as many female referees involved as possible.[4] Simultaneously, you have female referees working on men's games.

Kamikawa: There is one female referee working as the Referee in the Japan Football League (JFL).[5] Of course, we assess the performance of female referees to determine if they can be assigned to men's games. But before that, if a female referee wishes to work on a men's game, she needs to pass the fitness test requirement set for male referees that work on those men's games. This is one of the conditions. They have to meet this criterion. Otherwise, she would not be able to keep up with the play and to maintain the proper work rate. Men's games are more demanding physically.

Kiuchi: Do you think the JFA has enough female referees now? Or do you need more?

Kamikawa: We don't have enough.

Kiuchi: Is the number going up?

Kamikawa: Yes, it is. We have more and more female referees, but there are many that quit.

Kiuchi: In the U.S., I see a similar trend. The number is large, but many quit. Women are involved in soccer much more in the U.S. than in Japan.

Kamikawa: That is true. I have had the same observation about women's involvement in soccer in the U.S. But men's national team does well, too.

Kiuchi: Yes, it is a very good team. But when soccer is compared to other sports, it does not match up with their popularity.

Kamikawa: That makes sense. There are many other sports that seem to capture fans' attention.

Kiuchi: They have baseball, basketball, ice hockey, and football.

Kamikawa: True.

Kiuchi: I would like to get back to your experience in the U.S. a bit more. You spent a month there. After that, you have been to the U.S. multiple times. Based on your observation, what do you think will happen with soccer in the U.S.? Today, soccer is often referred to as the fifth sport. But you have witnessed soccer in the U.S., as well as in the rest of the world. You have played soccer, but you have also refereed soccer globally. You are now assessing referees internationally. So I wonder if you have any take on whether or not soccer can be a more stable part of American culture. This can be purely your personal thought.

Kamikawa: I was in the U.S. for a limited amount of time. But as I see American soccer from Japan, an ocean away, as far as soccer is concerned, Americans seem to get very excited about it only for a short period of time and lose interest in it quickly. It's the same with women's soccer. That is something difficult for me to grasp. Maybe this is where you can see American pride. They want to be, and have to be, number one in the world. So maybe until men's national team wins the World Cup or at least makes it constantly to the top four, soccer won't be more popular in the U.S. I must admit, though, I'm not certain how popular MLS is today. What is the average attendance per game?

Kiuchi: It is just shy of 20,000.

Kamikawa: So not much has changes since I was there.[6]

Kiuchi: Not very much. But the league has been expanding.

Kamikawa: That is true.

Kiuchi: I hear that FIFA does not like the fact that the U.S. top professional league has three non–American teams playing in it. The team in Vancouver now has a rivalry against Seattle. Or you have two teams from

California that are sharing the home stadium. That is another rivalry. But on average, the attendance seems to float between 15,000 and 20,000. Of course, some games can attract 40,000 people. When it comes to women's professional league, there was the WPS. But it was dismantled. There will be another league starting 2013. But as you say, when it comes to soccer, things don't seem to last for a long time.

Kamikawa: With regards to women's soccer, it is difficult to find sponsors. That is a challenge. For men's soccer, even if it is the fifth sport, local communities are supporting their teams. This is a positive thing. If they can continue their efforts, soccer may be the fifty sport today. But it may become a more popular sport. There are many children playing soccer. So in the future, I think soccer will grow in the U.S. But for Americans, being ranked at least third or fourth in the world seems to be a prerequisite for an explosive popularity growth.

Kiuchi: Women's national team has been doing well. I was actually in Japan when we beat the U.S. to win the World Cup in Germany. My friends were happy for me.

Kamikawa: The U.S. beat us in the Olympics, though. And when I think about it, the U.S. has many immigrants from Latin American and European countries. So there is a big possibility that soccer will grow much more there. The more I think about my stay in the U.S., the more I remember how fun it was. I saw a local soccer league game for Mexican immigrants. It was not just players. The referees were also Mexican. That is an independent league. I understand such leagues continue to exist today.

Kiuchi: How often do you have a chance to visit the U.S. these days?

Kamikawa: Not very frequently. The last time was when I was in Chicago two years ago. I often change planes in the U.S., but I do not get to visit the U.S. as much as I want to.

Kiuchi: There are Japanese referees that participate in tournaments in the U.S., though. I know some JFA referees working on games in Dallas or Florida.

Kamikawa: That is very true. It would be great if I could visit again. But I do remember, though, that when I was there, the time differences within the country was not easy to adjust to.

Kiuchi: From Los Angeles to New York, you have four hours of difference.

Kamikawa: I made two trips from West to East. I jogged on random streets. The last game was in Tampa. It was a good game.

Kiuchi: So you had six MLS games, in addition to the A-League game in Milwaukee?

Kamikawa: That is correct. Hideo Nomo was with the Dodgers. So I was able to go watch an MLB game, the day after my own match.

Kiuchi: Did someone from the U.S. Soccer Federation accompany you?

Kamikawa: When I went to the baseball game, I had my old friend who lived there with me. But the rest of the time, I was almost always on my own.

Kiuchi: There was no pick-up at the airport?

Kamikawa: It was actually a funny story. I landed in Los Angeles. I waited for my pick-up. I waited. And I waited. But nobody showed up. I knew the name of the hotel where I was supposed to stay. But as you know well, the same hotel chain usually has a hotel by the airport and another in the downtown area. I cannot recall which hotel it was. But I had no idea if I was supposed to check-in at the airport hotel or the downtown branch. So I called the one by the airport. But the receptionist on the phone had no clue. I decided to take a shuttle bus to go there just to see what would happen. At the hotel reception, I gave them my name and said, "Major League Soccer." But the MLS did not ring any bell in their mind. In Japan, if you say, "J-League," they will know what you are talking about. But not in the U.S., at least at the time. My broken English did not help, either. But they checked their guest list and found my name. A few hours later, I got a call explaining that someone was waiting for me for hours but could not find me. He was a FIFA assistant referee, by the way. But it was fun. At night, he took me to Santa Monica for dinner. When I went to my last game in Tampa, Joe Machnik who worked for the MLS, rented a convertible for us at the airport. The night before the game, we went to the beach and had some beer to relax. We also had oyster for dinner, I still remember. This may sound irrelevant to soccer. But soccer allowed me to experience the U.S. and American culture. So I am grateful for that. I also had a chance to participate in a MLS referee conference call. It was an exciting experience. I introduced myself over the phone and listened in to the conversation. After the call was over, I thought I placed the receiver back properly, but I suppose I didn't. The next morning, when I was checking out of the hotel, the bill had over $1,000 for the distance call charge. Nobody spends $1,000 on a call, you know. But anyway, the trip was a series of first-times.

Kiuchi: That was not your first trip abroad, was it?

Kamikawa: It was my first as a referee. I had been abroad as a player. When I worked for the Bellmare,[7] I accompanied its youth team to Italy. So I refereed their training matches. But those were not sanctioned matches. I still appreciate the willingness of the U.S. Soccer to let me work in their league when I was not even a FIFA official yet. Furthermore, as I said, I made that huge mistake on my first game. But when I think about it, it has been a while since American referees appeared in the World Cup.

Kiuchi: There are two referee crews with U.S. referees that are on the preliminary candidate list for 2014.

Kamikawa: I hope they will be selected. On the women's side, Margaret Domka was here in Japan and had a good presence in the game.

Kiuchi: She was actually leading my referee clinic a few weeks ago.

Kamikawa: In the U.S., do current referees work as instructors?

Kiuchi: Yes, they do. Top-level referees are trained by other top-level officials.

Kamikawa: Do they also assess other referees?

Kiuchi: Yes, they do. They often help out at the grassroots level or the next generation of top-level referees at regional or national tournaments.

Kamikawa: That is an excellent idea. Our professional referees in Japan should be more active in instructing and assessing. In many ways, that kind of exchange is very American. But I think we can integrate it in Japan, as well.

Kamikawa's experience and reflections are multi-layered. On one level, he explained his initial confusions about procedural differences between Japan and the U.S., as well as American soccer's exceptionalism manifested in its deviation from FIFA's Laws of the Game, including the implementation of the shoot-out and a counterintuitive use of the game clock. Although the shoot-out has not been a part of MLS's competition rules for over a decade, there are numerous signs of similar deviations in American soccer. FIFA's annual publication, *Laws of the Game*, states:

> Subject to the agreement of the member association concerned and provided the principles of these Laws are maintained, the Laws may be modified in their application for matches for players of under 16 years of age, for women footballers, for veteran footballers (over 35 years of age) and for players with disabilities [3].

Permitted modifications are: "size of the field of play," "size, weight and material of the ball," "width between the goalposts and height of the crossbar from the ground," "duration of the periods of play," and "substitutions" (3). This is to say that as a FIFA member association, U.S. Soccer is not allowed to make other changes without "the consent of the International Football Association Board" (3). However, it is not common for Under 18-year-old games to allow unlimited substitutions. In some areas, referees are required to show a yellow card or a red card to bench personnel when a disciplinary action is taken, even though FIFA stipulates that cards are only shown to players, substitutes, and substituted players. Kamikawa clearly touches upon this issue.

On another level, Kamikawa also addresses cultural differences around soccer. During his first stay in the U.S., he noticed the amount of efforts each team makes to entertain its fans. In 2008, J-League sent representatives of each team as a group to the U.S. to study and learn how American sport teams entertained their fans and local communities. Allowing some fans to step on the field during the halftime for a game, for example, was not common in Japan until recently. Kamikawa's observation speaks to, probably market-driven, but a different way in which sport is contextualized in American lifestyle.

The presence of ethnic leagues, the emphasis on women's soccer, and other topics also shed light on what soccer means in the U.S. For many that have lived inside the U.S., these may not be surprises. For example, as of 2007, the U.S. had approximately 4,187,000 registered soccer players. It was ranked second behind Germany with 6,309,000 players and ahead of Brazil with 2,142,000 players. As for male players, top three remained the same respectively with 5,438,000 players, 2,517,000 players, and 2,115,000 players. But when it comes to the number of female players, the U.S. ranked far ahead with 1,670,000 players. This was double the number of Germany, ranked second, with 871,000 players. The third was Canada, with 495,000 players (FIFA, "Big Count" 13). This heavy participation of women in soccer is clearly a unique characteristic of American society.

It is also remarkable that in many ways, Japanese soccer is trying to learn from American experience. This is not just about fan services. Kamikawa was impressed to hear about current elite referees' active engagement in referee development. In Japan, as he hinted in the interview, instructors and assessors are mostly retired officials. There are exceptions, but it is unlikely to see a current FIFA referee volunteering to mentor youth referees at a regional tournament in Japan. In the U.S., it is common. A few days prior to officiating an international match, a referee might teach a clinic for future elite referees at a local community center. Japan is known traditionally for its rigid hierarchical structure. Even to this day, a status crossover is unlikely to happen. Kamikawa, however, recognizes that there is something for the JFA to learn from American social acceptance of peer mentorship.

Notes

1. In the JFA's referee grade system, the Class 1 category is the national list. Class 1 referees officiate national-level matches. This grade is the minimum requirement to officiate in any professional games. Some of these referees are recommended by the JFA's Referee Committee to be on FIFA's referee list.

2. The A-League was a men's professional soccer league that operated between 1995 and 2004. It later became United Soccer League Division 1.

3. The Class 4 category is equivalent of U.S. Soccer's Grade 9. It is the introductory level of referees.

4. The Nadeshiko League is the top women's soccer league in Japan. Although the leagues is not a professional league, some players are professional.

5. JFL is the third-tier soccer league in Japan, after J-League's Division 1 and Division 2. It is the top amateur league.

6. The average attendance in 2007 when Kamikawa was in the U.S. was 14,619. In 2011, the average was 17,872.

7. The Bellmare is a J-League team for which Kamikawa used to work until he became a full-time professional referee in 2002.

Works Cited

Bartkowiak, Mathew, and Yuya Kiuchi. *Packaging Baseball: How Marketing Embellishes the Cultural Experience*. Jefferson, NC: McFarland, 2012. Print.

Federation International Football Association. "Big Count." *FIFA Magazine*. July 2007. Web. 21 Jan. 2013.

_____. *Laws of the Game*. Zurich, Switzerland: 2012.

Kamikawa, Toru. *Heijoushin* [*Presence of Mind*]. Tokyo: Koudansha, 2007. Print.

Major League Soccer. "About Major League Soccer." *MLS Press Box*. Major League Soccer. Web. 21 Jan. 2013.

_____. "1997 Full Season Stats." *Major League Soccer*. Major League Soccer. Web. 21 Jan. 2013.

Conclusion

Nine authors and two interviewees from various disciplines and with diverse backgrounds have demonstrated the common belief that soccer is not American is a myth. Youth soccer is popular. Many women play soccer. Academics and the sport seem to mix better in the U.S. than elsewhere. Statistical evidence based on television viewing suggests soccer is increasing in popularity. Furthermore, the argument that soccer will never be popular in a country of American football, hockey, basketball, and baseball is invalid because it already is popular.

Playing soccer, watching soccer, and talking about soccer is a significant part of American life, but the game may still carry its old stereotypes. In other words, if "American" is defined as "white English-speaking U.S.-born heterosexual adult male," then soccer may not be American. Therefore, to picture soccer as un–American is to subscribe to this outdated definition of what it means to be American. If this exclusive view can be thrown away and a more inclusive idea about the U.S.— that which includes non-whites, non–English speakers, immigrants, those with various sexual preferences, and youth — can be adopted, an obvious question is "What is not American about soccer?"

Therefore, examining soccer and understanding its cultural and social significance is to unearth prejudices that continue to exist in the U.S. The U.S. may have elected and re-elected an African American president. The country is supposed to be welcoming to immigrants. But if a sport is considered non–American because European immigrants and Latinos predominantly play the game, we do not have a post-racial or color-blind society. If soccer is considered less worthy because the women's national team tends to do better than men's national team, what does that say about gender equality and prejudices? Soccer, just like any other examples of popular culture, exists within a context. As the essays included here have showed, soccer serves as an access to the true zeitgeist that sometimes is concealed within collective misrepresentation and misunderstanding.

About the Contributors

Dwight Branch works in marketing research and consumer insights for Communispace in Boston. He has led proprietary consumer research studies for companies in such industries as sports and fitness apparel, hospitality, telecommunications, and alcoholic beverages. He has also worked in the news media industry with *Metro* Boston and with Boston Globe Media, publisher of the *Boston Globe* and Boston.com.

Danielle Sarver Coombs is an assistant professor in the School of Journalism and Mass Communication at Kent State University in Kent, Ohio. Her work can be found in a variety of publications, including the edited volume *Soccer and Philosophy*, the *Journal of Public Relations Research*, *Sport in Society*, and the *International Journal of Sport Communication*. She has also co-edited *American History Through American Sports* and *We Are What We Sell: How Advertising Shapes American Life... And Always Has* (both with Praeger).

Benjamin James Dettmar is an assistant professor at Adrian College in Michigan. He is completing a Ph.D. in American studies at Michigan State University. He is an editorial assistant for the *Journal of Popular Culture* and a staff member of the University Archives and Historical Collections. His dissertation focuses on the city of Detroit, and its seven failed bids to host the summer Olympics. He has published on the Olympic Games, baseball, soccer in the U.S. and sexuality in sport.

Glen M.E. Duerr is an assistant professor of international studies at Cedarville University in southwest Ohio. He received a Ph.D. from Kent State University. He is also a former semi-professional soccer player and has spent time in virtually every "minor league" in North America including the United Soccer League (USL) Pro system with the Cleveland City Stars, USL's Premier Development League with Cascade Surge, the Pacific Coast Soccer League's Fraser Valley Action, and the Canadian Soccer League's Vaughan Shooters.

Alex Galarza is a Ph.D. candidate in the Department of History at Michigan State University. His research examines soccer clubs and urban life in Buenos Aires during the 20th century. He is the recipient of a Fulbright IIE Award and a João Havelange

Research Scholarship and is also co-founder of the Football Scholars Forum, a soccer think-tank that collaborates online to discuss and develop fútbol scholarship, and the co-editor of *gradhacker.org*.

Andrew M. Guest is a social scientist and faculty member at the University of Portland, Oregon, with academic interests in child, youth and lifespan development, particularly as related to sports and other types of activities. He is especially fascinated by cultures of soccer, having experiences as a player, coach and scholar in locales ranging from Michigan and Oregon to Malawi and Angola. He has also been the editor for four editions of *Taking Sides: Clashing Views in Life-Span Development*.

Cedrick G. Heraux is an assistant professor in the Department of Sociology and Criminal Justice at Adrian College, Michigan. He holds a Ph.D. in criminal justice from Michigan State University. His primary research interests relate to the sociology of violence, particularly in the contexts of sport (soccer) and police behavior. His work has previously been published in the *Journal of Criminal Justice*, and *Justice Quarterly*.

Toru Kamikawa is the chair of the Japan Football Association Referee Committee and a member of the Referees Committee of the Fédération Internationale de Football Association (FIFA) and the Asian Football Confederation (AFC). He travels internationally as a referee inspector and assessor to evaluate top officials and has officiated in more than 700 official matches including 236 J-League games and 84 international games. The AFC Referee of the Year in 2002, he participated in the World Cups of 2002 and 2006 (at which he officiated the bronze medal match between Germany and Portugal).

David Keyes is a Ph.D. candidate in the Department of Anthropology at the University of California, San Diego. His dissertation examines the growth of youth soccer out of immigrant communities into the American mainstream in the second half of the twentieth century and the integration of the children of immigrants into youth soccer today. He is also the editor of *XI*, a North American soccer quarterly.

Yuya Kiuchi is an assistant professor in the Writing, Rhetoric, and American Cultures Department at Michigan State University. He is the author of *Struggles for Equal Voice* (SUNY Press, 2012) and co-author of *Packaging Baseball* (McFarland, 2012). He has translated several books from English to Japanese, and is working on a monograph that examines the contemporary history of African American images in Japan. He serves on the editorial review board of the *Journal of Popular Culture* and is a sports area co-chair of the Popular Culture Association and American Culture Association.

Dennis J. Seese is a research librarian at American University and freelance writer and journalist based in Washington, D.C. He earned an MLIS from the University of Pittsburgh. His soccer musings have been published on *ESPN FC*, *In Bed with Maradona* and *SB Nation*, where he is a staff writer and editor for the Real Madrid blog, *Managing Madrid*. He has also been published in the *Huffington Post*, *Library Journal*, *Educational Media Review Online (EMRO)* and *Education Review*.

Cliff Starkey is an instructor of literature at Prince George's Community College in Largo, Maryland. He received a master's degree from Kansas State University, and has taught literature and media studies at various colleges in the Midwest and the Washington, D.C., metro area.

Index

Abramovich, Roman 77–78
Abu Dhabi United Group 78
A.C. Milan 85
academia 2, 7, 95, 115, 179–180, 184–190 passim, 205
Acosta, Ralph 14
Adebayor, Emmanuel 78
Adu, Freddy 102, 117n10
Africa 25, 26, 30, 32, 64, 100, 152; *see also* World Cup
African Americans 43, 45, 46, 205
Agüero, Sergio 78
Akers, Michelle 164, 166, 167, 175
Altidore, Jozy 102
amateur soccer 4, 28, 110, 151, 153, 156, 182, 190
American Broadcasting Company (ABC) 61, 76, 105, 106, 107, 116, 163
American football 3, 25, 29, 46, 98, 103, 147; as most popular American sport 71, 84, 96, 100, 161, 205; and television 97, 113
American Soccer League (ASL) 56, 152
American Youth Soccer Organization (AYSO) 4, 9–10, 13–23, 154–155; *see also* youth
Americanization 10, 11, 15–16, 21, 22, 30, 80, 105
Ángel, Juan Pablo 93
Anschutz family 145
anti-soccer 49, 51, 53, 59–60
Argentina 7, 21, 179–183, 187, 190
Armando, Alberto 180–181
Arsenal F.C. 29, 74, 77, 78, 80–81, 85, 95, 100, 111, 129
A.S. Roma 86
Asia 43, 100, 109, 152, 197

Asian Football Confederation (AFC) 7, 193–194
ASL *see* American Soccer League 56, 152
Australia 32, 144, 168
AYSO *see* American Youth Soccer Organization

Bale, Gareth 73
Baltimore (city) 104
Barcelona (city) 29, 109; *see also* F.C. Barcelona
Barry, Gareth 78
baseball 1, 5, 19, 46–49 passim, 54–56, 111, 113–114, 201; as most popular American sport 2, 10, 18, 46–47, 52, 71–72, 81, 92, 96, 100, 110, 114, 116, 150, 154, 161, 181, 195, 199, 205; and the Olympics 110; and soccer 5, 39, 43–44, 46–47, 49, 52–54, 56, 60–62, 155–156; *see also* Major League Baseball (MLB); World Baseball Classic (WBC)
Basen, Tom 17
basketball 6, 17, 29, 36, 37, 47, 49, 58, 97, 99, 110, 114, 117n14, 150, 166, 197, 205; as most popular American sport 2, 49, 71, 84, 96, 100, 116, 144, 154, 161, 199, 205; *see also* National Basket Association (NBA); Women's National Basket Association (WNBA)
Beck, Glenn 45, 47–48, 50
Beckenbauer, Franz 101, 106
Beckham, David 6, 91, 92–93, 101, 112–113, 135, 137n21, 150
Beijing 110, 171
Belgium 104, 126, 129
Best, George 101, 106

Bethlehem Steel F.C. 104
Blackburn Rovers F.C. 64, 74
Blatter, Sepp 63, 136
Boca Juniors 180–182
Bocanegra, Carlos 25
Brazil 117, 131, 132, 171, 203; and women's soccer 59–60, 64, 169, 173; and World Cups 104–107 passim
Budweiser 110, 168
Bundesliga 89; *see also* Germany
business 5, 26, 54, 63, 65, 67, 72, 77, 79, 86–87, 89, 91, 92–93, 158, 175, 182

cable television 7, 71, 170, 184
Cahill, Tim 93
Canada 88, 144, 146, 150, 156, 176, 203
capitalism 5, 47, 52, 71–73, 77, 79, 80–81, 89, 100, 104, 170, 176
Celtic F.C. 122, 125, 137*n*7
CenturyLink Field 85, 90
Chastain, Brandi 56, 113, 115, 164, 166–167, 169
Chelsea F.C. 74, 77–81, 85, 100
Chicago (city) 11, 50, 101, 153, 193, 200; *see also* Chicago Fire
Chicago Fire 96, 133, 145, 146, 148; *see also* Chicago (city)
China 100, 152, 155, 162; and women's soccer 114, 163–164, 168–169
Chivas USA 117*n*11, 133, 145, 147, 148, 153; *see also* Los Angeles
class 13, 17, 35, 99, 129; middle class 44, 58–59, 115, 180–181; upper class 98–99; upper-middle class 30, 35, 36, 156; working class 124, 128–130, 156, 188
Club Atético River Plate 180, 182
club soccer 3, 11, 31, 33, 37, 39, 102, 153, 183; and Argentina 180–182; and Europe 29, 72
college 2–5, 25–26, 28–40 passim, 73–75, 103–104, 111, 144, 155–156, 183, 189, 190, 198; *see also* education
Colorado Rapids 148
Columbus Crew 102, 133–134, 146–147, 149
communism 5, 52, 72, 117*n*9
community 2, 4, 5, 11, 25–31, 33–36, 39–41, 58, 86, 101, 129, 137*n*7, 179–192 passim, 198, 200, 203; and immigrants 6–15 passim, 18, 21–22, 67, 104, 146, 151–153, 176, 180, 183
consumerism 12–13, 47–48, 65, 67, 86; and soccer 54, 61–63, 92, 128, 181, 184, 186, 190

contract 78, 92, 168; and media 76, 106, 145; and players 25, 30, 73–74, 78, 92, 113, 137*n*21, 168, 174
Crespo, Hernán 78
Cruyff, Johan 101

Davies, Charlie 102
D.C. United 96
derby 86, 135, 137*n*6
designated player 74, 133, 137*n*21
Detroit 4, 54
Development Academy 31–34, 41*n*4
DiCicco, Tony 165, 167–168
domestication 4, 9–23
Donovan, Landon 6, 73, 92, 102, 135
Dorrance, Anson 162
Drogba, Didier 78
drug 110, 112, 173
Duff, Duncan 14

EA Sports 64
education 4, 26–41 passim, 41*n*5, 156, 161, 185; *see also* college
elitism 26–27, 31–41 passim, 41*n*5, 192, 203
endorsement 114, 134, 166, 172, 174–175
England 25, 28, 41*n*3, 52, 72–81 passim, 89, 97, 104, 105, 137*n*21, 138*n*32, 144; and national team 25, 40, 61, 97, 101, 104, 117*n*7, 127; as soccer's birth place 121–122; and violence 124–136 passim, 137*n*17, 137*n*18
English Premier League (EPL) 55, 61–63, 72–81, 84–86, 100, 102, 108, 138*n*31, 184
EPL *see* English Premier League
Erdos, Steve 14
Escobar, Andrés 112, 132
ESPN 3, 57, 61–62, 67, 71–72, 76, 77, 97, 99, 106, 107–110, 112, 117*n*11, 174, 184; and Luker on Trends/ESPN study 49, 51, 57, 61; and World Cup 72, 109–110, 116, 163, 170
ESPN2 117*n*11, 163, 184
ethnicity 10–23 passim, 96, 101, 151–153, 203; *see also* immigration
Euro Cup 84, 157
Europe 2, 5, 6, 16–17, 30, 51–53, 88, 95–98, 100, 102, 107, 109, 116*n*2, 117*n*9, 117*n*10, 137*n*16, 137*n*31, 184, 189; immigrants from 38, 151–153, 200, 205; leagues in 25, 32, 52, 55, 71–81 passim, 84, 85, 89, 93, 96, 100, 103, 108, 124–136 passim, 153; teams in 28–29, 71–81

Index

passim, 84, 96, 100, 103, 108, 124–136 passim, 153; violence in 17, 121–136 passim; *see also* Union Européen de Football Association (UEFA)
Everton F.C. 77, 100
exceptionalism 28, 96, 100, 143–144, 161–162, 202

Falls River 152
family 3, 4, 10, 13, 16, 19–23 passim, 33, 35–38, 44, 112, 132, 151, 156, 176
fans 6, 29, 48, 57, 84, 89, 95–96, 102, 105, 110, 117n8, 136n2, 147, 180, 185–191 passim, 199; and China 100; and Europe 73, 79, 80–81, 89; and Japan 196–197, 203; and MLS 5, 62, 64, 67, 72, 85–89, 91–92, 107–108, 149–154 passim, 197, 203; and other sports 19, 65, 89, 90, 97–100; and referees 1, 17; and violence 16, 17, 20, 112, 122–136 passim, 138n22; and women's soccer 160, 163–164, 171, 176
F.C. Barcelona 29, 64, 80, 85, 88, 89, 96, 102, 109, 110, 173; *see also* Barcelona (city)
F.C. Bayern Munich 61, 80, 89
F.C. Dallas 148
Fédération Internationale de Football Association (FIFA) 1, 7, 52, 63–64, 79–80, 109–110, 131, 136, 145, 150, 162–166 passim, 172, 189, 192–203 passim; *see also* World Cup
femininity 46–47, 59–61, 95, 115, 165–166, 173–174, 176; *see also* gender; homosexuality; masculinity
Ferguson, Sir Alex 80
Fernandes, Tony 79
Feyenood Rotterdam 126, 137n13
FIFA *see* Fédération Internationale de Football Association
Figo, Luís 92
film 92, 95, 110–113, 117n7, 186
fitness 17–18, 198
Football Scholars Forum 7, 179, 183, 186, 188–189
Foudy, Julie 166
Fox Soccer Channel (FSC) 72, 76, 107, 144
France 41n3, 79, 105, 109, 128; and national team 109, 171, 186; and violence 124–131 passim
Friedel, Brad 102
Frings, Torstein 93, 138n22

FSC *see* Fox Soccer Channel
Fulham F.C. 77

Garber, Don 48, 135, 145, 146, 149
Gatorade 166, 168
gay *see* homosexuality
gender 3, 13, 46, 59, 176, 205; *see also* femininity; gender; masculinity
Germany 32, 53, 89, 97, 109, 126–127, 137n18, 38n22, 151, 152, 186; World Cups in 7, 169–170, 192, 200, 203; *see also* Bundesliga
Gerrard, Steven 25
Ghana 40, 61, 117n10
Glasgow 29, 104, 122, 125
GLASL *see* Greater Los Angeles Soccer League
Glazer family 72, 78, 89
globalization 27, 30–32, 40, 46, 100–102, 110, 173
Golden State Soccer League (GSSL) 21
Greater Los Angeles Soccer League (GLASL) 13–15; *see also* Los Angeles
GSSL *see* Golden State Soccer League 21
Gulick, Luther 28

Hamm, Mia 56, 114, 116, 163, 166–167, 172
Hanauer, Adrian 87, 89, 91
Henry, Thierry 64, 91, 93
heteronormativity 5
high school 1–2, 4–5, 25–42, 105, 113, 154–156, 183, 198
hockey *see* ice hockey
Holden, Stuart 102
homosexuality 57, 165, 173
hooligan 6, 121–138
Horan, Lindsey 40
Houston Dynamo 90, 102, 117n11, 135, 145, 148, 149
Hughes, Bill 13–16, 18
Hunt family 145

ice hockey 18, 110, 165; as most popular American sport 2, 71, 72, 84, 96, 100, 116, 144–145, 161, 199, 205; *see also* National Hockey League (NHL)
IFAB *see* International Football Association Board
immigration 4, 6, 30, 58, 59, 103, 151–154, 157–158, 176, 180, 184, 200, 205; and Los Angeles 13–14, 22; and MLS 144, 153; soccer as immigrants' sport 6, 9, 11, 29, 152, 153, 183; statistics on 151–152;

and women 7; and youth 6, 14, 28, 30, 143; *see also* ethnicity
India 53, 144, 152
individualism 4, 25–41 passim, 67
injury 17, 18, 122, 125–127, 192
Inter Milan 61, 85
International Football Association Board (IFAB) 122
International Olympic Committee (IOC) 109–110
Internet 76, 81, 103
intramural soccer 155, 181
Ipswich Town F.C. 126
Ireland 92, 96, 127, 152
Italy 52, 85, 126, 193, 201; and national team 97, 105, 109; and violence 16, 20, 124, 126, 131, 136n1, 136n5, 137n17; *see also* Serie A

J-League 7, 192–203 passim
Japan 7, 109, 128, 170, 192–203 passim; and national team 1, 65, 114, 161, 169, 170–171, 202; and the World Cup in 2002 100, 128, 192
Juventus F.C. 86, 126–127

Kansas City 32–33, 146, 148, 194; *see also* Sporting Kansas City
Keane, Robbie 92–93
Kearny Scots 152
Kleinatis, Alfred 195
Klinsman, Jürgen 32
Kraft family 145

LA Galaxy 75, 90–92, 117n11, 133, 135, 137n21; *see also* Los Angeles
Latino 21, 30, 43, 45–48, 52, 56–58, 67, 102, 153, 205
S.S. *Lazio* 124, 136n5
Leeds United A.F.C. 80, 126
Leicester City F.C. 105, 129
Ligue Un 92
Little League baseball 46, 155
Liverpool F.C. 25, 72, 77, 80, 104, 121, 126–127, 137n15, 137n16, 137n17
Ljundberg, Freddie 93
Logan, Doug 132–133, 145
London 29, 122, 125, 137n9; and Olympics 7, 26, 160, 170–171
Los Angeles 9, 13–23, 25, 107, 131, 146, 147, 152, 194, 200–201; *see also* Chivas USA; Greater Los Angeles Soccer League (GLASL); LA Galaxy

Major League Baseball (MLB) 49, 52, 54, 55, 64, 86, 92, 99, 109, 113, 149, 196; *see also* baseball
Manchester City F.C. 74, 77–79, 81
Manchester United F.C. 72, 74, 78, 80, 81, 85, 89, 100, 109, 136n2
Mariotti, Jay 108
marketing 55, 86, 168; and MLS 49, 59, 62–63, 67, 90, 150; and women's national team 172, 174–175
Márquez, Rafael 93
masculinity 46–47, 53, 59, 60, 111, 113, 129, 155, 165, 172, 174; *see also* femininity; gender; homosexuality
Matthäus, Lothar 101
McClean, Ted 14
McDonald's 110, 168
media 6, 16, 17, 25, 50, 63–68 passim, 96, 97, 106, 115, 117n10, 161–171 passim, 184, 186; anti-soccer and 45, 65, 108; and violence 122–136 passim
meritocracy 26, 28, 40
Mexico 30–31, 60, 102, 105–106, 112, 144, 151–153, 158, 175, 200
Miami Fusion F.C. 138n29, 145–146
Millennials 43–44, 48, 56–58, 67; *see also* youth
Millwall F.C. 125–126, 137n9, 137n12
minorities 43, 47, 57, 87, 108
MLB *see* Major League Baseball
MLS Cup 57, 68, 91, 92, 135, 150
MLS Direct Kick 107
Montreal Impact 90, 133, 145, 148, 149
Morgan, Alex 161, 169, 172, 174

NASL *see* North American Soccer League
Nasri, Samir 78
National Basket Association (NBA) 49, 51–52, 54, 57, 61, 66, 72, 74, 75, 81, 86, 99, 146, 149, 150; *see also* basketball
National Broadcasting Company (NBC) 62, 72, 76, 93, 113, 160, 162, 171
National Collegiate Athletic Association (NCAA) 43, 104, 115
National Hockey League (NHL) 51, 86, 146, 149–150
National Premier Soccer League (NPSL) 156
National Soccer Coaches Association of America (NSCAA) 33
National Women's Soccer League (NWSL) 114, 116n4, 175, 176
nationalism 10, 12, 121

NBA *see* National Basket Association
NBC *see* National Broadcasting Company
NCAA *see* National Collegiate Athletic Association
Netherlands 126–129, 131
New England Revolution 90
New York 28, 104–105, 146, 152, 162, 194–195, 200
New York City FC 146
New York Cosmos 101, 105, 131
New York Red Bull 85, 91, 133–135, 146, 148
New Zealand 144
NHL *see* National Hockey League
Nike 99, 115, 160, 166, 168
North American Soccer League (NASL) 56, 71, 72, 87, 101, 104–6, 131, 146, 154, 184
Norway 168, 170
NPSL *see* National Premier Soccer League
NSCAA *see* National Soccer Coaches Association of America
NWSL *see* National Women's Soccer League

Obama, Barack 43–46, 50, 55–59 passim, 67, 157
ODP *see* Olympic Development Program
Old Trafford 128, 136n2
Olympic Development Program (ODP) 31, 36
Olympics 50, 110, 114, 131, 162, 165; and men's national team 50, 53; and women's national team 4, 7, 26, 160–162, 168, 170–176 passim, 200; *see also* International Olympic Committee (IOC); Olympic Development Program (ODP)
Onyewu, Oguchi 102
O'Reilly, Bill 43–45, 61

Paris 126, 186
Paris Saint-Germain F.C. 124, 136n4, 40, 79, 92
PDL *see* Professional Development League
Pelé 101, 105–106, 131, 166
Philadelphia Union 117n10, 135, 138n30, 145, 148
Pittsburgh 104
popular culture 6, 47, 54, 99, 115, 116, 117n6, 179–180, 205
Portland Timbers 84–85, 87, 90, 92, 135, 145–149 passim
Portugal 112, 128, 130–131, 192

Preston North End F.C. 122
privatization 19
Professional Development League (PDL) 156
PSAL *see* Public Schools Athletic League
Public Schools Athletic League (PSAL) 28–29; YMCA 28, 181

Quarterly XI 186, 208
Queens Park Rangers F.C. 77, 79, 122

race 99
Rangers F.C. 29, 125, 137n7
Rapinoe, Megan 161, 171–173
Real Madrid C.F. 80–81, 85, 89, 92, 111, 124, 136n3
Real Salt Lake 57, 91, 133, 145, 147
referee 1–3, 7, 17, 19, 113, 162, 192–204
Robben, Arjen 78
Robinho 78
Rome, Jim 59, 62, 108
Rooney, Wayne 73
rugby 10, 103, 122

safety 4, 10, 13, 16–18, 20–21, 23
salary 74, 77, 80, 137n21, 174
San Jose Earthquakes 133, 145, 148
satellite television 7, 72, 81, 184
Scotland 104, 112, 125, 152
Scottish Cup 125
Serie A 85–86; *see also* Italy
Shea, Brek 73
Shevchenko, Andrei 78
The Simpsons 112–113, 116n1
soccer mom 2, 30, 46, 59–61, 67–68, 163
soccer-preneurs 5, 72, 77, 81
social media 67, 86, 157, 170
socialism 5, 52, 71–81 passim
Solá, José Luis Sánchez 153
Solo, Hope 161, 169, 171, 172–173, 174–175
South Africa 25–26, 32, 64, 100
South America 30, 100, 152, 156–157, 180, 197
South Korea 100, 109, 128
Soviet Union 111, 127
Spain 85, 102, 124, 144
sponsorship 28, 35, 38, 92, 96, 98, 100, 106, 110, 123, 137n10; and women's sports 168, 172, 175, 200
Sporting Kansas City 133, 146, 148; *see also* Kansas City
Sports Illustrated 33, 54, 64, 66, 164–166, 174

Stierle, Hans 14, 16, 18
suburbanization 3, 4, 9–10, 13, 17, 19–23, 30, 35–38, 44–46, 58–61, 101–102, 115, 148, 150, 156–157, 180
Super Bowl 75, 92, 98–99, 109, 116n5, 170

Tampa Bay Mutiny 138n23, 145, 146
television 6, 61–62, 71–72, 81, 100, 105, 106, 136, 143, 145, 149, 165, 173, 184; and ratings 55, 61–62, 64, 92; and viewership 76, 84, 107, 170, 171, 205
Tévez, Carlos 78
Thompson, Tim 15
Time Warner 106
Title IX 29–30, 67, 114, 155, 161–162, 165
Toronto FC 145, 147–148
Tottenham Hotspur F.C. 86, 105, 126, 137n13

Union Européen de Football Association (UEFA) 79, 80, 126, 137n13; Champions League 61, 78, 108–109, 127–128, 130
United Soccer Leagues (USL) 87–88
United States Football Association 96
U.S. men's national team 2, 96, 160, 168, 170, 199; and education 4, 26; and Olympics 50; and World Cups 4, 40, 60, 114, 133, 164
United States Soccer Federation (USSF) 32, 131, 133
United States Soccer Football Association (USSFA) 15–16, 21
United Stated Youth Soccer Association (USYSA) 154–155
U.S. women's national team 2, 7, 65, 96, 116, 160–176 passim, 199–200; and education 4, 26; and 1999 World Cup 56, 114, 115, 160–176 passim; and 2011 World Cup 4, 26, 58, 65, 114, 160–176 passim, 199–200
university *see* college
USL *see* United Soccer Leagues
USSF *see* United States Soccer Federation
USSFA *see* United States Soccer Football Association
USYSA *see* United States Youth Soccer Association

Valderrama, Carlos 101
Vancouver Whitecaps FC 84, 87, 138n30, 145–149 passim, 199
Verón, Juan 78
violence 6, 16–17, 20, 46, 121–137, 162

Wambach, Abby 161, 169–175 passim
WBC *see* World Baseball Classic
West Ham F.C. 125–126, 134, 137n9
Wigan Athletic F.C. 77, 80
WNBA *see* Women's National Basket Association
Women's National Basket Association (WNBA) 114; *see also* basketball
Women's Professional Soccer (WPS) 114, 116n4, 171, 200
Women's United Soccer Association (WUSA) 114, 116n4, 167–168, 171, 175
World Baseball Classic (WBC) 108, 109–110, 117n13, 192; *see also* baseball
World Cup 1–3, 26, 39, 40, 48, 72, 96, 109, 150, 157, 184, 192, 199; in 1930 104; in 1950 101, 104, 117n7; in 1966 97; in 1970 105; in 1978 181; in 1986 60, 106; in 1990 40; in 1991 161, 164; in 1994 56, 71, 76, 84, 100–107 passim, 116n7, 116n2, 117n8, 117n12, 127, 131–132, 137n20, 144–147 passim, 164; in 1998 128, 137n20; in 1999 56, 114–115, 160–176 passim; in 2002 2, 100, 128, 131, 133, 144, 192; in 2006 61, 76, 109, 111, 117n13, 144, 192, 200; in 2007 173; in 2010 4, 25–26, 45, 50, 61, 64, 76, 100, 109, 114, 116; in 2011 59, 65–66, 114, 160–176 passim; in 2014 93; in 2015 176; in 2018 76; in 2022 76, 100; *see also* Fédération Internationale de Football Association (FIFA)
World War I 122, 154
World War II 4, 9, 11, 13, 20–23, 29, 122, 153–154
WPS *see* Women's Professional Soccer
WUSA *see* Women's United Soccer Association

X Games 57, 71
xenophobia 124, 130

youth 2–6, 9–23 passim, 25–41 passim; 46, 57–59, 63, 68, 72–73, 96, 102, 116, 124, 143–144, 154–158, 161, 167, 182–182, 192, 197–198, 201–204 passim, 205; *see also* American Youth Soccer Organization (AYSO); United Stated Youth Soccer Association (USYSA)

Zidane, Zinedine 92, 111, 113

www.ingramcontent.com/pod-product-compliance
Ingram Content Group UK Ltd.
Pitfield, Milton Keynes, MK11 3LW, UK
UKHW041953140426
5217IPUK00015B/778